A Study Guide for the Operator Certificate of Professional Competence (CPC) in Road Freight 2018

Second edition

A Study Guide for the Operator Certificate of Professional Competence (CPC) in Road Freight 2018

A complete self-study course for OCR and CILT examinations

Clive Pidgeon

KoganPage

First published in Great Britain and the United States in 2016 by Kogan Page Limited
Second edition published 2018

2nd Floor, 45 Gee Street	c/o Martin P Hill Consulting	4737/23 Ansari Road
London	122 W 27th Street	Daryaganj
EC1V 3RS	New York, NY 10001	New Delhi 110002
United Kingdom	USA	India

www.koganpage.com

© Clive Pidgeon, 2016, 2018

The right of Clive Pidgeon to be identified as the author of this work has been asserted by him in accordance with the Copyright, Designs and Patents Act 1988.

ISBN   978 0 7494 8193 3
E-ISBN 978 0 7494 8194 0

British Library Cataloguing-in-Publication Data

A CIP record for this book is available from the British Library.

Library of Congress Control Number

20170151861

Typeset by Integra Software Services, Pondicherry
Print production managed by Jellyfish
Printed and bound by 4edge Limited, UK

CONTENTS

Introduction 1

01   Civil law 9

Introduction to contracts 9
Contract components 10
Contracts and conditions of carriage 13
Convention Relative au Contrat de Transport
      International de Marchandises par Route (CMR) 17
Transport auxiliaries 24
Self-test example questions 26

02   Commercial law 29

Introduction 29
Sole traders 30
Partnerships 32
Limited companies 36
Company registration procedure 39
Directors' roles and duties 43
Company secretaries 44
Auditors 45
Annual general meetings 45
Shareholders 46
Business closures 48
Summary 51
Self-test example questions 52

03   Social law 54

SOCIAL INSTITUTIONS 55

Trade unions 55
The Advisory, Conciliation and Arbitration Service
      (ACAS) 59

The Central Arbitration Committee (CAC) 60
Employment Appeal Tribunal (EAT) 60
Health and safety 61
National Insurance (NI) 81
Rights of employees 82

DRIVERS' HOURS, RECORD KEEPING AND DCPC 100

EU Drivers' Hours Regulations (EC Regulation 561/2006)
    and Working Time Regulations (RTD) 100
The European Agreement on International Road
    Transport (AETR) 106
British domestic drivers' hours rules and Working Time
    Regulations (HAD) 106
Mixed EU/AETR and GB domestic driving 110
Tachographs 112
Operators' roles and responsibilities 121
Breakdown of equipment 122
Inspection and calibration 123
Drivers' record books and record keeping 123
Related offences, penalties and DVSA powers 125
Driver Certificate of Professional Competence
    (DCPC) 128
Self-test example questions 131

04   Fiscal law 137

Value-added tax (VAT) 137
Motor vehicle taxation (VED) 140
HGV Road User Levy 144
Other charges 145
Income tax for the self-employed 152
Employed staff income tax and NI 152
Business taxation – corporation tax 153
Recovery vehicles 153
Trade licences 155
Self-test example questions 157

05   Business and financial management 160

Business transaction documents 161
Payment of accounts 162

Short-term financing 164
Long-term financing 165
Financial accounts and financial ratios 165
Budgets and cash flow 174
Operational costing 178
Depreciation 183
How organizations are structured 187
Management definitions 188
Grievance and discipline 190
Market research and marketing 191
Data protection 194
Public relations 195
Insurance 196
Information and communication technology (ICT) 201
Incoterms 202
Self-test example questions 205

06   Access to the market 210

Operator licensing 211
The Operator Compliance Risk Score (OCRS) 223
Traffic Commissioners' powers and related offences 225
Documentation for operating internationally 227
International freight movements 230
Customs procedures 231
The Schengen Agreement 236
Self-test example questions 239

07   Technical standards and technical aspects of operation 246

UK maximum weights and dimensions 247
European and international weights and dimensions 251
Abnormal indivisible loads (AILs) 253
Vehicle and equipment criteria 257
Vehicle type approval 260
Plating and testing 261
Construction and use (C&U) and lighting regulations 265
Emissions and noise 273
Vehicle maintenance 274

Load safety 279
Transport ancillaries 281
Dangerous goods 285
Perishable foodstuffs 295
Waste 296
Livestock 298
Phytosanitary issues 301
Self-test example questions 302

08   Road safety 307

Driver licensing 307
Driving tests and Driver Certificate of Professional
    Competence (DCPC) 312
International driving permits 315
UK traffic rules 317
European rules 322
Drivers' daily ('first use') checks 331
Road traffic accidents/collisions 333
Security of goods 335
Planning international journeys 337
Self-test example questions 340

Answers to self-test questions 346
Online resources 370
Index 371

Introduction

Welcome to this self-study book, which has been specially designed and produced to offer a cost-effective alternative way of studying for, and passing, the Operator Certificate of Professional Competence in road freight examinations.

This book is designed to be used in several different ways:

- It can be used to study for the Operator Certificate of Professional Competence (CPC) in road freight operations, as a stand-alone self-study book.

- It can be used as pre-reading to gain some insight into what will be required if, and when, you decide to take your CPC.

- It can be used to assess your knowledge prior to sitting the CPC examinations.

- It can be used by existing CPC holders to update their knowledge and understanding.

- It can be used as a handy revision tool prior to sitting your CPC examinations.

- It can be used as a convenient revision book for people who have time at work, during breaks and so on, or have time during work-related nights out or away from base.

- It can be used as a reference book by managers and drivers.

- And it can be used also to assess whether you, or your sponsor, feel it is necessary to commit 7–10 days away from work studying one of the many courses offered in CPC, many of which cost £1,000–£1,500 per course, per delegate.

From the list above, it is clear that this book, amongst other things, is specifically designed to give you all the knowledge and understanding you will need to sit and pass the examinations for a Certificate of Professional

Competence (CPC) in road freight without committing a substantial amount of money or, as explained above, to supplement other training or to assess whether or not the CPC is actually for you.

This book covers the entire CPC syllabus, as laid out in EC Regulation 1071/2009, to a depth that will enable you to answer all the set examination questions and includes all the factual notes you will need to pass your exams. It does not, however, provide every administrative detail in relation to registration for the examinations, as you will be expected to arrange for your own examinations. The book meets the needs of those who wish to take either of the two most popular routes currently available within the UK to pass the CPC: the Oxford Cambridge Royal Society of Arts (OCR) examinations route and the Chartered Institute of Logistics and Transport (CILT) examinations route.

Throughout the book there are summaries of key learning points, spaces for you to make notes and self-test sections to enable you to measure your understanding of each of the sections.

The book only contains information that is drawn directly from the CPC syllabus and from which the examination questions will be composed. Throughout there are examples explaining many of the issues, but if you are uncertain about any of the elements then you will need to go over the material again, perhaps ask a manager or work colleague for clarity, or research the issue in more depth. Please do not try to 'wing' the examinations on the day, because it doesn't work and you will have wasted your money. You will also benefit from downloading past examination papers from either of the awarding organizations, and details are provided below.

As mentioned previously, to enable you to make the best use of this book during any study time that you may have, you will find lists of some of the 'key' items from each subsection as well as spaces available for you to make notes. Please note that whilst these lists will help you they are not exhaustive, as examination questions, particularly the multi-choice or short-answer questions, are randomly drawn from any single part of the syllabus.

In order to pass the certificate you will need to learn from each part of the set syllabus. The European Union (EU) standardized syllabus covers the following eight mandatory subject areas, which are all included in this book:

1 Civil law – including contracts and contracts of carriage.

2 Commercial law – including businesses and business structures.

3 Social law – including social institutions, health and safety, work-based legislation, drivers' hours and record keeping, and the Driver Certificate of Professional Competence (DCPC).

4 Fiscal Law – including value-added tax (VAT), vehicle excise duty (VED) and other taxation.

5 Business and financial management of the undertaking – including documents, accounting, cash flow, budgets, costings, staff management, marketing, insurance, IT and International Commercial Terms (Incoterms).

6 Access to the market – including operator licensing and international operations.

7 Technical standards and technical aspects of operation – including weights, dimensions, construction and use, vehicle maintenance, dangerous goods, perishable foodstuffs, waste and livestock transport.

8 Road safety – including driver licensing, driving tests, road traffic accident procedures and European links and road networks.

In order to keep the book both manageable and not too lengthy, whilst it does give you the basic knowledge you need to pass the examinations you are also strongly advised to download the publications listed below. These publications contain additional details and further explanations and examples relating to details you will need for your examinations. They are also an excellent source of information that is essential to supporting your CPC study programme:

- Goods Vehicle Operator Licensing Guide (GV74);
- Rules on Drivers' Hours and Tachographs (GV262);
- DVSA Guide to Maintaining Roadworthiness.

These are all available free to download from the government website (www.gov.uk), but ensure that you download the latest versions in order to develop good knowledge and understanding of the core areas covered by these publications. Please also note that the DVSA Guide to Maintaining Roadworthiness is used as the 'benchmark' publication, used by the awarding bodies when they produce examination material and examination questions relating to the inspection and maintenance of commercial vehicles. The other two guides also provide valuable information on statutory procedures and legal compliance and, given their value and the fact that they are free to download, should be studied closely.

As already mentioned, the two most popular routes to gain your CPC are the Oxford Cambridge Royal Society of Arts (OCR) examinations route and the Chartered Institute of Logistics and Transport (CILT) examinations route:

- Oxford Cambridge Royal Society of Arts (OCR)

  This involves completing a multi-choice question examination (RH1) of 60 questions of two hours' duration. The multi-choice examination addresses all areas of the syllabus, with a pass mark of 70 per cent (42/60). You are also required to sit a case study examination (RH2) of two and a quarter hours' duration (15 minutes is given for 'reading time'), requiring longer answers to between six and eight questions, with a total of 60 marks available. The case study questions are related to core subjects (for example, drivers' hours, operator licensing, finance/costings, and vehicle maintenance), and require a pass mark of 50 per cent (30 marks). You are required to answer all the set questions on the case study paper, which is an 'open book'-type examination, where you will be allowed to take reference material (such as this book and any downloaded material) into the examination room.

  The multi-choice examination is available either online or by attending a paper-based examination at a nominated OCR examination centre. The OCR examinations are held quarterly (March, June, September and December, normally on the first Friday of each of those months) but the multi-choice examination can be taken 'on-demand', if required. It should be noted that the OCR route is seen by many as the route to take if the candidate simply needs to acquire a CPC and does not intend to undertake any further studies or related learning, although it does require in-depth knowledge of many of the subject areas. Contact OCR on 02476 851509 or visit their website (www.ocr.org.uk) for further details and, when you are preparing to sit the examination, to download past case study papers from the same site.

- Chartered Institute of Logistics and Transport (CILT) examinations

  These consist of two examinations each of two hours' duration where the candidate needs to answer 20 short-answer questions and three out of four longer-answer questions, two of which are compulsory. To pass the exam you must achieve an overall pass mark of 50 per cent. This 50 per cent is made up of a pass mark of 40 per cent for paper one and 60 per cent for paper two. These examinations are held every two months at centres approved by the CILT. Paper one covers subjects in 1, 2, 5 and 6 in the list of subject areas above, whilst paper two covers subjects in 3, 4, 7 and 8.

  The CILT examination route also provides an opportunity to progress onto further studies for those candidates seeking professional or career development. Contact the CILT on 01536 740100 or visit their website (www.cilt.org.uk) for further information about the CPC or career development. The CILT also provides a book of sample CPC questions for people intending to sit their examinations.

The OCR case study and the CILT examinations are 'open book', which means you are able to take with you reference books, guides, text books and so on to use during the examination, but there is insufficient time during the examinations to use the 'open book' to produce sufficient correct answers to all the set questions, without some previously acquired depth of knowledge. The OCR multi-choice examination can be paper-based or completed 'on-screen' at approved examination centres. Both sets of examinations, either OCR or CILT, also provide both National and International Professional Competence. You can find your nearest CPC approved examination centre by either contacting OCR or the CILT or by searching on the internet.

It may seem that the syllabus is extensive and that the examinations are somewhat daunting but both examination bodies do allow some degree of flexibility in relation to handwriting, spelling and grammar, for example, and where English may not be a first language. Other types of assistance are available where there may be a special need but any enquiry needs to be sent to either OCR or the CILT.

You may also have noted the comment that you will definitely need to gain a good degree of knowledge and understanding before entering for the examination. Having to demonstrate both knowledge and understanding is required by the EU Regulation, which sets this qualification at what is known as Level Three standard, hence the requirement, which unfortunately is not negotiable. This self-study guide and the documents you need to download (as noted above) are sufficient to give you the knowledge and understanding required but it does take effort and commitment from you, and there is no 'easy fix'.

The content of the book is written to reflect the order in which the syllabus has been developed and the order in which the examination questions are set. This will help you to relate to what part of the syllabus any question is asking you to respond to and help you more easily relate to the appropriate section of this book when in the examination. It also reflects the same sequence of content that you will find in any other, much more expensive, study material.

To help you, where there are slight differences in the content required by each of the awarding bodies these will be noted in the text. Do not forget that both organizations (OCR and CILT) supply past papers or sample questions to help you prepare for the examinations and these should be used so that anyone preparing to take the examinations can assess the standard of difficulty of typical questions and their own readiness to sit the examination. As stated, these past papers and sample questions are available from the organizations themselves.

At this point, thanks must be given to the Chartered Institute of Logistics and Transport (CILT UK) for supplying information that enabled the book to be written in order to accurately reflect not only the requirements of the EU Directive but also the content and sequence of the CILT's comprehensive study material.

Before we start the first chapter we need to gain some background knowledge relating to the EU. This is important for any person intending to take the OCR examination route as there are multi-choice questions that relate to the information below.

The points below, although useful, are not widely examined by the CILT, although if you intend to take the CILT examinations you will be expected to know the extent of the EU and the difference between the EU and the European Free Trade Association (EFTA) (see below).

The key points you need to know are:

● The EU currently consists of 28 countries. These are:

Austria*	Italy*
Belgium*	Latvia*
Bulgaria	Lithuania*
Croatia	Luxembourg*
Cyprus*	Malta*
Czech Republic	Netherlands*
Denmark	Poland
Estonia*	Portugal*
Finland*	Romania
France*	Slovakia*
Germany*	Slovenia*
Greece*	Spain*
Hungary	Sweden
Republic of Ireland*	United Kingdom

_____

* These are countries in the eurozone.

The EU administration is as follows:

● First, there is the EU Council of Ministers which votes on EU policy, with member states having different numbers of votes depending upon their size. The council is made up of heads of state of the EU member states. There is a permanent president, who serves for a term of 2.5

years, and it is the minister of transport of the president's member state who chairs policy meetings and sets priorities for the future six months.

- The EU Commission makes proposals to the EU Council of Ministers to consider. The Commission is made up of single representatives from each member state.

- The European Economic and Social Committee is made up of members who serve for renewable periods of five years. There are 350 members who give opinions on policy proposals from bodies across the EU that are intended to be evaluated or assessed by the Commission and the Council.

- The European Parliament, which sits for three weeks every month in Brussels and one week every month in Strasbourg, is made up of members (MEPs) who serve five-year terms. The European Parliament debates laws and, in conjunction with the Council, passes laws. They also monitor the other EU administrative bodies such as the Council and debate the EU's budget.

Note: The European Parliament cannot pass laws without the EU Council of Ministers but does advise the council on intended legislation.

- The European Court of Justice, which is currently made up of 28 judges (one per member state) has 11 advocates general who act to advise the Court. The Court sits in Brussels and holds plenary sessions and smaller Grand Chamber sessions (of 13 judges). All decisions need to be unanimous because the Court's main role is to interpret the 'Treaty of Rome', which is one of the foundation treaties of the EU itself.

- The EU Common Transport Policy was formed in response to the Treaty of Rome. It is aimed at removing trade barriers and trade restrictions between member states. It also harmonizes many transport-related laws and regulations, limits excessive harmful competition and aims to create a more professional transport industry.

- The EU Single Market was created by the Single European Act. It was aimed at removing additional barriers to trade relating to customs procedures, fiscal restrictions, legal standards, the free movement of goods and people, and economic growth across the whole of the EU.

- The European Economic Area (EEA) is a free trade area that comprises all the EU member states plus Iceland, Liechtenstein and Norway.

- The European Free Trade Area (EFTA) is another free trade area made up of all the EU member states plus Iceland, Liechtenstein, Norway and Switzerland (although Switzerland did not join the EEA). This means that these 32 countries form a free trade area with preferential trade conditions.

Note: Free trade areas are not customs areas and are subject to a limited number of customs controls with the EU.

Please also note that the EU in its current format is still used for examination purposes as 'Brexit' has not, as yet, been finalized.

We will now move on to begin the first area of required study, civil law.

Civil law

01

The regulations state that in order to be deemed competent in this area of study the learner must be:

- familiar with the main types of contract used in road transport and with the rights and obligations arising therefrom;
- capable of negotiating a legally valid transport contract, notably with regard to conditions of carriage;
- able to consider a claim by his or her principal regarding compensation for loss of or damage to goods during transportation or for their late delivery, and to understand how such claims affect his or her contractual liability;
- familiar with the rules and obligations arising from the Convention on the Contract for the International Carriage of Goods by Road (CMR Convention);
- familiar with the different categories of transport auxiliaries, their role, their functions and, where appropriate, their status.

We address each of these below.

Introduction to contracts

In order to understand the nature of contracts we need to begin by understanding a little about the structure of the law and the specific law that governs them.

Traditionally, in the United Kingdom we introduce and pass laws either by Acts of Parliament, known as statute (breaking these laws is classed as a 'crime') or through sets of standards that have become accepted as appropriate actions and customs within civil society as a whole. This is known as common law and breaking common laws results not in crimes but what are known as 'torts' (these are known as 'delicts' in Scotland). These types of civil offences are normally subject to the alleged guilty party being sued for damages. The term 'damages' indicates that any sum awarded is done so to make good any damage done, for example, to the victim's status, reputation or business.

Both statute and common laws apply to transport businesses and have done so for many years. For instance, vehicle speed limits are clearly a statutory issue, whilst claims for loss or delay of goods may be a common law issue.

However, more recently, we find that the transport industry, and industry as a whole, also needs to comply with laws emanating from the EU. Many of us may be less familiar with the structure and hierarchy of these laws but modern managers must learn to raise their awareness of EU legislation, including intended legislation, and to make whatever preparation and changes are required in order to accommodate it when it is introduced and impacts upon their business.

One of the key points about EU legislation is that it comes in the form of regulations and also in the form of directives. With a regulation, every member state is bound to comply in full with the terms of the regulation. With directives, each member state must, in general terms, comply but is able to make adjustments in order to make the directive align with other rules or regulations within the country concerned or fit into their own social structure.

Throughout this module you will be learning about many legal obligations and constraints that affect both general businesses and road haulage businesses. Some of the principal obligations to any business result from working with suppliers and customers and revolve around contractual obligations.

Contract components

Because contracts are an integral part of any business, transport or otherwise, we will all encounter them at some time or another and we need to understand exactly what they are. A contract can simply be defined as 'a legally binding agreement'. Other, more lengthy, definitions include 'a voluntary, deliberate and legally binding agreement between two or more competent parties' (BusinessDictionary.com) but the meanings are much the same when we break down contracts into their individual elements. In any case, a legally binding contract does not have to be written down, recorded, signed, witnessed or dated: verbal agreements can suffice as proof that a contract has been formed.

Although contracts can be formed by word of mouth (and usually a handshake) they do need to follow a pattern and contain seven certain components in order for them to be deemed 'legal'. As a transport manager or vehicle operator you need to know what these components are and how they combine into the formation of a contract. These points are also required for your examinations: they will be examined for whichever examination route you decide to take.

The seven components of a legally binding contract are:

1 There must be an initial 'Offer' made by an offeror to an offeree. The offer needs to be specific and have at least some outline terms. So something like 'Can you take these 26 pallets of animal feed from Bristol to London on 24 March?' would constitute an offer made and specific terms. If the question was 'Are you free to do a job some time next week?' then there are no specific terms and a contract would not be formed or be able to be legally enforced.

2 Providing that the initial offer is not withdrawn at this stage, the next component of a contract is 'Acceptance'. All the offeree needs to do to accept is to give a positive (affirmative) response to the offer made from the offeror. It is vital that acceptance is relayed to the offeror or there is no acceptance. However, it must be noted that acceptance is deemed to have been made once any letter, signed form, or other document enters the postal system, whether or not it has been delivered. This fact has led many organizations to write in 'cooling off' periods in case doubts do occur after acceptance.

3 The third component is a little difficult to explain as it is termed 'Consideration'. Consideration is required if a contract is to be deemed legally binding and is based upon a common law principle that only transactions and bargaining can be supported in law, not simple promises. In short this means that both parties need to gain, or lose, something by forming a contract. In basic terms, in our example above the haulier would gain and the offeror would pay. It could be argued that both would also gain but, irrespective, both parties would be affected. Another example might be a hire purchase agreement where the hirer gets access to the goods while the hire purchase company receives payments more than totalling the purchase price but needs to administer the agreement and takes a risk. Both these examples mean that the contracts would be deemed legal, in relation to consideration being present.

4 The fourth component is also somewhat oddly named: 'Capacity'. Capacity relates to the ability of a person to enter into a legally binding contract. In business terms this means that contracts cannot be deemed legal if any person attempting to form a contract is:

- under 18 years of age;

- of unsound mind; or

- under the influence of alcohol or drugs so that they simply do not know what they are doing.

It should also be noted that to protect themselves, registered companies limit their 'capacity' by setting limits of authorization for different levels of management, and different roles, within the 'objects clause' of the Memorandum of Association (see Chapter 2 on commercial law).

5 The next component we need to consider is 'Intention'. There must be an intention, by all the parties concerned, to form a legally binding relationship. It is not allowed to 'hoodwink', or fool someone into forming a contract if they never intended to do so. Where someone is misled into an attempt to form a contract, all that is formed is an agreement, which is not a legally binding relationship and is therefore not a contract.

6 The next required component is that every contract must in itself be 'Legal'. If a contract is related to any unlawful act or breaking the law then it would not be deemed to be legally binding. For example, any contract offered that would mean the driver exceeding their driving hours or having to exceed speed limits in order to keep to schedule would not be a legally binding contract. In a similar vein, it is also strange when we hear references to 'contract killers'!

7 The last required component is 'Formalities'. This means that, if the contract specifies conditions such as taking a certain route, using specified overnight stop locations or using certain vehicles, for example, then any deviation from those requests, or any other terms and conditions that were itemized in the contract, would break the terms of the contract because these 'formalities' had not been observed.

All of the seven components above need to be in place and applied if a contract is to be deemed legal and binding under law. Should any component be either missing, or not adhered to, then the party to the contract who feels they have in some way suffered excessively, or have not been treated in line with the agreed contract (damaged), can sue for damages in a civil court.

Next we move on to examine the transport-specific contracts that we encounter most regularly within the transport sector.

Key points you need to know

- The difference between statute and common law.
- The definition of a contract.
- That contracts can be verbal only.
- All seven components of a contract and full details relating to them.

Notes

....

....

....

....

....

....

....

....

....

Contracts and conditions of carriage

The most common form of contract encountered in the transport industry is undoubtedly a contract of carriage. Whilst many operators have their own contract terms many others use the terms of the contracts of carriage that have been developed by either the Road Haulage Association (RHA) or the Freight Transport Association (FTA). These conditions of carriage are often printed on the rear side of delivery notes and invoices; they clearly state the conditions relating to the proposed or completed work, and act to form a legally binding contract. The conditions within the contract will address issues such as:

- payment terms and discount or penalty arrangements;
- actions in the event of loss or damage of the goods;

- levels of liability in the event of loss or damage;
- any additional specific requirements relating to other issues such as demurrage or punctuality.

In order to meet the requirements of this qualification we need to understand the two types of carriers that may be encountered when entering into a contract of carriage. These are:

- *Private carriers* (such as Eddie Stobart and other general hauliers) who can select who they want to work for, what they want to carry, when they can do the work and how they carry out the work. In fact they are what we know as hauliers, who limit their liability to work-related activities.

- *Common carriers* who have to carry any items presented to them and who cannot limit their liability to work-related issues – they are fully liable at all times. Common carriers may be liable for damages if they refuse, without sufficient justification, to carry a customer's goods on normal scheduled routes between declared locations, and they may be faced with unlimited liability for any loss of or damage to goods in transit. Examples include UPS and FedEx.

We also need to learn about the component parts of the contracts and conditions of carriage, including what the conditions actually cover, levels of liability, how conditions relate to subcontractors, the rules relating to exemption clauses and the duties of principals and agents. These are all covered below.

The two most used conditions of carriage are those that belong to the RHA and FTA (the FTA has now combined with the Chartered Institute of Purchasing and Supply (CIPS) to produce their conditions of carriage although they are still widely referred to as the FTA conditions). Both the RHA and FTA conditions cover areas such as:

- acts outside the control of the carrier: floods, storms, war, unexpected delays (sometimes referred to as force majeure);
- negligence or improper actions by the sender, or any person involved with preparing or loading the goods that was also outside the control of the carrier;
- inherent vice of the goods (this means that if the goods were actually broken or faulty when they were loaded, the carrier is not liable);
- limits of liability (currently £1,300 per tonne);
- collection and/or delivery requirements (in relation to times and delays);

- lien (see below);
- subcontractors (also see below).

Lien

Lien requires an explanation because it is the right of a haulier to retain goods until the agreed contracted price has been paid by the customer. If payment is not made, lien then gives the haulier the right to unload the goods and sell them, taking what is owed, including any unloading costs, and returning any balance to the customer.

Subcontractors

Subcontracting within the UK between UK operators is also covered by domestic conditions of carriage because subcontractors are treated differently on most international journeys, which are carried out under CMR conditions of carriage. We will cover CMR shortly.

For domestic purposes, when a subcontractor is used it is the original carrier who remains responsible overall for ensuring the contract is carried out legally and within any agreed terms and conditions. In short, if you engage a subcontractor while operating under the RHA or FTA conditions of carriage it is you that will be held responsible if things go wrong.

In addition, in relation to using subcontractors, the original carrier is not obliged to tell the customer how much the subcontractor is charging but they must ensure that the subcontractor is properly insured to carry out the work. The subcontractor is also bound to have the correct insurance and carry out the subcontracting in a 'diligent' manner.

Finally, should the first subcontractor subcontract to a second subcontractor and there be a problem with the second subcontractor, it would be the first subcontractor who would be liable to the customer, and not the original carrier.

Exemption clauses

Exemption clauses effectively limit the level of liability set within a contract of carriage. For example, they may exempt the carrier should goods become damaged because of a delay at the delivery point caused by industrial action at the customer's premises, or they may exempt partial liability in cases of the driver being unable to check the load at the time of collection.

The key fact about exemption clauses is that they have to be 'properly communicated' to the customer before the work is carried out. They cannot be suddenly 'sprung' on a customer if things go wrong. They are normally part of what we know as the 'small print' on a contract. Whilst they may be used, for them to be legal they too must be reasonable and fair, and cannot be used to protect the carrier from failing to perform in a legally binding manner.

Principals and agents

Principals and agents are terms used in contracts of carriage to identify the parties involved and thereby provide areas and levels of responsibilities for each. A principal is the person requiring the agent to act on their behalf in relation to forming a contract. For example, freight forwarders often act as agents for their customers (principals).

Once appointed, and the roles and responsibilities of the agent have been agreed, an agent is normally able to make contracts on behalf of the principal. Providing that they do not act outside the terms of any properly formed agency agreement, and exceed their authority, the agent will be entitled to some form of commission based on either the value of the goods or an agreed fixed fee.

Both the principal and the agent have specific duties and responsibilities under an agency agreement. The principal must:

- agree to be bound by the agency agreement;
- accept liability for any claim against a legally binding contract;
- indemnify the agent from claims and liabilities when carrying out their duties;
- indemnify the agent for any expenses incurred in relation to properly carrying out their duties;
- pay the agent any agreed fixed fee or commission.

In turn, the agent must:

- act within the terms of the specific, agreed agency agreement;
- carry out their duties with due care and diligence;
- agree to be subject to the control of the principal and to act on their behalf;
- avoid any personal conflict of interest between the principal and themselves;
- ensure monies received are promptly passed on to the principal.

Key points you need to know

- The difference between private and common carriers.
- Items covered under conditions of carriage.
- Level of liability.
- Definition of lien.
- Liability and responsibility relating to subcontractors.
- Communication of exemption clauses.
- Duties and roles of principals and agents.

Notes

....

....

....

....

....

....

....

....

....

....

We now move on to cover international conditions of carriage. These are often referred to as CMR but the CMR agreement is actually somewhat more complex and also covers other areas. However, for these examinations we will concentrate on the issues related to CMR that may appear in any of the set examinations.

Convention Relative au Contrat de Transport International de Marchandises par Route (CMR)

CMR acts to provide a set of standard conditions for moving goods internationally. It is a convention that is overseen by the United Nations Economic Commission for Europe (UNECE) and is applied when goods are moved from, or to, one or more of the countries that are signatory to the convention. The countries concerned include all EU member states and European Free Trade Area (EFTA) countries (the EFTA countries are Iceland, Liechtenstein, Norway and Switzerland) and other countries such as Russia, Turkey, most Central Asia countries and countries in the Balkans region. (The title of the convention is written in French as are most of the UNECE conventions we examine throughout the book.)

CMR only applies to goods that are carried for hire and reward. It does not apply to goods moved as 'own account' goods, such as those goods produced by a manufacturer who would, for example, move them to a plant abroad for further processing or assembly. Neither does CMR apply to goods that are postal items, funeral consignments or domestic furniture removals. In addition it does not apply to goods moved between the UK and Republic of Ireland and/or Northern Ireland.

The convention clearly lays out the duties of the sender, the carrier and the recipient of any international consignment that is carried by road, or by road/rail, road/sea, providing that the goods are not at any time removed from the vehicle (unloaded for transhipment, for instance). In practice this means that a container that remains on a trailer going from the UK to France would be under CMR, but if the trailer was unloaded at Dover and taken to France independently then CMR would not apply. In these cases, international maritime law would generally apply to the sea crossing, and local French law would apply once the container was in France.

CMR consignment note

All goods carried under the convention must travel along with a CMR consignment note. This note does not have to be in any statutory format or layout but it does have to have certain sections where information has to be entered. For example, there must be spaces on the note where the size of the consignment, its weight or numbers of items can be recorded and there needs to be details of the sender, carrier and recipient. There also needs to be a 'reservations box' for the receiving driver to note any reservations he/she may have about the load, such as any damage, or if they were unable to check the load upon taking it over, or any other uncertainties relating to the consignment in question.

For examination purposes, you also need to know that there are often some optional 'boxes' used on CMR notes for recording a 'special interest'. This is used when high-value goods are being moved and the carrier agrees to pay a higher level of compensation than would normally be paid

FIGURE 1.1 CMR consignment note

LETTRE DE VOITURE INTERNATIONALE	CMR	INTERNATIONAL CONSIGNMENT NOTE

Sender (name, address, country) Expéditeur (nom, adresse, pays) **1**	Sender's/agent's reference Reference de l'expéditeur/de l'agent	**2/3**
Consignee (name, address, country) Destinateire (nom, adresse, pays) **4**	Carrier (name, address, country) Transporteur (nom, adresse, pays)	**5**
Place and date of taking over the goods (place, county date) Lieu et date de la prise on charge des marchandises (lieu, pays, date) **6**	Successive carriers Transporteurs successifs	**7**
Place designated for delivery of goods (place, country) Lieu prévu pour la livraison des marchandises (lieu, pays) **8**	This carriage is subject. notwithstanding any clause to the contrary, to the Convention on the Contract for the International Carriage of Goods by Road (CMR) Ce transport est soumis nonobstant toute clause contraire à la Convention Relative au Contrat de Transport International de Marchandises par Route (CMR)	

COPY 1 SENDER
COPY 2 CONSIGNEE
COPY 3 CARRIER

* NB FOR
DANGEROUS
GOODS
INDICATE
PROPER
SHIPPING
NAME
ADR CLASS
ITEM NO
AND LETTER
IF ANY
UN NO

Shipping marks and nos; no and kind of packages; description of goods* Marques et nos; no et nature des colis; designation des marchndises* **9**	Gross wieght **10** (kg) Poids brut (kg)	Volume **11** (m3) Cubage (m3)

Carriage charges Prix de transport **12**	Sender's instructions for customs Instructions de l'expéditeur (optional)	**13**
Reservations Réserves **14**	Documents attached Documents annexés (optional)	**15**
	Special agreements Conventions particuliéres (optional)	**16**
Goods received Marchandises reçues **17**	Signature of carrier **18** Signature du transporteur	Company completing this note **19** Société émettrice
		Place and date; signature **20** Lieu et date; signature

(see below for normal liability). Another box is used to declare any pre-agreed time limits within which the goods need to be delivered. If this second box is not present, or not used, and there are no pre-agreed time limits, the convention applies 'reasonable times' for delivery (these are also discussed below).

The consignment notes themselves normally come supplied as four-part forms that are coloured red (sender's copy for retention), blue (consignee's copy to go with the goods), green (carrier's copy to go with the goods) and black (a further copy for the carrier to retain at base).

Should the consignment note be lost, destroyed or otherwise fail to turn up, the convention will remain in force. This prevents issues relating to fraudulent claims and other abuses of the convention.

Limits of liability

Once operators are working under the terms of the convention, they are protected from excessive claims for compensation for the loss of the goods by the convention, which limits the amount able to be claimed if the goods themselves are lost or damaged. Claims relating to the goods are limited to a figure of 8.33 special drawing rights (SDRs) per kilogramme unless a 'special interest' (see above) has been declared. SDRs are, in reality, valued as a 'basket of currencies' specifically designed to provide limits of compensation under the terms of the convention, and are not directly related to any particular currency. Their value is published daily in the financial press and a single SDR is usually valued between £1.20 and £1.30 (this can be lower when the value of the pound falls on international currency markets). This normally makes the level of compensation between £10.00 and £10.80 per kilogramme. This would make the liability between £10,000 and £10,800 per tonne as opposed to the figure of £1,300 per tonne for domestic carriage. This fact and the rules of the convention are why hauliers operating under CMR must take out CMR insurance in case of claims for the goods.

It should also be appreciated that a typical 25-tonne load under domestic conditions of carriage would be valued at £32,500 for compensation purposes, whereas a 25-tonne load under CMR would be valued at between £250,000 and £270,000! (Further, any load carried under CMR is subject to a maximum value of 330,000 SDR.) It should also be noted that under the terms of CMR, the figure of 8.33 SDRs cannot be lowered.

Having covered the documentation to be used and the level of liability for the goods, let's now look at specific responsibilities and liabilities of persons involved with moving goods under the terms of CMR.

Sender's responsibilities and liabilities

The sender has several responsibilities, including ensuring that the goods are properly packaged and labelled. They are also responsible for the accuracy of the documentation relating to the consignment, and that it clearly identifies the carrier, clearly describes the goods, and identifies any dangerous goods to be moved.

In relation to packaging, it is the sender who is liable for damage or costs if the packaging is deemed insufficient or inappropriate. In relation to documentation, the sender is still responsible even if it is the carrier who fills out the CMR note. However, if there are problems, the sender is able to terminate the contract at any time during which the goods are in transit.

Carrier's responsibilities and liabilities

The carrier also has responsibilities and is deemed to be liable for the total or partial loss of the goods while under their control, or for any damage to them, from the time the goods were collected until the time they were delivered. It is also the responsibility of the carrier to use vehicles, trailers and equipment that are in good condition. Using a trailer with a damaged roof, for instance, would make the carrier liable if the goods were damaged because of a leak. However, carriers do have some defences to prevent them from false or spurious claims, providing that the carrier is able to prove such things as:

- There was fault or neglect by the person claiming (often the cause of spurious claims).
- Any loss or damage was due to circumstances beyond the carrier's control (ie the vehicle carrying the goods encounters flash floods).
- Defective packaging/marking (as a cause of the problem).
- Incorrect instructions given (especially in relation to handling or perishability).
- Inherent vice of the goods (ie the goods were already either broken or defective).
- Damage by moth or vermin (including mice, rats, foxes and feral cats).
- Poor handling by the sender or anyone engaged by the sender (either loading or unloading).
- The use of a flat trailer, if agreed (if a flat trailer is authorized by the sender then they cannot claim if the load becomes exposed to the elements, providing that the sheeting used was in good condition at the time of despatch).

Whilst the carrier is not liable under the items above, the convention does make the carrier liable for delay, loss or damage under some circumstances. These are important and are outlined below:

- The carrier is liable for delay if the goods are not delivered within the time limit that was agreed by the sender and carrier, or within what the convention calls a 'reasonable time' if no time limit has actually been agreed. It is also to be noted that claims for delay are limited to the sum of the actual carriage charges and not the value of the goods themselves. Where the goods are delivered but subject to a delay, under the convention, claims must be submitted in writing within 21 days of the eventual delivery.

- In relation to the loss of the goods, the carrier is liable if the goods are not delivered within 30 days of an agreed date or within 60 days of collection if there was no agreed date.

- In cases of total loss, partial loss and/or damage the carrier is only liable to pay compensation if the claim is made in writing immediately if the loss or damage is evident at the time of delivery, or made in writing within seven days if the loss or damage is not evident at the time of delivery.

In all cases of loss, damage or delay, or any other issues that might arise from the carriage of goods under the convention, any claims must be submitted in writing within one year of the carriage having been carried out unless the claim against the carrier alleges 'wilful misconduct' in which case the time limit for claims is extended to three years.

Unlike domestic conditions and contracts of carriage, the issue of the liability of sub-contractors, or 'successive carriers' as they are termed under the Convention, is treated differently and the Convention clearly lays down the rules relating to the roles and liability of any successive carriers. These are that:

- Any successive carrier taking control of a consignment must give the previous carrier a dated and signed receipt and enter their details on the CMR consignment note and enter any 'reservations' in the reservations box.

- Where the whole movement of the goods is covered by a single contract, each successive carrier will be held liable for whole movement.

- Where the loss or damage of the goods is proven to be because of the actions or inactions of a single carrier, that successive carrier shall be wholly liable for the loss or damage.

- Where the damage or loss is proven to be because of the actions or inactions of two or more carriers, each carrier concerned will pay according to their level of reward in relation to the overall carriage charges.

- Where the loss or damage cannot be apportioned to any specific successive carriers, all hauliers involved will pay in proportion to their level of reward in relation to the overall carriage charges.*

- Should any successive carrier become insolvent or bankrupt, all the other hauliers are deemed liable to have to pay any outstanding compensation in proportion to their level of reward in relation to the overall carriage charges.

---

* Where there are claims relating to these final two bullet points, the Convention prevents any claims from any of the successive carriers that the claim is invalid, or incorrect, once the compensation figure has been decided by a court.

Unwitting CMR

This term is used to describe the situation where a domestic haulier 'unwittingly' (unknowingly) becomes involved with a movement that is controlled by the terms of the CMR Convention.

This situation most commonly occurs when domestic hauliers are either delivering or collecting unaccompanied trailers, either loaded trailers or trailers carrying containers, to or from ports in the UK. The danger is that, because CMR applies to the whole journey, providing the goods are not unloaded the load is still 'in transit' and the domestic haulier will need CMR insurance to cover the SDR value of the consignment. As explained above, if the goods or the container have been unloaded from a vehicle then they would be classed as a domestic movement and the RHA or FTA level of liability would suffice.

Key points you need to know

CMR is one of the key areas for the CPC examination and you will ALWAYS be examined in it in some way or another. It is also very often used to compile case study (OCR) or long-answer (CILT) questions and you need to have thorough understanding of all the points outlined above. In particular:

- where CMR applies;

- the consignment note;

- levels of liability;

- roles and responsibilities;

- time limits for delay and loss, claims;

- 'unwitting CMR'.

Notes

....

....

....

....

....

....

....

....

....

....

Transport auxiliaries

As you may have noted from the outline syllabus at the beginning of this chapter, we now need to discuss the roles of what are termed 'transport auxiliaries'. These are organizations that act, in some way or another, to support the road freight transport sector. For syllabus and examination purposes we need to briefly discuss the roles of clearing houses, groupage operators, freight forwarders and warehouse and distribution operators:

- Clearing houses are organizations and businesses that do not normally operate their own vehicles, but they do act to provide operators with customers who need goods moving. Traditionally, the types of work offered by clearing houses would be termed 'return loads'. In principle, clearing houses act as a point of contact between those requiring transport and those able to provide it.

- Groupage operators are also often referred to as 'consolidation services'. They provide the means for customers with less than full loads, or even individual items, to move their goods as cost-effectively as possible by pulling together 'grouped' loads of smaller consignments into larger unit loads. Smaller consignments are often referred to as Less than Container Loads (LCL) by both groupage operators and freight forwarders (see below). By doing this they can then trunk the smaller consignments as a complete load, which is often a scheduled service, reducing costs to their customers. Once the loads have been sent to a suitable location they are then broken down into their original component size ready for final delivery. The breaking down of these grouped loads is known as 'break bulk'.

- Freight forwarders are businesses and organizations able to offer services such as groupage and break bulk, but who are also able to offer many more services, up to and including everything that a potential customer, requiring any amount or type of goods moving, may require. Typically they can pack goods, prepare documentation (including customs clearances), especially where specialist documentation is required, arrange insurance, provide transport, provide distribution, provide containers, carry out cost comparisons, undertake warehousing and offer agents. Whilst there are many freight forwarding organizations that operate domestically there are also many companies who offer global services, such as P&O and Maersk.

- Warehousing and distribution are services offered by both smaller operators, perhaps operating in a niche market, and multinational third-party logistics providers (3PL) operating globally. They are most commonly found working under contract for retail chains where they take bulk loads into storage in the warehouse, pick orders for individual outlets and then use transport (either their own or contracted, or a mixture of both at peak times) for final distribution to the stores.

This final short subsection completes the needs of the set syllabus in relation to civil law.

Key points you need to know

- The roles and differences of the auxiliaries above.
- The difference between a clearing house and a freight forwarder.

Notes

....

....

....

....

....

....

....

....

....

....

Self-test example questions

As this is the first chapter it is probably worth pointing out that the OCR scenario papers (long questions) require you to answer six to eight questions but the CILT long questions only require you to answer three long questions per paper, which is a maximum of six questions.

In addition, the questions used at the end of each of the chapters are only for demonstration purposes and, although the answers themselves are correct, actual examination questions and required answers may be different.

It should also be noted that the number of questions for each chapter reflects the importance both the CILT and OCR put on the subject area. For instance, you can rightly expect more questions on Operator Licensing than on Civil Law.

OCR-type questions (multi-choice)

1 Which of the following groups of people do not have the capacity to enter into a legally binding general business contract?

   a People under the age of 18.

   b People of unsound mind.

   c People under the influence of alcohol or drugs so that they simply do not know what they are doing.

   d People under the age of 21.

2 Why would a driver need to use the 'reservations box' on a CMR note?

   a To inform the customer of a late delivery.

   b To inform the customs of duty that needs to be paid.

   c To record that they were unable to check the load at the time of collection.

   d To record a 'special interest' relating to the consignment.

3 i) Clearing houses are organizations and businesses that do not normally operate their own vehicles, but they do act to provide operators with customers who need goods moving. ii) Groupage operators provide the means for customers with less than full loads, or even individual items, to move their goods as cost-effectively as possible by pulling together 'grouped' loads of smaller consignments into larger unit loads. These statements are:

a (i) True (ii) False.

b (i) False (ii) False.

c (i) False (ii) True.

d (i) True (ii) True.

OCR case study-type question

This subject area is not widely examined by OCR in their case studies but they do sometimes ask about the seven components that make up a contract, or for you to explain the limits of liability and time limits for loss and delay under CMR as part of a given scenario relating to a specific load.

Note: It is almost impossible to write a sample case study 'long question' because a different scenario is used for each examination. The best advice is to download past 'Unit Four' papers from the OCR website (type in that you want CPC past papers and follow the links) and work through the scenario questions contained within them. The same website also provides sample 'past papers' of multi-choice questions, should you wish to download them.

CILT-type questions (short answer)

1 Briefly discuss the main groups of people who are not able to enter into legally binding business contracts.

2 Briefly explain the purpose of the 'reservations box' on a CMR note.

3 Briefly describe the services provided by clearing houses and groupage operators.

CILT-type question (long answer)

Discuss the essential components that go together to form a legally binding business contract.

The CILT only provides sample papers to members and so the CILT 'sample' questions (both short answer and long answer) are examples of the types of questions and subject areas that the CILT will examine.

Once you are happy that you can answer questions such as those above then please feel free to move on to the next chapter, which examines commercial law. However, if you are unsure or not certain about any of the content, or any of the 'key points you need to know', then please revisit until you feel that you have a full grasp of the material and what is required. Please also remember that these were only sample questions.

Commercial law

02

The CPC syllabus requires that, in relation to commercial law, you should be:

- familiar with the conditions and formalities laid down for plying for trade and the general obligations incumbent upon transport operators and the consequences of bankruptcy;
- able to demonstrate the appropriate knowledge of the various forms of commercial companies and the rules governing their constitution and operation.

In order to be able to meet these requirements you will need information about business issues including sole traders, partnerships, forming private limited companies, forming public limited companies, bankruptcy, insolvency, roles of directors and roles of auditors. All that you will require for your examination in relation to commercial law is contained in this chapter.

We begin by looking at the first requirement, which relates to the conditions and formalities for 'plying for trade'.

Introduction

In order to 'ply for trade' you need to start a business. Businesses come in all shapes and sizes:

- *Sole traders* are people who run businesses by themselves and are usually described as 'self-employed' although, whilst they may 'run' the business and own it, they might employ some staff. In real terms it is very easy to set up a business as a sole trader and it can often be done without the need to borrow massive amounts of funds. However, a sole trader's level of liability does extend to the whole extent of their personal wealth. (Basically, if they go bankrupt they can lose their home, car, everything.)

- *Partnerships* are formed where two or more people join together to operate a business for the benefit of themselves and their partners. Partnerships can be 'unlimited', as is the case with sole traders, or they can limit their liability as is the case with 'limited companies'.

- *Private limited companies* are where private individuals have a private business that is registered at Companies House. Registering the company makes it a legal entity, which because it is an 'entity' is able to limit its liability to the value of the company and not the owners/directors. Private limited companies can only sell shares to family or friends; they cannot sell shares to the public at large.

- *Public limited companies* are normally larger organizations that operate in many similar ways to private limited companies but are able to sell shares to the public at large.

The above are all forms of businesses plying for trade but we need to examine the differences between them in detail, discuss how they can be set up, examine the requirements and the roles and responsibilities of business operators, business auditors, shareholders and liquidators, and other professional services that support and administer businesses.

We begin by looking at sole traders.

Sole traders

The main thing to remember is that sole traders do not operate their businesses with anyone else. They may have staff, as mentioned above, but they are solely in charge, which is why many people choose to run businesses in this way.

Becoming a sole trader is relatively easy; all you need are the funds to start and you can trade freely. In the case of transport, all you need is an operator's licence ('O' licence) with sufficient funds to meet the requirements of the licence and the funds for the deposit or purchase of items such as the vehicle, fuel and insurance. In real terms that makes transport quite an easy area in which to operate a business, which is why it is an industry where many 'owner-drivers' can be found. Whilst it is an uncomplicated way to start a business, it is also easy to cease trading; all you need to do is stop. There are no formalities.

Many sole traders find success because they deal directly (face to face) with their customers and are able to develop strong business links and trust with them. In addition, the more work a sole trader performs, the greater are the rewards. They are not bound by salary caps or grading and, if successful, are often able to expand their business through recommendation and word of mouth, and may actually employ staff of their own if the business grows sufficiently.

The benefits, however, are accompanied by some disbenefits, not least that if a sole trader does not perform well or lets down a customer, this can be communicated by customers and the sole trader may well have to cease trading as the work 'dries up'. In addition, because of the ease of access into becoming a sole trader, it is a very competitive area of business. This is largely due to the fact that many sole traders are small businesses. In turn, this can make attracting support and funding from banks and financial institutions difficult, particularly given the need for financial reserves in relation to 'O' licensing and/or if trying to expand a fleet of vehicles.

The main disbenefit, however, must be that the sole trader cannot limit their liability and, if they go bankrupt (sole traders go bankrupt, limited companies go into liquidation) they can lose everything 'up to the limit of their personal wealth'.

Other disbenefits include the fact that sole traders need to work to earn. 'No work = no money' and so sickness and holidays can prove costly and long-term illness may force closure. In cases where the sole trader may need to hire someone to cover for them, or employ someone to serve existing customers, there can also be problems because some customers expect the sole trader themselves to be the one to serve them (perhaps as they have for several years) and may resent the 'new face' or feel that they have been relegated to a poorer standard of service. In addition, as a sole trader you normally pay income tax and National Insurance Contributions (usually Class 2 and also possibly Class 4, depending on profit made) which are more than the Corporation Tax a Limited Company would pay.

Other disbenefits relate mainly to transport businesses where a sole trader may be the named holder of the 'O' licence and, should they go bankrupt, they will no longer be deemed to have 'good repute', which will bar them from having another 'O' licence for five years and, should they die, the 'O' licence can become invalid and the business may have to close, suffering whatever penalties may be imposed by failing to serve existing customers.

Key points you need to know

- The main benefits and disbenefits of being a sole trader.

Notes

....

....

....

Partnerships

Partnerships are actually governed by a very old Act of Parliament, which is still in force. However, there are no statutory formalities in forming a partnership; all that needs to happen is that 'two or more people operate a business with a view to returning a profit'. This means that two sole traders could actually operate as a partnership if they joined together to undertake some work, without them actually being aware that a 'partnership' had been formed. Because of this, and the associated dangers, anyone entering into an arrangement with another person(s) aimed at returning a profit should complete a 'Deed of Partnership', which will protect all the 'partners'. A Deed of Partnership should also be completed where anyone knowingly wishes to enter into a partnership with another individual.

A Deed of Partnership provides all stakeholders with details aimed at clarifying the degree of partnership involvement and the term of the partnership. (Many new partnerships opt for a provisional short term in order to see how the partnership is actually working before committing themselves to a longer term.)

The Deed of Partnership provides seven main items, including:

1 The names, addresses and other details of the partners.

2 The name under which the partnership intends to trade.

3 The level of funding each partner commits to the partnership.

4 The ratio of profits and losses that will be acceptable to the partners.

5 How the accounts will be recorded and retained.

6 A statement about individual partners being liable for any actions taken that were outside of their authority.

7 The intended duration of the partnership.

By recording these points the partners will be protecting themselves and each other in the event of any possible disputes or disagreements that may occur when a verbal agreement to form a partnership is used and there is 'nothing in writing'.

Once any partnership is operating all partners have duties, liabilities and rights. Some, or all, of these may be contained in the detail on the Deed of Partnership. However, where a Deed of Partnership is not drawn up these duties, liabilities and rights can be found in the old Partnership Act of 1890, and are still legally enforceable today.

Partners' rights and duties

- No fundamental or major change can be made to the business without the consent of all partners.
- No shares held by any partner can be transferred to another person (including another partner) without the approval of all the other partners.
- No new partners can enter the business without the approval of all the other partners.
- All partners must be permitted to participate in the management of the business.
- Any disputes are to be settled by a majority vote of all partners.
- Partners cannot draw salaries, they must draw dividends, which should be related to expected future profits.

Partners' liabilities

- The partnership, as a whole, must accept all and any liabilities incurred by any of the partners legally acting on partnership business.
- Any partner, acting outside the actual partnership business, who generates a profit is liable to pay the money to the partnership, unless otherwise agreed.
- Each partner is jointly liable for any debts incurred by the partnership business during any time that they were a partner.
- Where a partner cannot meet their share of any debt incurred by the partnership, the other partner(s) must make up that shortfall.
- If a partnership commits a civil wrong, a tort (or delict) can be brought in a civil court, against either the partnership business or any individual partner.

- For any liability incurred where a partner may be under the age of 18 (a minor) the liability must be accepted by the other partners.
- All partners have unlimited liability to the total of their 'personal wealth' unless an LLP is formed (see below).

Where a partner does not actually contribute to the running of an unlimited liability partnership but has provided funding for the partnership (for example, if a parent provides funds to set up a partnership), they are known as a 'sleeping partner'. Sleeping partners do not participate in the actual running of the business and neither do they take dividends based on profits. They are, however, fully liable along with all the other partners for any debts, should the partnership get into trouble.

Because unlimited liability partnerships are seen as something of a risk, some partnerships are established where the liability can be limited. These types of partnerships are often related to businesses providing support services such as auditing, accountancy and legal support.

These 'limited liability partnerships' are treated in a very similar fashion to limited companies, insofar that they fall under the control of Companies House (see below), except that they have LLP after their name and not Ltd, and the partners are referred to as 'members' not partners.

In these 'limited liability partnerships' any 'member' who had provided funds but took no active part in running the business, or received no form of profit from the undertaking, would also limit their liability, unlike sleeping partners in unlimited liability partnerships. This fact, the terms 'partner' and 'member' and the general limited or unlimited nature of liability, are what sets apart an unlimited liability partnership and a limited liability partnership (LLP).

In all partnerships, both unlimited liability and limited liability, every partner or member is treated as an agent of the partnership and, as such, has the duty to perform in line with the duties of an agent. In practice this means that they must act only within their authority and must always endeavour to perform their duties in a diligent manner. Failing to do either of these things will mean that it is the partner in question who will be liable for any liabilities caused by them and not the partnership as a whole.

Because most partnerships are subject to a definite term and some partnerships are formed for specific reasons, they often need to be dissolved. There are five main ways that this can happen and that you must understand. A partnership can be dissolved:

- if it would be against the law to carry on the partnership;
- on a date agreed for the partnership to cease;

- if all the partners agree that the partnership should finish;

- if a partner dies or becomes bankrupt;*

- when a judgement to dissolve the partnership is made by a court.**

---

* Where a partner dies or goes bankrupt the other partners may carry on the partnership, but a new Deed of Partnership will need to be drawn up.

** A court is able to dissolve a partnership if the application to dissolve it is made by one or more of the partners. The reasons behind such applications may be a major disagreement, one of the partners becoming too ill to carry on, poor profitability, actual losses incurred, or some other justifiable reason.

Clearly there are benefits in forming partnerships, not least the ability to carry out more work and joint funding and, in some cases, being able to limit liability, but because all partners have rights and liabilities for their actions these can sometimes be seen as constraints, or disbenefits.

Whilst it is a fact that many properly formed partnerships work, and work well, a lot depends on having a definitive Deed of Partnership to protect all concerned.

Key points you need to know

- The contents of a Deed of Partnership.

- Partners' rights, liabilities, sleeping partners.

- The difference between unlimited liability and limited liability partnerships.

- How to dissolve a partnership.

Notes

Against the law to carry on, on a date agreed to cease, if all parties agree to finish, dies or BANKRUPT, COURT JUDGEMENT.

Limited companies

We now come to the more complex area of plying for trade, the issue of forming a limited company. This is often done because a business wants to limit its liability but, as we will see, there are other reasons for wishing to form a company.

If we begin by examining how companies are able to limit their liability then things should become a little clearer. A company is able to limit its liability because a company is treated as an 'entity' in legal terms; just like a person, it is seen as an 'individual'. Because it is an 'individual' then it is a different 'individual' from the 'individuals' actually running the company. This means that they are not liable for the actions of the company. In turn, it means that if a company gets into financial difficulty, it is only liable up to the extent of its personal wealth (which is what the company is worth), thus enabling the directors to protect their own personal wealth. (Shareholdings by directors or other shareholders are seen as part of the company and would form a part of the wealth of the company.)

Whilst limited liability is certainly a key point, there are, as discussed above, many more reasons for wishing to form a company, such as:

- A company is regarded as a 'corporate body' and, as such, has a corporate identity that can often act to promote the company and give a positive image.

- A company can sell shares to gain additional funding and financial reserves.

- A company does not pay income tax as a sole trader would – it pays 'corporation tax', which is a business tax set at a lower limit than income tax.

- A company is able to own assets such as land, buildings and even vehicles.

- Because a company is an 'individual' it can also enter into legally binding contracts.

Whilst the above probably represent the main beneficial reasons for forming small companies, there are, as in life, some disbenefits. The main ones being that:

- The costs of setting up a company can be considerable in relation to the application and registration.

- Once formed there are ongoing re-registration and annual accountancy costs.

- Companies can be deemed to be guilty of both breaches of contract and some criminal acts, not least corporate manslaughter.
- Under UK law, the details, including financial details, are recorded at Companies House and are open to scrutiny by the public at large, naturally including customers and competitors.

Again these are just some of the main disbenefits and, in the case of a single person with no employees forming a limited company – which they are perfectly at liberty to do – the costs and administration might be seen to outweigh the benefits. The deciding factor is normally limiting liability to protect personal wealth.

When considering limited companies, there are two types of limited companies. These are: private limited companies and public limited companies. We now deal briefly with each in turn before we move on to forming companies.

Private limited companies (ltd)

A private limited company:

- must have at least one director;
- must have a registered name that ends in 'ltd';
- can only sell shares to family, friends or persons selected;
- cannot sell shares to the public (perhaps via the stock exchange);
- must declare that they do not sell shares to the public on their annual return (known as a Confirmation Statement) to the Registrar of Companies at Companies House;
- must produce annual accounts, which if they do not have a company secretary must be endorsed by a chartered accountant.

Public limited companies (plc)

Public limited companies are very similar to private limited companies, insofar as limited liability is concerned, but there are several major differences that you need to know. These are that plcs must:

- have a company name that ends in 'plc';
- have a minimum of two directors;
- have at least two members (who could be the directors);
- have a company secretary, in addition to the directors, who must hold a minimum qualification laid down in the Companies Act;

- have at least £50,000 (or euro equivalent) of authorized share capital to trade;

- must have issued at least the £50,000 (or euro equivalent) of share capital;

- must state that it is a plc on its Memorandum of Association (see below).

Most plcs are large companies that began life as private limited companies but, as they became more and more successful, decided to apply for plc status in order to sell shares to the public at large and attract investment to further expand. In reality, when they do this they become largely public owned, which as we will read later does have its own problems. However, before a private limited company can become a plc, a resolution needs to be passed by the directors/shareholders and an application made to the Registrar of Companies.

Once the change to plc has been granted the new plc is 'listed' on the stock exchange and able to trade shares. The 'listing' process requires all new plcs to provide the stock exchange with details and particulars of the company, which the stock exchange then publishes.

Key points you need to know

- The benefits and disbenefits of forming a limited company.

- The two types of limited companies.

- The similarities and differences between the two types of companies.

Notes

....
....
....
....
....
....
....
....
....
....

Company registration procedure

Now that we know the similarities and differences between ltd and plc, we need to examine how to begin the process of registration.

In order to begin the process of registration of either a private limited company or a public limited company an application form (form IN01) needs to be completed. Where a limited liability partnership is to be formed a form LL IN01 is to be used. All the necessary forms and help are available from Companies House in Cardiff (for companies in England and Wales), Companies House in Edinburgh (for companies in Scotland) or Companies House in Belfast (for companies in Northern Ireland). Companies House has a website enabling most applications to be done electronically. Further information and guidance pamphlets, which you may find useful in your studies, are available from www.companieshouse.gov.uk.

Whether the application is done electronically or by using the post, form IN01 acts as the application form to supply Companies House with certain details, including:

- the company name (which must not be either risqué or seem to be discriminatory in any way);
- the location of the company and the registered address of the office;
- the type of limited company (public or private, including details of whether or not any issue of shares has been made);
- details of any and all directors and other company officers (such as a company secretary), including people with significant control of the company (voting rights or more than 25 per cent of the shares);
- a Standard Industrial Classification (SIC) code which is a code Companies House uses to identify the type of business sector the company will belong to;
- a statement of capital and proposed shareholding by the directors;
- a statement declaring whether or not model Articles of Association are to be adopted when the company is registered (Articles of Association are outlined below).

In addition to completing form IN01, the applicant also needs to submit several other documents to be sent with it:

- Memorandum of Association

    A Memorandum of Association is a document containing statements from each person involved that they do actually intend to form a limited company and be a part of it. Where the applicants declare that there will be share capital, each of the applicants must also sign to agree to take at least one single share in the company, should it be formed. Once all the applicants involved have signed the Memorandum of Association it is ready to accompany the IN01.

- Articles of Association

   The Articles of Association also need to be completed and submitted. The Articles of Association form what is commonly called 'The Company Rule Book' because they explain how the company will operate and how it will be managed. Many applicants choose to use a 'model' set of articles, which simplifies matters and ensures that the declared articles are seen as suitable by the Registrar of Companies.

The Articles of Association are said to define the 'objects' of the proposed company. In this respect the 'objects' refer to things such as:

- the type of business that is being proposed and what sector of business it will operate within;
- details of the directors;
- how the directors will be rewarded;
- the extent of authority of the directors;
- the types of shareholders;
- the rights of shareholders;
- how the required annual general meetings will be managed.

Once the IN01 and these two documents are completed there are two additional forms that need to be filled in before the application can be submitted:

- form 10, which provides details about the location (address) of the company's registered office;
- form 12, which is a statutory declaration stating that all the conditions laid out in the Companies Act have been met in relation to the application to form a company.

Once all these five documents – IN01, Memorandum of Association, Articles of Association, form 10, form 12 – have been completed they can be submitted along with the fee to Companies House. However, the company cannot actually legally trade until Companies House has issued a Certificate of Incorporation giving details of the company name, company number and date of incorporation. Once the company has this it is then able to trade. It must not trade, under any circumstances, until this Certificate of Incorporation has been received.

If the application relates to the formation of a plc and not a ltd company, then once the Certificate of Incorporation has been issued, a plc still cannot trade until a Trading Certificate – confirming that the company does in fact have at least £50,000 (or euro equivalent) of issued share capital – has also been issued. Once able to trade, a company is said to be a registered company. This means that they need to maintain a register of certain information.

Note: During the time that an application to form a plc is being processed it is normal for the company to develop a prospectus. A prospectus is usually a brief history of previous employment or positions held of any of the directors, and how potential investors may invest in the company if they wish to do so. A prospectus needs to be approved by the Financial Conduct Authority (FCA) before it can be used, which is why they are usually drawn up by brokers or underwriters.

Company stationery

Once registered and trading there is also a requirement under the Companies Act that requires companies to have company stationery that is in a set format. To meet this format requirement all registered companies must have stationery that provides details of:

- the address of the company registered office;
- the registration number of the company held at Companies House;
- whether the company is registered in England, Wales, Scotland or Northern Ireland.

Note: Whilst there is no requirement under the Companies Act for details of directors to be included on company stationery, the Companies Act does state that if a single director puts their name on it then all the directors must also provide their names.

The company register

All trading companies are required to keep a register relating to company activity. This is another statutory requirement under the Companies Act. The register must contain certain items of information including:

- the dates that each person purchasing shares became a shareholder;
- the names, addresses and occupations of each shareholder;

- the number and types of shares held by each shareholder;
- full details of how shares can be transferred;
- full details of any mortgages, debentures or charges against the company.

Along with the register, and often incorporated into it, every company needs to maintain:

- a set of company accounts;*
- a register of directors (see below);
- a book of annual general, and/or extraordinary meeting minutes.

---

* Company accounts need to be submitted annually to Companies House and retained by a ltd company for a minimum of three years and by a plc for a minimum of six years. Also, as we will see later, all companies registered for VAT must retain records (accounts) for a minimum period of six years.

Key points you need to know

- The registration process.
- The forms used and their purpose.
- The differences between ltd and plc when registering and before trading.
- Accounts procedures.

Notes

FORMS - INO1 - MEMORANDUM of ASSOCIATION - ARTICLES of
ASSOCIATION - FORM 10 - FORM 12

Having covered the application, registration and some of the early trading requirements, we now need to move on to the statutory rules and duties, under the Companies Act, relating to the people who manage and/or own companies: directors, company secretaries, auditors and shareholders. We begin with company directors.

Directors' roles and duties

A company director who is properly identified on the Memorandum of Association or voted into post at an annual general meeting (AGM) has certain obligations towards the company. These roles make them:

- accountable to the shareholders for the proper and efficient running and performance of the company;
- responsible for the ethical and professional performance of the company;
- responsible for the safety of their employees;
- required to use their skills and act in good faith at all times;
- responsible for ensuring that the employees' interests are properly safeguarded;
- bound not to make any secret or illegal/unfair profit;
- banned from 'insider dealing';*
- not allowed to borrow money, as a loan, from the company;
- deemed liable for any negligence by the company.

---

* In general terms, insider dealing is where a person uses confidential information from inside a business to buy or sell shares for personal gain.

This list really ensures that directors have a 'duty of care' in relation to the company they are 'directing'. However, if they are sued for any breach of duty, the onus is on the prosecution to prove that it was the director who was responsible and, if so, it is the director and not the company who can (sometimes) be personally liable.

In addition to the top-level list of directors' responsibilities there are certain specific duties they need to perform to comply with the Companies Act. These duties are mainly aimed at ensuring that directors make considered judgements in relation to business management, such as considering:

- any long-term consequences of any proposed decisions;
- the impact of the company's operations, on both the community and the environment as a whole;
- how their actions may impact upon the interests of the company's employees;
- the need to maintain effective business relationships with suppliers, customers and other stakeholders;
- the need to maintain a positive image in relation to standards of business conduct;
- the need to ensure their actions are fair to all concerned.

As mentioned earlier, every company needs to maintain a directors register. The directors register must provide details of:

- every director's full name (including any former names);
- every director's date of birth;
- every director's nationality;
- every director's personal address;
- every director's business address;
- every director's declared occupation.

The directors register is required to be made available for viewing to company members (without any charge) or to anyone who wishes to view it (for payment of a fee). The register will normally be kept at the registered office of the company but, in any case, its location must be made known to the Registrar of Companies. The Registrar of Companies must also be informed if any details within the directors register are changed, altered or amended.

Company secretaries

Whilst there is no requirement for a private limited company to appoint a company secretary, all plcs must have a company secretary and, as mentioned earlier, company secretaries are also bound by details contained within the Companies Act. In cases where a private limited company does choose to appoint a company secretary, the duties of the secretary are:

- to ensure that, at all times, the company is able to meet the requirements of all legislation, including the Companies Act;

- to compile and maintain all company registers;
- to organize all company meetings and keep a record of the minutes;
- to ensure that the records of meetings and any resolutions passed are available for inspection at the company's registered office;
- to ensure that the records of meetings and any resolutions passed are retained for 10 years.

In the case of plcs only, the company secretary must also:

- be suitably qualified in an appropriate profession (such as being an accountant, barrister, solicitor or chartered secretary); or
- be able to demonstrate sufficient prior experience as a company secretary.

Let's now move on to the role of an auditor because, unlike directors, company auditors are totally independent from the company.

Auditors

Auditors are appointed at the AGM by a vote held by the shareholders. The company auditor has a duty to provide an independent report to inform the shareholders of the true financial position of the company. The auditor actually has a duty to the shareholders, and not to the directors or the company itself, to carry out this task.

In cases where the company is a plc or a private limited company with a turnover exceeding £6.5 million, as well as having to produce an independent report, the auditor must also be totally independent from the company concerned.

Having now examined the people involved with companies and their roles and responsibilities, and having mentioned AGMs, we need to examine briefly the role of an AGM as this is also included in your syllabus.

Annual general meetings

The main purpose of an AGM (other than it must take place under the Companies Act) is to allow the directors to give a summary of performance and a view towards the next 12 months, and for the auditor to present his/her findings to assembled shareholders.

As a part of the AGM, the company accounts (balance sheet; and profit and loss account) will also be presented before being 'signed off' by the directors. (A single director can sign off for a ltd company but at least two directors need to sign off for a plc.)

The AGM is also an opportunity for shareholders to raise issues and, if necessary, to take votes on proposed courses of action, up to and including reappointing or changing the auditor for the following year, replacing directors or even closing the company itself.

At an AGM, shareholders are normally allowed to vote either by post or in person, but some companies do accept proxy voting, providing that proper authorization is given to allow the proxy to vote on another person's behalf.

Once again we have mentioned shareholders and so, as before, it is only correct that we now discuss the issues you need to know in relation to shareholders and shares.

Shareholders

People who buy shares are known as shareholders and usually (if they retain the shares) these shareholders will expect to receive an annual 'dividend' (either a cash sum or some free additional shares) in return for their financial support of the company in question.

Because of their support in a company, shareholders, as we know, are able to vote at the AGM and have sufficient power to completely overturn any plans or strategic aims of a company if they feel it is not in their best interest. This often makes for a volatile relationship between shareholders and directors seeking things such as change or additional investment.

As we will see later, the shareholders also have considerable power when a failing company has an option to close.

Shares

Shares in companies are bought by people seeking to invest in the company and are traded by people seeking to buy at one price and sell at a higher price. Each 'share' actually represents a 'share' of the total value of the company.

The total amount of shares any company may offer for sale is known as the company's total share capital. This sum is initially declared on the IN01 when the company is first registered and needs to be amended if it is raised or lowered. In addition, before the total share capital can be changed all the existing shareholders must have agreed that this is what they want to happen (this may well be agreed by a vote at the AGM, for instance).

Shares do differ in their nature. We see some shares that are seen as long-term, relatively safe investments: for example, shares in large institutions such as banks and Royal Mail. Other shares are more volatile, such as shares in future markets or new technology. These shares may return much higher dividends but the associated risks are much greater – there is even a chance that these shares may even 'crash and burn', which would result in the shareholder losing everything.

Whilst there are obviously different types of shares, the two main types that we need to focus on are known as 'ordinary shares' and 'preference shares'.

Types of shares

Ordinary shares are the type of shares that are usually held by ordinary shareholders. They not only give the shareholder the right to vote at the AGM but they also offer the chance of a dividend. The dividend payable will normally be related to a percentage of the total profit of the company. This means that if the company does well the dividend can be high but, if the company fails to perform as expected, the dividend can be much lower than expected, and the holder of ordinary shares will get very little. Should a loss be reported, the ordinary shareholder may get nothing at all. (This is often the start of action by shareholders to replace some, or all, of the management team at the following AGM.) Because of the risk that a shareholder may not be rewarded as expected, they can select to purchase preference shares.

Preference shares are seen as a 'lower risk' option for shareholders. Preference shares pay out a fixed dividend irrespective of the level of profit of the company. However, like ordinary shares, there may be no dividend if the company fails to make any profit and a loss is reported. Because there is less risk, providing some sort of profit is reported, preference shareholders usually have no voting rights at the AGM. (Please note that this is 'usually' the case but, where preference shareholders do have voting rights, it must be clearly declared in the company 'Rule Book', the Articles of Association.)

As a summary statement, and not an absolute rule, the two types of shares give shareholders different options to meet their needs, with more aggressive, active shareholders mainly selecting ordinary shares whilst older, less active investors may find the lower-risk preference shares more to their liking.

Key points you need to know

- Directors' roles.

- The content of a directors register.

- The criteria to be a company secretary.

- An auditor's role.

- The purpose of an AGM.

- The rights of shareholders.

- The difference between ordinary and preference shares.

Notes

....

....

....

....

....

....

....

....

....

....

As we get towards the end of this section on commercial law we can see that it has tried to follow a progressive pattern from types of businesses, application, registration and operation of limited companies, shareholding and share types. We need to finish this section by now looking at how businesses close down, either voluntarily, or when compulsory closure is the only option. We also briefly examine the roles of certain individuals involved in the closure of companies.

Business closures

First let's look at the process of voluntarily closing down a small business such as a sole trader or an unlimited liability partnership. When an individual ceases trading they either do so voluntarily (simply ceasing trading or by an IVA) or go bankrupt.

Individual voluntary arrangements

In cases where creditors agree, an individual voluntary arrangement (IVA) can be made. This is an agreement between the creditors and the sole trader that allows the sole trader to pay their creditor debts by regular payments over a period of time until the debts are cleared. The sole trader may carry on trading while this is being done.

The IVA must be arranged by an insolvency practitioner who contacts all the creditors and, providing creditors who are owed at least 75 per cent of the total debts agree, the insolvency practitioner calculates what the payments should be and the period of repayment. The sole trader then makes payments to the insolvency practitioner who passes the money on to the various creditors, including any creditors who did not actually agree to the IVA being implemented.

The insolvency practitioner is paid a fee for setting up the IVA and a fee for administering it. The insolvency practitioner also enters the IVA on the IVA Register, where it will stay for three months after all debts have been paid. Should the payments not be made as agreed, then the IVA will be cancelled and compulsory actions may follow.

Company closures

When a company ceases trading, the term used is that the company is 'wound up'. The winding up of a company can be either voluntary or compulsory but, where it is compulsory, some elements contained within the Insolvency Act come into play and, in all cases of winding up, the company will be completely deleted from the Companies House 'Register of Companies'.

There are three ways to wind up voluntarily:

- Members' voluntary winding up: this is where the shareholders pass a resolution calling for the voluntary winding up of a company that is still solvent. If this is accepted then the directors ask the Registrar of Companies for a 'Statutory Declaration of Solvency', which is filed by the Registrar. This declaration states that the company is able to meet all its liabilities and is still solvent but is simply requesting to be wound up. The company can then appoint a liquidator to oversee the winding-up process.

- Creditors' voluntary winding up: this is used in situations where a company is actually insolvent and cannot meet all its liabilities, and the directors will hold an extraordinary general meeting with all the creditors to make sure they are aware of the situation. Following this meeting the creditors will nominate a liquidator to oversee the winding up.

- In a similar way to an IVA, companies that are insolvent can use a company voluntary arrangement (CVA) to pay creditors over an agreed fixed period of time. A CVA also relies on creditors owed a minimum of 75 per cent of the total debts to agree to the arrangement. This is usually done by the insolvency practitioner calling a meeting of all creditors. Once the CVA has been agreed, the company is classed as 'solvent' and can carry on trading providing it makes the payments to the insolvency practitioner, as agreed. In cases where the creditors cannot agree, or payments are not made, then the company may – in the same way as an IVA – go into voluntary winding up or compulsory winding up.

As the voluntary winding up of a sole trader business and the three methods of voluntarily winding companies up have been covered we must now examine the compulsory procedures.

Compulsory winding up

Most companies are compulsorily wound up because they become insolvent (they cannot pay all their debts). In relation to being unable to pay debts, the Insolvency Act states that where a company cannot pay its debts, non-payment can be claimed if a company fails to pay a creditor who is owed more than £750 and who has made a statutory demand for payment, but has not been paid to their 'reasonable satisfaction'. As you might imagine, this type of definition could be easily used by organizations such as banks, loan companies, building societies and financial institutions. Where this is the case, the courts will appoint a liquidator to manage the disposal of company assets and distribute whatever funds can be raised (see below).

Other reasons for compulsory winding up tend to be linked to the Registrar of Companies who can compulsorily wind up a company that either does not trade within 12 months of being registered or that ceases to trade for a period of 12 months. In addition, compulsory winding up applies to any plc where the number of members falls below two and any plc that has its Trading Certificate withdrawn or withheld.

As we now know, liquidators are appointed to dispose of company assets where a company is compulsorily wound up. Their roles and responsibilities form part of the syllabus and are outlined below.

Liquidators' roles and responsibilities

Liquidators (known as licensed insolvency practitioners) are appointed by courts and have their duties laid out in the Insolvency Act. An appointed liquidator not only has the task of selling whatever assets the company may have but they must also follow a clearly laid out set of priorities when it comes to distributing the funds that are raised. As you may note, these do tend to favour certain sectors of the business and public sector, whilst somewhat disadvantaging the smaller investors who can probably least afford to lose monies. However, the priorities are below:

1 The liquidator's fees and any expenses incurred.

2 Secured creditors (where assets were purchased with a secured loan).

3 Preferential debts (VAT, PAYE and outstanding employee wages).

4 Unsecured debts (trade creditors supplying fuel, tyres, etc).

5 Debts with a 'floating charge' (typically things like bank overdrafts).

6 Shareholders (usually preference shareholders receiving payment before the ordinary shareholders).

It is worth noting that if the shareholders, who are the lowest priority, get paid in full then the company would not have been insolvent in the first place, as all debts are paid! In any case, once all the recoverable funds have been distributed the liquidator must then apply to the court for the company to be dissolved and for him/her to be released from their term as liquidator.

Summary

This section on commercial law may appear to be somewhat complicated but it is a part of the syllabus that you are required to know and an important part should you be considering starting a business, forming a partnership or forming a registered company. In the next chapter we move on to cover the social aspects of business under social law.

Key points you need to know

- Members' and creditors' voluntary winding-up processes.
- IVA and CVA procedures.
- Reasons for compulsory winding up.
- Liquidators' roles and payment priorities.

Notes

....
....
....
....
....
....
....
....
....
....

Self-test example questions

OCR-type questions (multi-choice)

1 Which of the following are said to be a disbenefit of operating as a sole trader?

   a As a sole trader you can never form a limited liability partnership.

   b As a sole trader you still require an external nominated transport manager, other than yourself.

   c As a sole trader you are required to declare yourself as a director of the business and fulfil the duties of a director.

   d As a sole trader you cannot limit your liability and if you go bankrupt you can lose everything 'up to the limit of your personal wealth'.

2 A company voluntary arrangement (CVA) is an arrangement to:

   a Pay creditors who are owed a minimum of 75 per cent of the total debts over an agreed period of time.

   b Pay creditors over a flexible period of time, providing that the creditors are owed at least 50 per cent of the total debts.

   c Pay creditors who are owed a minimum of 90 per cent of the total debts over an agreed fixed period of time.

   d Pay creditors over a flexible period of time while the insolvency practitioner seeks agreement from Companies House to pay creditors at least 60 per cent of all the outstanding debts.

OCR case study-type question

See past papers referred to in Chapter 1.

CILT-type questions (short answer)

1 Briefly describe the disbenefits of operating as a sole trader.

2 Briefly explain the term compulsory voluntary arrangement (CVA) and how it operates.

CILT-type question (long answer)

Discuss the different roles of a company auditor and a company secretary and explain the difference between ordinary shares and shareholders, and preference shares and shareholders.

Once you are happy that you can answer questions such as those above then please feel free to move on to the next chapter, which examines social law. However, if you are unsure or not certain about any of the content, or any of the 'key points you need to know' then please revisit until you feel that you have a full grasp of the material and what is required. Please also remember that these were only sample questions and both OCR and CILT can provide actual examples.

Social law

03

The syllabus requires that, in relation to social law, you need to be familiar with:

- the role and function of the various social institutions that are concerned with road transport, including trade unions; employment tribunals; the Advisory, Conciliation and Arbitration Service (ACAS); the Central Arbitration Committee (CAC); health and safety arbitrators; and employees' rights;

- the employers' social security obligations relating to current legislation in respect of health and safety; discrimination; employment protection; employment rights and more;

- the rules governing work contracts for the various categories of worker employed by road transport undertakings (form of employment contracts, obligations of the parties, working conditions and working hours, paid leave, remuneration, employment rights): full- and part-time employees; self-employed; agency staff; transfer of undertakings; remuneration and itemized pay statements; holiday entitlement; statutory payments; dismissal and unfair dismissal; notice to terminate employment; working time regulations and more;

- the rules applicable to driving time, rest periods and working time, and in particular the provisions of EU Regulation 165/2014 (this regulation replaced the old EEC Regulation 3821/85 in March 2015), Regulation (EC) No 561/2006, Directive 2002/15/EC and Directive 2006/22/EC, and the practical measures for applying those provisions; practical arrangements for implementing these regulations, including community regulations: the working week; driving time; breaks; daily and weekly rest periods; emergencies. Domestic hours' law: the working week; driving time; rest periods; emergencies. Tachograph legislation and operation: points of law; the records; driver and employer responsibilities; enforcement and inspection; calibration and sealing; malfunctions and more;

- the rules applicable to the initial qualification and continuous training of drivers (Driver CPC) and in particular those deriving from Directive 2003/59/EC.

Clearly, this is a large section of the overall syllabus, so we split it into two parts. First, we cover social institutions and employment issues. In the second part, we move on to address drivers' hours, tachographs and Driver CPC elements for which you will need the GV262, mentioned in the Introduction.

SOCIAL INSTITUTIONS

The term 'social institutions' applies to the many organizations and bodies that serve to represent people, protect their rights and keep them safe and free from exploitation. For the purposes of the syllabus we need to look at five industry-specific institutions, including:

- trade unions;
- the Advisory, Conciliation and Arbitration Service (ACAS);
- the Central Arbitration Committee (CAC);
- the Employment Appeal Tribunal;
- health and safety bodies.

Trade unions

Most people are well aware of the roles of trade unions, not least the role of representing their members in negotiations with employers and at times when members may feel aggrieved over work-related issues. The term 'recognized trade union' is also frequently used when referring to trade unions and all the 'recognized' part of the title means is that the trade union in question is 'recognized' by the employer as the one that the employer will negotiate with or deal with in relation to them (the trade union) representing the workforce. Members of other trade unions who may also work at a particular location will certainly enjoy any benefits brought by the recognized trade union but they will not be seen as 'recognized' trade union members by the employer.

It should be noted that, in many cases, trade union membership has diminished since the Conservative Government passed the 1992 Labour

Relations (Consolidation) Act, which effectively reduced the power of the trade unions particularly in relation to taking strike action and picketing premises. Whilst it did remove some rights of trade unions it also gave individual trade union members, and workers not wishing to belong to a trade union, rights and choices, not least by the abolition of the 'closed shop'. The term 'closed shop' referred to workplaces where only members of a certain union could be employed and non-union members could not be employed.

The 1992 Act also reaffirmed rights, and gave new rights to trade union members and trade union officials. We look at these in turn below.

Trade union members

Members of a recognized trade union are entitled to reasonable time off from work in order to properly participate in trade union activities, eg meetings or votes. However, this time off work does not have to be paid time off. There is no statutory right to payment for such time off although, in many cases, and in order to foster good relations in the workplace between employers and trade unions, small meetings and short periods of time off may be paid at the discretion of the employer.

Another right that members have is the right to take industrial action and to strike. The criteria for calling strikes were addressed in the 1992 Act and the position now is that before a strike can be called the trade union must notify the members that it intends to hold a ballot to decide on whether or not to take strike action. These ballots are normally postal ballots, although they must be open to scrutiny in order to ensure that they are fair and properly carried out. The ballot must normally go to at least 50 per cent of union members likely to take action. In the public sector, in addition to the 50 per cent at least 40 per cent of members entitled to vote must also endorse the proposal.

In order to be deemed fair, there needs to be a separate ballot at each individual depot or site and there must be a majority in favour or against strike action at every depot or site. Joint ballots where multi-site action is proposed are not allowed. If there is a vote for strike action the trade union must inform the employer, at least 14 days before the strike takes place, that it intends to take strike action, and the action itself must take place within four months of the date of the ballot.

Trade union officials

The 1992 Act also clarified the rights of trade union officials. In many ways it actually reduced many of their existing rights before that time. However, the 1992 Act did mean that recognized trade union officials, including shop stewards and area representatives, are now entitled to what is termed 'reasonable time off work with pay' in order to attend relevant training in trade union duties or roles and responsibilities and in order to carry out their designated trade union roles, including being involved in representing employees in negotiating with employers. In the cases of both training and representing employees the time off must only be taken to undertake activities that are appropriate to the particular trade union role or post.

Finally, in order to represent properly the members of a trade union, trade union officials from recognized trade unions have an absolute right to request, and be given, any information they require in relation to entering into 'collective bargaining'. This is where the trade union officials enter into bargaining with employers on behalf of their members. Providing the request is reasonable and relevant, should an employer refuse to give the required information the trade union concerned can make a complaint to the Central Arbitration Committee (CAC – see below). Should this happen, and the complaint is upheld, the employer will have to provide the information requested. The recognized trade union having a right to information is based on the right, under the 1992 Act, that the recognized trade union has to be able to represent its members from an 'informed position'.

In some cases, particularly where emotions may be running high, there may need to be a certification officer appointed to ensure that the employees are being fairly and honestly represented by a trade union that is not under the influence of the employers, any other trade union or any politically motivated body. The certification officer is responsible for ensuring that the trade union is in fact acting independently (termed an independent trade union) and is not being influenced in any way, for example in relation to discussions or intended industrial action.

Picketing

Should strike action, or other industrial action, actually take place the 1992 Act also defines the actions that can be taken in relation to the picketing of premises. This amendment in the Act was as a direct result of violence on picket lines, that is, the intimidation of workers not wishing to join in the industrial action concerned and the use of 'flying pickets' and 'secondary action'. Flying pickets were groups of workers and trade union members who travelled around different sites where action was taking place in order to represent the trade union concerned. However, they were somewhat 'taken over' by militant factions and became the catalyst for violence, confrontation and political extremism. Secondary action was where pickets would picket premises not directly involved with the dispute, such as suppliers and customers, in order to try to escalate the issues.

Although the right to picket has been a right enjoyed for many years, picketing must be peaceful and must not involve any criminal activity or wrongdoing such as threats, assault, trespass or damage to property. In order to ensure that picketing is now carried out peacefully a Code of Practice has been drawn up by the Department for Business, Innovation and Skills (BIS) clearly outlining how picketing should be conducted. It states three main principles that the picketing must comply with:

- Picketing can only be undertaken in 'contemplation or furtherance of a trade dispute'.

- Picketing can only be undertaken by a person 'attending at or near their own place of work'.

- Picketing should only be carried out to peacefully 'obtain or communicate information or peacefully persuade a person to work or not to work'.

The Code of Practice goes on to state that all picketing activity should be overseen and controlled by a competent official of the recognized trade union involved and that a 'picket line' should consist of no more than six people. The competent official must give their details to the police, carry a letter of authorization from the trade union and wear an armband or badge to enable them to be identified. The Code of Practice further allows recognized trade union officials to picket at sites where they may be visiting in order to represent or give advice and support to a member.

The BIS Code of Practice is available on the gov.uk website and is free to download, should any reader wish to learn more.

Key points you need to know

- What a recognized trade union actually is.

- The rights of trade union members.

- The rights of trade union officials.

- The role of a certification officer.

- The Picketing Code of Practice criteria and picketing controls.

Notes

_____

_____

_____

_____

_____

_____

_____

_____

_____

The Advisory, Conciliation and Arbitration Service (ACAS)

ACAS is a body that has been established in order to:

- help to improve the working relationship between employers and trade unions;
- act as a single point of contact when trade unions and employers cannot bring about a resolution to an industrial dispute without the need for some assistance or guidance;
- provide independent advice;
- provide up-to-date information;*
- provide high-quality training;
- provide information and advice on both industrial relations and other matters relating to personnel.

---

* ACAS produce their own Codes of Practice covering issues as far ranging as 'harassment at work' to guidance for employers, employees and trade unions considering starting negotiations in relation to a situation in the workplace.

In 2014, ACAS was given the task to review all cases where an employee, or employees, feel they have been unfairly dismissed and wish to be heard at an industrial tribunal, before the case can be heard by the tribunal (an industrial tribunal is an independent body that has powers to adjudicate on what are termed fair and unfair dismissal). This new role was specifically aimed at reducing the numbers of frivolous and/or unsound cases being presented at industrial tribunals, and now means that the cases that are heard are far more likely to be able to be resolved, one way or another.

The Central Arbitration Committee (CAC)

CAC is the third of the industrial social institutions that we need to briefly examine in order to fulfil the requirements of the syllabus.

The (some would say unfortunately termed) CAC is a committee used by ACAS in cases where the 'statutory' recognition of a trade union, or trade unions, cannot be agreed by the employer or trade union(s) in relation to collective bargaining. The statutory recognition is also required in cases where legal proceedings may be instigated.

CAC is a completely independent body that is able to adjudicate on this statutory issue. It is a body with statutory powers to do so and is a permanent body, not one that is comprised of part-time or casual members. In addition to its main role CAC has other statutory and non-statutory roles, including:

- determining the results of disputes between employers and trade unions that are in dispute over the disclosure of information for collective bargaining purposes;
- resolving issues relating to information and consultation arrangements;
- establishing and operating European Works Councils;
- dealing with complaints about the level of involvement of employees in certain types of companies;
- providing voluntary arbitration upon request in order to settle or mediate in industrial disputes.

Employment Appeal Tribunal (EAT)

The primary function of this social institution is to act as a tribunal to hear any appeals that are clearly linked to statutory issues that have arisen following a decision by an industrial tribunal, such as an employment tribunal (looked at later in this section).

It is tasked to try to identify if the industrial tribunal decisions were correct and legally based. EAT is not there to act as a second line of appeals against points that are undeniably facts, and will not normally re-examine issues of fact. On rare occasions EAT will also hear appeals relating to decisions made by CAC or by a certification officer.

Note: In order to reduce the burden on the taxpayer, who already funds ACAS and CAC, any person who wishes to go to either an industrial tribunal or an employment appeals tribunal must (since 2013) now pay a fee, upon application, before the tribunal will be called. It should also be noted that additional fees may be charged in some cases.

Key points you need to know

- The role of ACAS.
- The role of CAC.
- The role of EAT.

Notes

....

....

....

....

....

....

....

....

We now need to move on to our final industrial social institutions, which are the bodies that oversee our health and safety at work, and the pieces of legislation controlled by them, in order to satisfy the requirements of the syllabus. In addition, we also need to cover the roles and responsibilities that employees and employers have in relation to compliance with the various regulations.

Health and safety

Health and safety within the UK is the responsibility of the Health and Safety Executive and, to a slightly lesser extent, the Environment Agency. We will look at these organizations in turn.

The Health and Safety Executive (HSE)

The HSE is the highest authority in relation to overseeing health and safety within the UK. It is an executive that is comprised of people who have knowledge and experience from many industry sectors. They come together, as required, depending upon the subject matter, and are led by a full-time chair of the board with nine serving board members. Beneath that most senior board level is a management board with a chief executive who also has nine management board members. It is the HSE that formulates strategy and the longer-term aims and objectives in relation to health and safety.

There are eight main roles that the HSE performs. These are:

- preparing new health and safety regulations;
- ensuring that there is sufficient information on health and safety issues and that it is made available;
- carrying out investigations into health and safety issues;
- consulting with various other bodies and parties, as required;
- holding enquiries into health and safety issues, as necessary;
- administration of the various health and safety regulations;
- compliance with the health and safety regulations;
- enforcement of the compliance with health and safety regulations.

The role of enforcement falls mainly to HSE inspectors.

The health and safety inspectors

The enforcement staff of the HSE have many powers to enable them to enforce compliance with health and safety regulations and to investigate when things go wrong.

To enable them to do this, where they feel that there may be some sort of danger at a place of work they have the power to enter those premises at any time, day or night. Once they have entered they have the power to question staff, seal off areas and remove items. Following on from that, they have the power to carry out investigations and to take whatever actions may be necessary to maintain or restore proper standards of health and safety.

Whilst the HSE clearly has many powers, it also has two principal enforcement tools: prohibition notices and improvement notices.

Prohibition notices

Where an HSE inspector has reason to believe that whatever activities are being carried out may result in either a serious danger to health or a serious risk of injury, the inspector will issue a prohibition notice.

Prohibition notices come into force with immediate effect and effectively stop whatever activities were causing the problem. These activities are not allowed to recommence until the inspector is completely satisfied that the risks and dangers have been either reduced to an acceptable level or removed completely. In order to do this the inspector may need to make several visits to the premises concerned in order to check progress and/or standards.

Where the risk and dangers are not so severe the inspector has another tool at their disposal to bring about improvements.

Improvement notices

Improvement notices are issued by HSE inspectors to correct situations where they can clearly see that some sort of lesser breach of the regulations is occurring, and is likely to continue to occur.

The improvement notice clearly identifies the regulation, or regulations, that are being breached and gives the company responsible a reasonable time in which to correct matters. After the 'reasonable' time has been agreed the improvements must be carried out within that time. The minimum time-scale for such corrective action is 21 days. Once this time is complete, the inspector will revisit the company to inspect the improvements and, if they are satisfactory, will lift the improvement notice. It should be noted that an inspector who has issued an improvement notice is also able to visit the premises while improvements are in hand in order to check progress and standards of work, if necessary.

Note: If an organization appeals to the employment tribunal against an improvement notice within 21 days of the improvement notice being issued, the appeal acts to 'suspend' the notice until a decision on the appeal has been reached.

The final body we need to examine in relation to health and safety at work is the Environment Agency.

The Environment Agency (EA)

The first thing to note about the EA is that it works closely with the HSE, as many health and safety breaches have a direct impact upon the environment, not least pollution.

The second point to note is that the EA is regionalized. To that effect we have various regional bodies, including:

- the Environment Agency for England;
- the Scottish Environmental Protection Agency (SEPA);
- the Environment Agency Wales (part of Natural Resources Wales);
- the Northern Ireland Environment Agency (NIEA, part of the NI Department of the Environment).

All these bodies remain responsible to the Secretary of State for Environment, Food and Rural Affairs. The primary roles of all the regional bodies are to protect and improve the environment, to promote sustainable development within their areas of authority, and to work together to bring improvements and sustainability to all areas of the UK.

All the regional bodies mentioned above are actually enforcement and licensing agencies to oversee, control and enforce emissions and standards, monitor rates of discharges into water courses and to issue licences that may be required for hazardous activities such as asbestos removal and waste handling. In relation to transport operations, the regional bodies inspect, among other things, fuel bunkering facilities, lorry washing water filtering and recycling equipment, waste transfers and disposal – all areas where pollution could be an issue.

In a very similar fashion to HSE inspectors, all regional Environmental Agency inspectors have similar rights of entry and rights to scrutinize documentation and working practices, in order to build cases of non-compliance with the licensing provisions or in causing pollution. Such are the powers of EA inspectors that offences where prosecutions are brought can carry fines of up to £50,000 or one year in jail if the case is heard by a magistrate, or up to five years in jail if the case is heard in a Crown Court.

Key points you need to know

- The role of the HSE.
- The powers of HSE inspectors.
- The functions of the EA.

Notes

....
....
....
....
....
....
....
....
....

Having now looked at the various health and safety bodies we can move on to look at the principal of 'joint responsibility' regarding employees and employers and the different pieces of health and safety legislation that we need to include to ensure that we have full coverage of everything that is required by the syllabus, including how health and safety needs to be managed in the workplace in order to comply with the relevant legislation.

Employees' responsibilities

The Health and Safety at Work Act 1974 (HASAWA) clearly states that employees have a duty to cooperate with their employers in carrying out the requirements and ensuring compliance with the HASAWA 1974. This means that they must comply with such things as wearing safety equipment, if they are instructed to do so to carry out their tasks in a safe manner, and not ignore instructions in order to 'cut corners'. In short, they have a duty to take care of themselves.

Employees are also responsible for the health and safety of 'any other persons who may be affected by their acts or omissions'. This means not only work colleagues but also members of the public, if the work activities could put them at risk.

The employees' element of the 'joint responsibility' is fairly straightforward but the responsibility for employers is somewhat more demanding, as set out below.

Employers' responsibilities

In a similar way that employees have a responsibility for the safety of people who may be affected by their work activity, so an employer, in order to meet their general obligations towards other people, must ensure that they organize the work in such a way that no one is put at any risk to their health and safety. This means that the employer needs to post signs warning of risks or dangers; enforce the use of protective equipment; enforce the use of safety equipment on machinery, eg guards; and ensure that anyone entering the site or depot is aware of what is required in terms of health and safety during their time at that specific location. This often means ensuring that visiting drivers, agency staff, sales representatives and others are given a short safety brief or issued with a short 'site safety guide'. Clearly this is all aimed at ensuring that employers are also responsible for the health and safety of any person who may be affected by work activities.

Because of the complexity of trying to write legislation that can be applied right across industry as a whole, many of the employers' responsibilities are itemized in general terms. If there is a health and safety issue, employers need to be able to prove that they have been, or are being, what is called 'duly diligent'. Unfortunately, how diligent 'duly' actually is, is often left for the courts to decide.

What the regulations say is that, in relation to organizing work (as opposed to actually carrying out the work), in order to be deemed 'duly diligent' an employer must generally ensure that they have:

- only established and operate safe systems of work (normally by risk assessment);
- provided a safe place of work (this also includes when staff may be working away from base);
- a properly maintained healthy working environment (heat, air quality, etc);
- provided safe access and egress to and from the place of work (eg clear fire doors, gangways, exits);
- provided suitable arrangements and facilities for the safe storage, use, transport and handling of any substances used at work (particularly dangerous goods);
- provided safe equipment (eg plant, vehicles, machinery);
- provided welfare facilities (toilets, wash rooms, showers, as appropriate);
- ensured employees (including temporary employees) receive sufficient training to ensure safety in the workplace;
- ensured sufficient supervision is on hand at all times in order to ensure safety.

We can see that the general nature of these responsibilities makes compliance something that needs to be regularly reviewed as tasks change, technology changes, and new staff arrive. In addition there are other formal requirements that fall under the responsibility of the employer.

Other, more focused requirements include such things as a safety policy statement, safety representatives and safety committees.

Safety policy statement

Every employer with five or more employees must develop and be able to produce a safety policy. They must also ensure that the safety policy statement is clearly communicated to all staff and properly reviewed and kept current.

The actual policy can be developed by the company concerned in order to fit the related activities. However, it must:

- state the company's commitment in relation to the provision of a healthy and safe working environment;
- clearly state the company's commitment to ensure that the specific items in the general policy can be achieved;
- clearly commit to carrying out tasks aimed at risk reduction, including training;
- provide details of who are the nominated health and safety contacts within the company and how they may be contacted.

Once the company has a properly formed and communicated health and safety policy, employers may be further responsible for seeing that safety representatives and safety committees are established, if they are requested, or required.

Safety representatives and safety committees

Employers must discuss health and safety with any nominated safety representatives. In unionized workforces, safety representatives should be appointed by the recognized trade union but, in non-unionized workforces, safety representatives can be elected from within the employees. In either case, providing suitable notice is given to the employer, the employer must allow them to inspect the workplace and any relevant health and safety documentation. In cases of non-unionized workforces the employer must still consult with anyone who is properly appointed as a safety representative – they cannot avoid this responsibility.

In addition to safety representatives being drawn from either the recognized trade union or the general workforce by a simple vote, there are guidelines as to who is eligible to be nominated. These guidelines state that only persons who have been employed by the company for at least two years, or have two years' experience in similar employment, should be eligible.

Employers also have further responsibilities, including:

- giving safety representatives sufficient paid time off for them to carry out their safety roles effectively;
- giving safety representatives sufficient paid time off for them to receive health and safety-related training;
- upon the receipt of a written request from at least two safety representatives to form a safety committee; this committee must be formed within three months of the date of request.

We can now see how health and safety is managed and controlled and so we can move on, below, to look at the legislation itself. We will discuss in chronological order the 'main' legislation you need to know about for your examination and then discuss more minor areas of legislation, which although 'minor' are still regulations that must be complied with.

Key points you need to know

- Employees' responsibilities.
- Employers' responsibilities.
- Safety policy criteria.
- Safety representatives' criteria.

Notes

....

....

....

....

....

....

....

....

....

....

Health and Safety at Work Act 1974 (HASAWA)

The 1974 Act may seem somewhat dated but it is the foundation for a considerable amount of the health and safety requirements we have today – in fact, so comprehensive are the principles contained within it that it has been used as a guide and benchmark by many countries around the world when developing health and safety standards. We mentioned the term 'principles' above because although it is comprehensive it is often non-specific, which in reality is its major strength and also the reason why it does not take a great deal to address it. That said, it is no secret that health and safety legislation appears to be introduced at quite a rate, with much of it coming from the EU. This will become more obvious when we examine the relevant legislation later in this section.

The HASAWA applies to almost all employers and employees in the UK and, as we know, does so by establishing a system of 'joint responsibility', irrespective of the actual sector of industry to which it is being applied. It was introduced to reform and repeal old legislation and to introduce new standards for health and safety. It also brought 'persons affected by workers' activities' into scope and covered both safe working conditions and welfare standards for workers. Finally, it set standards for controlling emissions; and for controlling, storing, handling and transporting dangerous substances – if this sounds familiar it is because these items form the 'due diligence' criteria for employers and are very important.

The HASAWA was probably the most significant piece of domestic health and safety legislation (although there is other domestic legislation relating to certain aspects of work). However, since joining the EU, it is that body that has produced much of the legislation we have in place today. Not least, the 1992 EU Directive.

The 1992 EU Framework Directive

This directive was aimed at improving the health and safety in a number of work areas. Because it applies to several areas and was composed of several smaller directives, these are generally referred to as the EU daughter directives. These include:

- workplace;
- work equipment;
- manual handling;
- personal protective equipment (PPE);
- display screen equipment.

Workplace

This directive sets standards for things such as air quality, lighting, temperatures, hygiene and cleanliness and minimum dimensions for work areas. It was introduced alongside a Code of Practice that also covered and expanded these general areas to include:

- floor surfaces (eg non-slip);
- the provision of seating;
- toilet and washing facilities;
- the provision of drinking water;
- adequate breaks from workstations;
- the provision of changing rooms;
- the security of any items that need to be stored above in elevated positions;
- the safety of windows (eg standards of glass and prevention of falling out).

Work equipment

This daughter directive covers the actual provision and use of equipment used in the workplace. It is principally aimed at ensuring that all work equipment, including mechanical equipment and even hand tools, are in good condition and that their use has been properly assessed in relation to any hazards or risks that may exist when the equipment is either being used, stored or not in use.

Note: Whilst risk assessments (looked at shortly) were not formally introduced until 1999, this daughter directive made it quite clear that using equipment that was not in good condition would be a contravention.

Manual handling

The 1992 daughter directive covering manual handling acts to ensure that 'as far as is reasonably practicable' employers do not allow manual handling tasks where an employee could be injured or placed at risk of injury. It was also introduced in order to reduce the levels of injuries caused by poor techniques and thereby reduce the cost to industry as a whole, for example with regard to time off, sick pay and temporary cover.

Where any manual handling tasks cannot actually be eliminated then they must be kept to an absolute minimum and, if at all possible, the employer must 'as far as is reasonably practicable' replace the manual handling element of the work with machines or equipment. In order to do this, there must be a proper assessment of the potential for injury of the task, and proper training and assessment of any equipment brought in to replace the manual handling task.

Personal protective equipment (PPE)

In relation to PPE, the daughter directive is quite simple – it requires:

- that it must be supplied if necessary and replaced when damaged or worn out;
- that employees issued with PPE must report any damage or loss of PPE to the employer;
- that all PPE must comply with any relevant standards of design or safety level;
- that it must be fit for purpose, insofar that it is in good condition and is able to be used to protect, as required;
- that PPE is always only ever used as a 'last resort' to protect an employee after assessing that the task it relates to cannot be changed or replaced.

Display screen equipment

In relation to using display screens, this daughter directive applies to workers who use screens for periods of more than one hour, each working day, or nearly each working day, and that workstations that have screens are assessed to eliminate risks or, if they cannot be eliminated, that they are – as far as possible – reduced in number.

In order to do this the employer may need to reduce any glare from the screens, ensure that there is adequate lighting, provide suitable 'posture friendly' seating and increase the sizes of fonts used for work documents.

Employers must also ensure that staff using screens are properly trained in their use and allow them regular breaks away from display screens in order to refresh their posture and rest their eyes. In respect of eyesight, employers must provide guidance on eyesight issues to staff and provide eyesight checks on a regular basis, if any employee requests so.

The Management of Health and Safety Regulations 1999

We have referred to the 1999 regulations already in this section. These are UK regulations that added specific requirements to the older 1974 Act and also formalized some things such as standards of assessing risks in the workplace following the introduction of the 1992 daughter directives.

The 1999 regulations apply to a total of 10 key areas of work, including activities and employees. These include:

- risk assessment;
- duties of employees;
- employee information;
- training;
- competent person;
- health surveillance;
- temporary staff;
- health and safety arrangements;
- emergency procedures;
- emergency services.

The items above are in no particular order, but as risk assessment has been mentioned perhaps that is as good a place as any to begin looking at the regulations in a little more detail.

Risk assessment

In addition to protecting people from work activities, as per the 1974 Act, the 1999 regulations stipulate that all employers (and the self-employed) must complete risk assessments for all their work activities involving employees and any other person who may be affected by work activities. These risk assessments must follow a certain format, be undertaken as ongoing activities, be reviewed when work activities or equipment changes and, in workplaces where there are five or more employees, any risk assessment that demonstrates any significant risk or hazard needs to be recorded and a record retained by the employer.

Many organizations now involve ordinary staff at work in risk assessment, by including their thoughts and feedback on tasks they perform daily in order to ask them if they think that tasks can be carried out more safely.

The HSE is the principal UK body that sets the standards for risk assessment. It produces a guide for employers that lays out the actions and sequence of actions deemed necessary to constitute a proper risk assessment. The guide, produced by the HSE, is free to download from the HSE website and is titled 'The Five Steps to Risk Assessment'. These steps are:

Step 1 – identify the hazards to workers.

Step 2 – decide who might be harmed and how they might be harmed.

Step 3 – evaluate the risks and decide on what precautions need to be taken.

Step 4 – record your findings and implement any action points arising from them.

Step 5 – review your risk assessments regularly and update as necessary.

Duties of employees

As we know, all employees have a duty to 'take care of their own health and safety and the health and safety of anyone who may be affected by their activities'. This means that they must also comply with instructions given by the employer relating to safety matters, safety instructions or safe systems of work and to inform the employer of any matters where, for example, safety standards or equipment are possibly allowing a hazard to remain in the workplace.

Employee information

As employees must comply with safety instructions, employers also have a duty under these regulations to provide to their employees any information found when carrying out risk assessments. They also need to inform their employees of who carried out the assessment, when it was undertaken, what was found and what actions were taken to remove or lessen the hazard. This is normally made available upon request by safety representatives or other members of staff.

Training

It is a duty of an employer to ensure that all employees receive health and safety training when first joining a company and then every time that changes in the workplace introduce new risks that need to be managed. Some health and safety training must also be repeated at regular intervals in order to keep knowledge current and, at times, to maintain some sort of standard of competence (in the transport industry it might be noted that Driver CPC training covering health and safety and some dangerous goods training for drivers can act in this way).

Competent person

Even though safety representatives are not compulsory, all employers covered by the 1999 regulations must nominate a 'competent person' to ensure that health and safety rules and standards are being complied with and that there is a suitable system of control in place. The 'competent person' can be either an external 'expert' or a suitably knowledgeable employee. In the case of the self-employed, it is deemed that the self-employed person needs to be the competent person in order to take care of themselves and others who may be affected by their work activities.

Health surveillance

Employers must ensure that the health of workers exposed to certain risks is regularly monitored and that proper records of these types of health checks are kept. This type of surveillance would typically apply to workers working in sites where toxic materials, including asbestos, are being used.

Temporary staff

All temporary employees – regardless of whether or not they are at work as seasonal staff, are acting as temporary cover or are agency staff – must be made aware of the risks and hazards in the workplace and of any skills that they may need to possess in order to operate safely (including licences for forklifts). Where appropriate, all temporary staff must also be made aware of any health surveillance requirements that may be applicable to their work.

Health and safety arrangements

The 1999 regulations added to the general employers' duties under the older 1974 Act insofar that, in order to ensure they offer a safe place of work, it is necessary for six requirements to be met. These are:

- Have a planned system of risk assessments. They cannot be random.
- Have proper control of the implementation of actions agreed to improve safety measures.
- Monitor to see how effectively risks in the workplace are being controlled.
- Periodically review the entire health and safety management system.
- Develop an appropriate safety structure within individual organizations.
- Develop, and communicate to the workforce, effective emergency procedures. (This may require the procedures to be produced in different languages.)

Emergency services

Finally, the 1999 regulations also state that all employers must ensure that there are effective and operational lines of communication with all the emergency services and emergency service providers, as required. Typical service providers may include the St John Ambulance, mine rescue or even bomb disposal units.

Key points you need to know

- The principle of joint responsibilities under HASAWA.

- What the EU daughter directives cover.

- The 10 areas of the 1999 Health and Safety Regulations.

Notes

....

....

....

....

....

....

....

....

....

For the syllabus, we now need to look at some additional 'domestic' legislation related to health and safety, as questions are asked about this legislation. In particular, we need to look at:

- The control of hazardous substances (COSHH) regulations.
- The reporting of accidents/incidents regulations (RIDDOR).
- Regulations covering smoking in the workplace.
- Regulations covering first aid.
- Regulations covering fire safety.
- Regulations regarding corporate manslaughter.

- National Insurance regulations.
- Employers' liability insurance regulations.

COSHH

The main purpose of the COSHH Regulations 2002 is to eliminate, reduce and control exposure of workers to hazardous substances. In order to do that, the regulations also classify the nature or type of hazard. These are:

- very toxic;
- toxic;
- harmful;
- corrosive;
- irritant.

These different types of hazards apply to all substances and also things such as vapours or airborne dust.

Under COSHH there is still the issue of 'joint responsibility' insofar that the employees must comply with any rules aimed at keeping them safe from hazardous materials; however, the bulk of the responsibilities for COSHH lie with the employer.

First, the employer must make suitable and adequate assessments of any hazards, and hazardous substances, before any employee is exposed to them.

Second, the employer must eliminate the use of any hazardous substances wherever possible. If it is not possible, the employer must reduce and control any exposure and issue personal protective equipment (PPE) only as a last resort if there are no alternative ways of controlling exposure.

Third, the employer must provide information, instruction and training about any hazardous substances. This training must be seen to be 'appropriate' for the substances and the staff concerned.

Finally, the employer must monitor staff exposure to hazardous substances and keep records of the monitoring carried out. Under some circumstances (as mentioned earlier) health surveillance of the employees concerned may need to be required.

The Reporting of Injuries, Diseases and Dangerous Occurrences (RIDDOR)

RIDDOR is only applicable for certain accidents and incidents. Many minor accidents will not be covered by RIDDOR although all accidents, even minor ones, need to be recorded in an accident book.

The following types of accidents and incidents are the ones that need to be reported in order to comply with RIDDOR:

- fatal accidents;
- accidents resulting in major injury – loss of a limb, eye, finger or toe requiring more than 24 hours in hospital;
- accidents requiring seven consecutive days to be taken off work;
- dangerous occurrences – eg leaks of any toxic substance, structural collapse, crane loads falling;
- most incidents relating to occurrences with liquefied petroleum gas (LPG) or natural gas (NG);
- some work-related diseases – eg asbestosis, silicosis.

Whilst the Health and Safety Executive (HSE) is in overall control of RIDDOR it is 'operated' from the HSE Incident Contact Centre (ICC) located in South Wales. In order to make a report to the ICC there are two different options available depending upon the circumstances:

- For accidents where there is a fatality, a major injury or a dangerous occurrence, the incident has to be reported immediately by phone to the HSE Incident Contact Centre or online to the ICC through the HSE website and a written report must be received by the HSE within 10 days of the incident.
- For accidents causing more than seven days' incapacity for work, immediate notification to the ICC is not required but a written report is still required within 15 days, not 10 days as for fatal accidents.

It needs to be clarified that when speaking about seven days' incapacity for work that the seven days applies to seven days following the day of the accident and includes weekends and bank holidays, irrespective of whether or not the worker involved would have worked on any of those days – the issue being that they could not work had they been asked to do so.

Because the ICC is only contactable by telephone or online, if a written hard copy report is required to be sent to the HSE then it needs to be sent to: RIDDOR REPORTS, Health and Safety Executive, Redgrave Court, Merton Road, Bootle, Merseyside, L20 7HS.

The details and reports of all accidents that are reported under RIDDOR must be retained for a minimum period of three years. And, although not reportable, RIDDOR also requires accident books to be used to record all minor accidents. Once an accident book is completely full it too must be retained for a minimum of three years.

Before we leave the rules of RIDDOR, it should be noted that where a reportable accident or incident involves a goods vehicle operating on the highway the Traffic Commissioners (TCs) must also be informed.

Smoking in the workplace

The Smoke-free (Premises and Enforcement) Regulations 2006 introduced the UK to a new raft of legislation. This 'no smoking' legislation applies to almost every 'enclosed' and 'substantially enclosed' public place and workplace:

- Premises are considered 'enclosed' if they have a ceiling or roof and (except for doors, windows or passageways) are wholly enclosed.

- Premises are considered 'substantially enclosed' if they have a ceiling or roof, but have an 'opening' in the walls, which is less than half the total area of the walls. The area of the opening does not include any type of door, window or fitting that is capable of being opened or closed.

Because of the two definitions above, it is now an offence to smoke indoors in a public place or a place of work and 'No Smoking' signs must be posted at the entrance to every building affected by this ban.

The regulations also apply to vehicles and vehicle cabs that are deemed to be 'places of work'. Within these 'smoke-free' vehicles an approved 70-millimetre diameter, 'No Smoking' sign must be visible in every compartment or cabin where people may be carried.

Contravention of the No Smoking Regulations results in different actions depending upon the type of contravention. Typically it involves:

- Fixed penalty notices for employees smoking in a place of work. However, if taken to court it can result in heavier fines being levied.

- Fixed penalty notices being issued to employers who fail to post 'No Smoking' signs when they are required. This too can result in heavier fines if taken to court.

- Fines being handed out to any person who is in a position to control smoke-free premises and fails to do so.

Because the fixed penalty notices above are classed as 'graduated' fixed penalties, the actual amount of the fixed penalty payment will vary according to the severity and circumstances.

Note: Since 1 October 2015 drivers who drive private cars in England and Wales, and have children under the age of 18 as passengers, can now also be fined £50 for smoking in the vehicle. In Scotland the fine is £100.

Before leaving the Smoking at Work Regulations we also need to note that e-cigarettes (personal vaporizers and electronic nicotine delivery systems) currently fall outside of the scope of the No Smoking Regulations above, but employers are advised by the HSE that they need to have a set policy in relation to their use at work and to consider other non-smoking employees as a part of that policy. This advice needs to be carefully followed as e-cigarettes are now licensed medicines and it is further expected that additional legislation will accompany this change.

First aid

First aid is covered by the Health and Safety (First Aid) Regulations 1981. These regulations, along with a complementary employers' guide to first aid in the workplace, ensure that, 'as far as is reasonably practicable', adequate and appropriate first aid equipment is provided. Once again the term 'as far as is reasonably practicable' crops up, leaving the actual interpretation up to the individual employer and making it quite difficult for many employers to be confident that they have gone 'as far as is reasonably practicable' in relation to satisfying the regulations.

What we do know is that the HSE feels that employers should train a minimum qualified first aid-trained staff to a ratio of 1:50 for normal (low-risk) work activity and that the term 'adequate and appropriate first aid equipment' means that employers should provide first aid kits in premises and, if appropriate, in vehicles and also provide, for example, fire extinguishers, fire hose reels and fire blankets as appropriate.

Fire safety

Since the introduction of risk assessments there is now no requirement for organizations to display a fire safety certificate for places of work. However, the risk assessments relating to fire safety must be carried out by a person deemed competent to do so and the organization must act on any recommended fire safety precautions and procedures that the competent person recommends following the risk assessment(s). The risk assessment(s) must also consider site visitors such as temporary staff, suppliers and the general public.

The local fire service, although no longer in charge of certification, will generally oversee and, if required, enforce compliance with the legislation. In so doing they will consider three major areas of fire safety:

1 Safe access and egress from buildings and areas in the event of a fire.

2 The appropriate numbers and types of notices, instructions and signs relating to a fire and the location and use of any fire equipment.

3 The operational effectiveness of any fitted fire detection or fire-fighting equipment on the premises.

Corporate manslaughter

Corporate manslaughter may not immediately seem to be a health and safety matter but, where employees lose their lives whilst at work, there are now regulations enabling the organization itself to be prosecuted. Before this law was introduced it was impossible to charge an organization for the manslaughter of an employee; only individuals could be charged with manslaughter, and in large companies it is always almost impossible to identify a single individual who was responsible. This law now means that any organization that causes the death of an employee through having ineffective safety standards, or has work practices that are not properly managed and a death results, is deemed to have failed in its duty of care to the individual concerned and, as such, can be prosecuted for the individual's manslaughter.

In Scotland the term 'culpable homicide' is used to describe this type of offence.

Other legislation

The different items of legislation above are only a sample of the complete range of legislative compliance that accompanies business operations. In addition, we must also consider areas such as:

- Noise, where the 2005 regulations require employers to carry out risk assessments, reduce noise levels as far as possible, provide information for staff and provide hearing protection to workers.

- Lifting Operations and Lifting Equipment Regulations (LOLER), requiring trained operatives, safe systems of work and periodic inspections and testing of equipment.

- Regulations covering compliance relating to electricity in the workplace, health and safety information, working at height and control of vibration.

National Insurance (NI)

National Insurance (NI) is a part of the payments made by employers to Her Majesty's Revenue and Customs (HMRC) to arrive on a specific nominated day within the following month. The collective term for all the 'stoppages' is 'employee contributions' and NI is one of these.

NI payments made by employers vary depending upon the amount the individual employee concerned earns and whether or not the employee works for a single, or several, employers.

The self-employed also have to pay NI but they have two options of what to pay:

- They can pay Class 2 contributions. Class 2 contributions can either be paid as part of an individual's Self Assessment tax bill or paid monthly by direct debit as a set contribution for every week the self-employed person carries out self-employment. They provide a minimal level of National Insurance such as a state pension, access to the NHS and, if applicable, the right to Employment and Support Allowance (ESA).

- They can pay Class 4 contributions. Class 4 contributions do vary according to the profit made by the self-employed person and are collected at the same time as the income tax payments are made. Class 4 contributions give the individual concerned the right to be eligible for a much broader range of benefits than are available under Class 2.

Employers' liability insurance

The final piece of domestic legislation we need to examine before we move on to employee rights is the legislation that ensures that employers take out employers' liability insurance to insure their workforce against injuries or death at work. In order to do this, employers must take out insurance with a minimum cover of £5 million.

Should they fail to do so or fail to display a copy of the certificate of insurance in the workplace they can be prosecuted. For failure to take out the insurance the fine is £2,500 for every day the business trades without insurance; for failure to display the certificate the fine is £1,000 for every day it was not visible. Whilst these figures are the maximum allowed under the regulations they are considerable amounts if contraventions have happened over a long period of time.

Key points you need to know

- Classes of hazardous substances under COSHH.

- Employers' responsibilities under COSHH.

- Types of accidents, reporting procedures and time off work criteria under RIDDOR.

- Rules and penalties for smoking at work.

- First-aider ratio.

- The main criteria for fire safety compliance.

- Where corporate manslaughter can be applied.

- The difference between employers paying NI and self-employed NI.

- The purpose of employers' liability insurance and associated penalties.

Notes

....

....

....

....

....

....

....

....

....

....

Now that we have covered the syllabus requirements for health and safety and employer compliance, we can again move on to now look at the rights of employees, including temporary workers, agency staff, self-employed workers, part-time workers and full-time workers.

Rights of employees

The different categories of workers, as noted above, share many common rights, although there are also some variations that we need to note as we go along. In particular, for this qualification we need to look at employee rights in relation to:

- terms of employment;
- working time;
- itemized pay statements;
- guarantee payments;
- payments and the minimum wage;
- statutory sick pay (SSP);
- employee involvement;
- minimum periods of notice;
- grievance and discipline;
- fair and unfair dismissal;
- redundancy;
- public duties;
- flexible working;
- maternity rights;
- paternity rights;
- parental/dependants' rights;
- provisions for time off;
- medical suspension.

Although it may seem like quite a long list, we do need to examine each one in turn in order for you to be properly prepared for your examinations.

Terms of employment

Because the law states that every employee must be given sufficient information in order for a legally binding contract of employment to be formed, employers must give employees written details (referred to as particulars) of employment. They must issue these particulars within two months of the employee commencing employment.

The statutory requirement is that the employer cannot discriminate against different types of employees. This means that every employee, either full-time or part-time, must be given particulars covering the following:

- the identity of the parties concerned (normally the employer and the employee);

- a brief job description and a job title;

- starting date of employment;

- a location, or locations, of where work will be carried out;

- a pay scale and the method and intervals of payment;

- working hours;

- holiday entitlement and sick pay arrangements;

- any reference to any previous employment that will count, under the transfer of undertakings (protection of employment) regulations (TUPE),* in relation to it counting as previous continuous employment;

- pension terms and conditions;

- the required period to give notice;

- the organization's grievance and disciplinary procedures;

- should the employee be promoted, or change roles, then the employer has a maximum period of 28 days in which to reissue new particulars of employment to reflect the new roles.

---

* TUPE protects employees from losing 'seniority' or length of service by making them entitled to claim for time spent in continuous employment with an employer when a company is taken over by another company and by ensuring that their original terms and conditions are protected.

TUPE is a complicated area of legislation but, in general terms, if an employee has a minimum of six months working for an employer and the job changes between two firms, a TUPE will be said to have occurred. It is also worth noting that TUPE is interpreted slightly differently in Scotland where the employees enjoy rather more flexibility in relation to the actual definition of a 'takeover'.

Working time

The Working Time Directive (WTD) mostly applies to non-mobile workers. It is referred to as the Horizontal Amending Directive (HAD). Whilst it mainly covers non-mobile workers it does also apply to mobile workers who are NOT working under EU Drivers' Hours Regulations (Regulation EC 561/2006).

In transport, the most common group of workers covered by the HAD are British domestic drivers (see below for the actual British domestic drivers' hours legislation). These are drivers who drive under 'domestic' rules and not EU drivers' hours rules and include drivers such as drivers driving goods vehicles not exceeding 3,500 kilogrammes gross vehicle weight; local authority drivers; gas, water and electricity service drivers; and other groups who we will identify later. The main point is that you will need to refer to the HAD rules below when considering compliance in relation to domestic drivers.

The HAD is overseen and enforced by the HSE and all records relating to hours worked must be retained by the employer for a minimum period of two years. Note that mobile workers, working under EU drivers' hours, are covered by the Road Transport Directive (RTD) and will be addressed later in this chapter.

The Horizontal Amending Directive states that:

- An average working week must not exceed 48 hours (an average working week is normally calculated by using a 17-week qualifying period to arrive at a weekly average).

- The qualifying period may be changed by a collective agreement with a trade union or employee representative body to a maximum of 52 weeks.

- Staff who complete a total of six consecutive hours' work must have a 20-minute break.

- Staff must have 11 consecutive hours' rest during each 24-hour period. This period must be 'consecutive' and must not be interrupted.

- Staff must have a minimum of 24 hours' weekly rest for every period of seven days.

- 'Night work' is defined as any period of seven hours, which includes any of the hours from midnight to 5 am.

- A 'night worker' is someone who normally works at least three hours at night, which count as 'night work' (as defined above).

- Night workers must only work a maximum of eight hours in any 24-hour period. The eight-hour maximum is also an 'average' time and is also calculated over whatever qualifying period is used to calculate an average working week.

- All workers who have completed at least 12 months' service are entitled to 5.6 weeks' (28 days') paid holiday each year.

- Employees with less than 12 months' service are entitled to holidays on a pro rata basis.

Itemized pay statements and equal pay

Every employee is entitled to an itemized pay statement. They can be downloaded online or obtained as a hard copy depending upon the organization concerned. They must show three principal figures: gross pay; deductions; net pay.

In order to reduce the 'gender' pay gap, in any pay rate there must be no difference that is based solely on gender. Please also note that, in support of this, there are currently discussions that are intended to result in businesses with 250+ employees having to make statutory declarations in relation to any differences in pay between men and women in their employment.

Guarantee payments

A worker who has been employed for more than one month is entitled to what are known as guarantee payments. These are payments made when an employee arrives at work but is told that there is no work to be done that day. The payments are not related to any agreed 'daily rate' or pay scale and are currently about £25 per day. They are only payable for being 'laid off' for up to a maximum of five days every three months.

Payment, the minimum wage and the living wage

The principle of a national minimum wage was originally established some years ago. However, the rates have naturally risen since then and usually rise annually, or even more regularly depending upon Budget announcements by the Chancellor of the Exchequer.

Different groups of employees are treated differently under this legislation. From 1 April 2017, the groups and related minimum rates of pay are:

- The rate (for 25+ year-olds) is £7.50 an hour.
- The rate for 21- to 24-year-olds is £7.05 per hour.
- The rate for 18- to 20-year-olds is £5.60 per hour.
- The rate for 16- to 17-year-olds is £4.05 per hour.
- The apprentice rate is £3.50 per hour.

Note 1: The national minimum wage rate now aligns with the national living wage rate for workers over 25.

Note 2: Under normal circumstances, the minimum wage rates are reviewed every October, whilst the living wage rate is reviewed every April.

Statutory Sick Pay (SSP)

SSP is normally paid by the employer and is not normally a government benefit other than in extreme cases where an employee is unable to attend the workplace for extended periods of time.

SSP is triggered by the employee informing the employer that they are sick and unable to come to work. For periods of sickness up to a maximum of seven days, self-certification is all that is required. For longer periods the employee must obtain a doctor's note (certificate) stating that the employee concerned is unable to work.

Payment of SSP by the employer does not begin from the original notification to the employer. The first three days of sickness, away from work during normal working days, are known as 'waiting days'. It is not until the employee has been off work for a minimum period of four consecutive days (three of which must be working days) that payments will be made.

Once payments begin a 'period of incapacity for work' (PIW) is established and payments will then be made to cover every normal working day that the employee is unable to work. These 'normal working days' are known as 'qualifying days'.

The rules state that SSP is only payable up to a maximum period of 28 weeks in any single PIW. This means that, should an employee be off work for longer than 28 weeks in a single PIW the employee, not the employer, will need to apply for the government-funded Employment and Support Allowance (ESA).

Employees who have claimed SSP and then return to work cannot claim SSP again until they have been back at work for a minimum of eight weeks.

Employee involvement

Many large organizations are committed, and obliged, to involve employees in processes involving improvements and changes in the workplace. Where this is the case, the companies concerned are classified by the numbers of employees.

Companies employing 50 or more employees must agree to enter into discussion with employee representatives, if asked to do so, in order to discuss how the flow of communication across the company might be improved and how the employees can become more involved in the decision-making processes.

Companies employing more than 250 employees must ensure that they include a statement in their company annual report that clearly states how the employees have been involved in relevant key business processes and decisions.

Periods of notice

Periods of notice are not always required. For instance, in cases of fighting or theft the employer may dismiss an employee 'on the spot'. There may, however, be repercussions. Instant dismissal is also an option for certain conduct-related issues, including persistent absenteeism or persistent lateness and, as has been documented by the media, for conduct outside the workplace that reflects badly on the organization.

Under normal circumstances, statutory minimum periods of notice will apply. These depend upon the length of 'continuous' service of the employee, as follows:

- less than one month's service – no period required;
- one month to two years' service – one week;
- two years to 12 years' service – one week for each complete year;
- 12 years or more – 12 weeks.

Note: The minimum periods above relate to notice given by the employer. However, employees who have completed more than one month's service must give their employer a minimum of one week's notice (all the figures above only relate to the statutory requirement and not any individual, or additional requirements laid out in any contracts of employment).

We have now covered the first eight of the 16 items included in the syllabus. Perhaps at this 'halfway' stage we should confirm understanding so far.

Key points you need to know

- Content of terms of employment and related timescales.
- HAD working, break and rest times (you need to know these in detail for drivers' hours compliance questions).
- The three main figures on an itemized pay statement.
- Guarantee payment timescale criteria.
- Minimum wage groups and rates, including the living wage.
- SSP entitlement criteria.
- Sizes of companies for employee involvement.
- Period of notice criteria, including employee criteria.

Notes

....
....
....
....
....
....
....
....
....

We now go on to cover the final group of employee rights, beginning with the grievance and discipline procedure and the right not to be dismissed unfairly.

Grievance and discipline

Under current employment legislation, all employers are bound to follow a set procedure in relation to grievance and discipline unless, as we discussed earlier, there are grounds for immediate dismissal. Where this 'normal' procedure is not adhered to, the employee has the right to take the employer to an employment tribunal. The simple three-step process is as follows:

- Step 1: the employer must send a written statement outlining the reason for the intended action and invite the employee to attend a meeting, where the employee is able to be represented, so that matters can be discussed.
- Step 2: following the meeting the employee must be told of any decision made by the employer, before any disciplinary action can actually begin.
- Step 3: the employee must be permitted to have the right to appeal the decision made.

Note: Even in cases of gross misconduct the employee still has the right to receive written reasons for their dismissal and to be told about their right of appeal.

Fair dismissal

There are several ways for an employer to 'fairly' dismiss an employee. As mentioned earlier, gross misconduct is one method and extended periods of sickness are another. The other ways mainly relate to underperformance or unethical conduct in one way or another.

For instance, an employer can dismiss an employee if they are incapable, in some way, of undertaking the job role or if they make false statements when applying for a job, such as claiming to have qualifications or experience that they don't have. This goes further insofar that an employee can also be dismissed for failing to gain qualifications required for a job, such as failing to gain a C+E Category licence, or an operator's CPC, when required to have one.

Employees can also be fairly dismissed because they simply cannot do the job expected of them to a satisfactory level (incompetence) and they can also be dismissed if, for some reason, they can no longer legally carry out the job they were recruited for, such as losing their LGV licence entitlement.

Unfair dismissal

In the same way that dismissals can be judged to be 'fair' they can also be judged to be 'unfair'. The various reasons for unfair dismissal are termed 'inadmissible reasons'. These are itemized in employment legislation and include when an employee is dismissed:

- on the grounds of race, gender or disability;
- for reasons relating to pregnancy;
- for leaving the place of work because of imminent danger;
- for asserting any of their statutory rights, such as rights under health and safety and employment regulations;
- for making a representation of health and safety in the workplace;
- after being brought in to cover for such things as maternity leave and the employer fails to make it absolutely clear that the employment is not permanent;
- having completed successive short-term fixed contracts totalling more than a 12-month period;
- for belonging to a particular trade union or refusing to join a particular trade union or for being involved with trade union activities outside of working hours;
- for taking part in properly observed industrial action;
- within 12 weeks of the beginning of any industrial action;
- for acting as a representative of the other employees in negotiations with the employer or employer organization.

Challenging the decision

The examples above are fairly clear-cut but, where the dismissal is challenged, things become a little more complex. Where the dismissal is challenged the employer needs to prove that there were 'substantial reasons' for the dismissal and that it was not simply a number of minor issues that built up over time, or personal issues or disagreements.

Where the dismissal is challenged it normally leads to an employment tribunal. Where the employee has been employed for at least two years they can request written reasons for the dismissal and, if this is done, the employer must supply the reasons within 14 days of the request.

It should be noted that the employment tribunal is also able to deal with employee complaints covering many issues where it is alleged the employer has acted improperly in some way or another. Examples include sexual harassment, gender discrimination, equal pay and disability discrimination.

Because of the rise in short-term contracts of employment, the authorities now permit appeals to be made by employees who have completed a series of consecutive short-term contracts. They now see this as 'continuous' employment providing that the series of short-term contracts extend to a period exceeding 12 months.

An employee normally has three months from the date of the incident to request a tribunal to be held. They do so by completing and submitting a form ET1. The employer then needs to complete a form ET3. Both the ET1 and the ET3 are then sent to the regional tribunal office and on to ACAS. Should ACAS be unable to find a solution that satisfies both parties then a tribunal will normally be called.

However, not all employees are able to request a tribunal for unfair dismissal. These include:

- members of the armed forces, the police and share fishermen;
- workers working outside the UK;
- independent contractors working under a specific contract;
- employees who started working for the employer after 6 April 2012 who have less than 24 months' service with that employer.

Employment tribunal structure

We mentioned the role of the EAT earlier, but before the EAT become involved there has to be an employment tribunal – it is the decision made at the tribunal that will later go to the EAT to be appealed. The structure and composition of an employment tribunal is as follows: the tribunal is overseen by a chairperson – this person is appointed by the Lord Chancellor and is always someone who is a member of the legal profession. The chairperson is joined by two other senior members, who are chosen to represent both sides involved in the appeal.

These three individuals are supported by other members who are appointed by the Secretary of State for Business, Innovation and Skills (BIS), and who will represent employer organizations and the Trades Union Congress (TUC).

In all cases, it is the role of the tribunal to insist that the employee proves that they were unfairly dismissed and not to make the employer prove that they were not. Where it is proven that an employee has been unfairly dismissed, the employee can ask to be reinstated. Clearly, this may not be a satisfactory solution for many reasons. Where it is felt that it is an unsatisfactory option then the employee is entitled to financial compensation to a level felt appropriate by the tribunal.

The tribunal assesses the level of the award based upon length of service, any financial hardship and any issues resulting from reinstatement not being suitable. There are three elements that can be used separately, or jointly, by the tribunal to set the level of the award. These are a basic award, relating to factors such as length of service, age, average wage or salary; a compensation award, relating to factors such as loss of earnings, pension rights and expenses; and an additional award, relating to the failure to reinstate.

If either the employer or the employee disagree with the decision of the employment tribunal, they have the right of appeal. This appeal is made to the Employment Appeals Tribunal (EAT) who will look at the original findings of the employment tribunal and make a final decision.

Redundancy

Redundancy is another complex area of employment legislation that requires employers and employee organizations to act in certain ways. We will try to summarize the main issues. First, it has to be recognized that redundancy can be defined as a situation where an employee is dismissed because:

- a business no longer carries out the type of business the employee was employed for;
- a business no longer carries out business in the place or location where the employee is employed;
- a business no longer requires the employee to carry out a particular type of work.

If one of these three circumstances is met then redundancy is classed as a fair reason for dismissal, providing that the employee(s) concerned have completed at least 24 months' employment with the employer since 6 April 2012. The 'fairness test' also relies on the fact that selection for redundancy is completely unbiased and not unfair in any way and that it does not discriminate in any way.

Basically, the actions required when making staff redundant rely upon the number of redundancies involved at each establishment. The term 'each establishment' is important (see below):

- Any employer intending to make fewer than 20 people redundant has no legal obligation or statutory commitment to notify either a workers' representative or a trade union of the intention to implement redundancies.

- Any employer intending to make 20–99 employees redundant within any 90-day period must consult with the appropriate staff or trade union representatives at least 30 days before the first redundancy is to take place. The employer must also give notice to the Secretary of State for BIS at least 30 days before the first redundancy.

- Any employer intending to make 100+ employees redundant within any 90-day period must consult with the appropriate staff or trade union representatives at least 45 days before the first redundancy is to take place. The employer must also give notice to the Secretary of State for BIS at least 45 days before the first redundancy.

The term 'each establishment' means that an unscrupulous employer could make 19 people redundant at 20 sites and not need to inform anyone of their intentions.

Redundancy payments

Employees who are made redundant are entitled to different levels of redundancy payments based on their age, length of service (up to a maximum of 20 years) and a statutory wage limit to a maximum of 30 weeks' wages.

The statutory payment levels are:

- one and a half weeks' pay for each full year that an employee is 41 years old, or older;

- one week's pay for each full year an employee is 22 years old, or older, but under 41 years of age;

- half a week's pay for each full year an employee is under 22 years of age.

Redundancy entitlement

There are additional entitlements relating to redundancy because employees with over two years' service are also entitled to 'reasonable' time off, with pay, to look for alternative employment.

However, although it is widely thought that all employees are entitled to redundancy payments and entitlements, some employees are not entitled. These include employees with less than two years' service.

In addition, workers made redundant who refuse a 'practical and fair' alternative position may also lose their right to redundancy payments. However, if they do accept a new position they are allowed up to four weeks to decide whether or not they are happy, or suited, to the new position and, if not, they can elect for redundancy without the loss of any benefits. In a recent change to the regulations, employees over the set state retirement age are now entitled to redundancy payments.

Note: It should be noted that the remaining employee rights (below) will be included in the examinations but, as the information relating to most of them is outline detail, they will largely appear in the OCR multi-choice exams or the CILT short-answer exams due to it being somewhat difficult to produce detailed answers from such 'outline' content.

Public duties

In addition to trade union officials being entitled to additional time off, employees who perform certain public duties are also able to be given additional time off work (either paid or unpaid) by their employer. The rules state that 'reasonable' time off should be made available for employees who perform duties for the 'public good'. These duties include being:

- a member of a health authority;
- a local councillor;
- a school governor;
- a member of any statutory tribunal (such as an employment tribunal);
- a magistrate (magistrates are also sometimes called justices of the peace);
- a member of the Environment Agency (EA);
- a member of the Scottish Environment Protection Agency (SEPA);
- a member of the General Teaching Councils for England and Wales;
- a member of a school council or board in Scotland;

- a member of the governing/management body of an educational establishment;
- a member of the prison independent monitoring boards in England or Wales;
- a member of a prison visiting committee in Scotland;
- a member of a Water Customer Consultation Panel in England and Wales;
- a member of Scottish Water.

In addition, many employers also grant some sort of additional time off for employees who, for example, serve as reserve firefighters or in the reserve armed forces, but there is no actual right for these employees to have additional time off, even though the duties may be classed as 'serving the public good'.

Flexible working

Once an employee has completed a minimum of 26 weeks' employment they are entitled to request 'flexible working'. Flexible working is often related to adjusting working hours around parental duties but also includes such things as changing shift patterns, working from home, reducing working hours, and job sharing. Every employer who receives a request for flexible working must act upon the request in a reasonable and appropriate manner or risk the possibility of an employment tribunal. However, if for good business reasons the request simply cannot be entertained then the employer may reject it.

Until this point we have covered employee rights that are available to almost all employees; we will now look at some employee rights that are only aimed at certain employees.

Maternity rights

The right to benefits, including time off from work, is available to both biological mothers and mothers who adopt a child. The actual entitlement to time off from work is comprised of antenatal leave and maternity leave. In addition there is the further right to maternity pay and the right not to be dismissed on the grounds of pregnancy or childbirth. We deal with each of these, and others, below.

Antenatal care (time off)

Any pregnant employee, regardless of time served, is able to request additional time off for antenatal care. This time off is paid time off. Because the employer must pay, they are entitled to ask for confirmation of the pregnancy from a medical practitioner and also to ask for proof of any appointments attended. In addition, the partner of the pregnant employee is also entitled to additional time off from work to attend up to two antenatal appointments, although the partner's time off is unpaid.

Maternity leave

Maternity leave is normally available for a minimum of 26 weeks. This 26-week period can be extended to a maximum of 52 weeks, upon request. However, if it is extended to 52 weeks then any time taken in excess of the 39-week qualifying period for Statutory Maternity Pay (SMP) will be unpaid.

After a period of maternity leave the female employee is entitled to return to work without losing seniority, pay, benefits, privileges or pension. Since 2008 the entitlement to retain benefits was extended to include such benefits as fitness club membership and even the ability to accrue holiday entitlement for up to the maximum 52-week period in spite of not actually working. The leave itself and the full range of retained benefits are simply down to the fact that maternity leave does not count as a break in service and so, as service is unbroken, the benefits of service must be retained.

When a child is adopted, any one of the two adoptive parents (including same-sex parents) may claim the same entitlement for maternity leave as a biological (birth) mother.

Female employees, or any adoptive parent who is on maternity leave, may, by agreement with the employer, be allowed to return to the workplace whilst on maternity leave for a period of up to 10 days. This time enables them to keep in touch with the workplace and work colleagues and is referred to as 'keeping in touch' days.

Additional regulations also apply that make it illegal for a mother of a newborn child to return to work within a minimum period of 14 days following the birth. This 14-day period is actually increased to 28 days in the case of factory employees. In addition, it is an offence for an employer to take on a new employee who cannot meet the 14-day or 28-day criteria.

Maternity leave requirements do not apply in every case. For instance, employers who have five or fewer employees may terminate the woman's employment instead of re-employing her. Where this is done, the employer must be able to justify the termination of employment insofar that it would not be reasonably practicable to re-employ the employee. This is another area where the employer may be drawn into an employment tribunal should they fail to make a proper case for the termination of the employment.

Maternity pay

Employers who pay Statutory Maternity Pay (SMP) are able to recover the money from the government by deducting it from the National Insurance (NI) contributions relating to the employee for the period of maternity leave, up to the maximum of 39 weeks, as mentioned above. However, it is paid at different rates depending upon the time it is taken. For instance, it is paid at a rate equivalent to 90 per cent of the average wage (before tax) of the employee for the first six weeks and then drops to the statutory normal rate (90 per cent of the average wage after tax is deducted) for the remainder of the period up to the 39-week cut-off point.

Note: The 90 per cent of the average wage after tax, which is paid for 33 weeks, is capped at about £140 per week if the average wage, after tax deductions, is actually higher than that.

Paternity leave

The father of a newborn child is entitled to either one or two weeks' paid paternity leave. This leave must be taken within a period not exceeding 56 days after the birth and cannot be taken on individual days. It must be taken in either a one-week or two-week block.

The old entitlement to extended paid paternity leave was generally abolished in 2015 although the authorities 'may' grant it under some circumstances, such as a situation where the mother is not in receipt of SMP, perhaps through being unemployed.

Shared parental leave

Where a child has been born on or after 5 April 2015 eligible mothers, fathers, adopters or partners can elect to share all, or some, of the time off work during the first year after the baby is born or placed for adoption. This right depends to some degree whether or not the two people involved with the birth or adoption qualify for maternity or paternity leave. In cases where there is only a single mother so the leave cannot be shared, then maternity leave and SMP (as described above) will apply.

To qualify for shared parental leave the female employee must have worked for the same employer for at least 26 weeks before the end of the fifteenth week before the week in which the child is due to be born. In addition, the person must have worked for at least 26 weeks in the 66 weeks leading up to the due date and earned at least £30.00 per week in 13 of these

66 weeks. In addition, the mother-to-be must inform the employer that they intend to share parental leave and they must do so at least eight weeks before any shared leave is taken.

Shared parental leave allows the leave to be taken either together or individually but it is limited to a maximum of 52 weeks, entitling each parent to up to 26 weeks each. Shared leave has to be taken in full weeks, not individual days. The leave can be taken as a full 26-week single period, or up to three separate periods totalling 26 weeks.

Unlike maternity leave, parents taking shared parental leave are actually entitled to 20 'keeping in touch' days each.

Shared Parental Pay (ShPP)

The same rules of eligibility apply to Shared Parental Pay (ShPP) as they do for Statutory Maternity or Paternity Pay (above). The rate of pay is also normally 90 per cent of the individual's average weekly pay, after tax has been deducted.

The rules do allow for ShPP to be paid in cases where the mother or adopter does not take the full entitlement of maternity or adoption pay or maternity allowance. In this case the outstanding entitlement can be paid to the mother or adopter as ShPP, providing that they are eligible.

Parental leave

Every parent, including same-sex parents, is entitled to take up to 18 weeks' unpaid leave for every child they have under 18 years of age. To qualify the parent must have been employed by an employer for a minimum period of 12 months and the periods requested must be agreed with the employer.

Dependants' leave

Regardless of the length of service every employee is entitled to 'reasonable time off' from work to attend a dependant relative (elderly or young) or to attend to some sort of personal or family emergency.

Medical suspension

Typically, employees who work in hazardous conditions or handle hazardous goods and materials can legally be suspended from work, with pay, for up to a maximum period of 26 weeks, if it is felt that there may be a danger to their health. In order to qualify for this medical suspension the employee must have completed a minimum of one month's employment with the employer concerned.

That concludes this somewhat complex section. Next we move on to another important area where both the employer and employee have duties, roles and responsibilities – drivers' hours and tachographs.

Key points you need to know

- Grievance procedure steps.
- Typical fair and unfair reasons for dismissal.
- Employment tribunal structure and procedures.
- Definition of redundancy.
- Redundancy notification procedures.
- Redundancy pay criteria.
- Flexible working criteria.
- Public duty time-off criteria.
- Antenatal, maternity leave and maternity pay criteria.
- Paternity leave criteria.
- Shared parental leave and pay criteria.
- Parental leave criteria.
- Dependants' leave criteria.
- Medical suspension criteria.

Notes

....
....
....
....
....
....
....
....
....
....

DRIVERS' HOURS, RECORD KEEPING AND DCPC

We now move on to very important parts of the syllabus: drivers' hours and tachographs. These are both areas where you will be expected to prove that you are competent for the examinations. To pass the examination you will need to be able to either produce legal schedules or procedures or to analyse schedules and procedures, including tachograph compliance procedures, or even produce instructions for drivers on drivers' hours compliance or tachograph operation and responsibilities. This is just one reason that you should download a GV262 (Rules on Drivers' Hours and Tachographs) from the gov.uk website and make sure you are thoroughly familiar with it – you will also be allowed to use the GV262 as a quick reference guide in the exam room. The notes below support the content of the GV262.

We begin with EU drivers' hours rules and the working time directive rules that also apply to these drivers, before moving on to examine other rules and regulations that apply to drivers not covered by the EU rules.

EU Drivers' Hours Regulations (EC Regulation 561/2006) and Working Time Regulations (RTD)

It should not be necessary to tell you how important these rules are in relation to operating a fleet of goods vehicles, and complying with the terms of the operator licence. It is absolutely vital you have a full and thorough understanding of these rules, as not only will you be examined on them in depth, you will be expected to comply with them in any role as transport supervisor, manager or operator.

These rules apply to drivers of goods vehicles within the EU in connection with a trade or business where the vehicle has a gross vehicle weight (GVW) exceeding 3.5 tonnes (3,500 kilogrammes) (including the weight of any trailer drawn). These rules also apply to the European Free Trade Area countries (EFTA): Iceland, Liechtenstein, Norway and Switzerland.

For clarity, some of the terms used in the regulations are defined below:

- Day: any period of 24 consecutive hours.
- Week: a period beginning at midnight Sunday until midnight the following Sunday.

- Fortnight: any two consecutive weeks.

- Driver: a driver is any person who drives the vehicle, even for a short period, or who is carried in the vehicle in order to be available for driving.

- Driving: the duration of driving recorded by the recording equipment (whether analogue or digital) or, when it is impossible to use the tachograph, manually by the driver.

- Period of availability: a period of availability (POA) is a period of time of waiting that is known in advance where the driver has a reasonable opportunity to spend the time as they wish. For instance, if a vehicle arrives at a site at 6.30 am and the sign on the gate says the site will open at 8 am, the driver can record this known time (1.5 hours) as a POA as he/she is able to do as they please, without moving the vehicle, until the site opens.

- Other work: all activities that are defined as working time under the Working Time Directive except driving. This also includes any work for the same or another employer outside the transport sector.

- Break: any period during which the driver may not carry out any driving or any other work and which is used exclusively for recuperation.

- Unforeseen events: provided that road safety is not jeopardized, a driver may depart from the EU Drivers' Hours regulations in order to reach a safe stopping place to ensure the safety of persons, the vehicle or the load. The reason behind the unforeseen events should be recorded on the driver's tachograph chart or printout – at latest upon arrival at the suitable stopping place. The driver must inform their employer of the breach of the regulations as soon as possible.

- Bonus schemes: bonus schemes related to distance travelled and/or the amount of goods carried are prohibited unless it can be proven that they do not endanger road safety.

These definitions are important because they determine things such as a 'day', 'week' and 'fortnight' in relation to how much work or duty can be performed within prescribed time limits. Let's now look at a summary of the rules themselves:

- Daily driving: a driver may drive for a maximum of nine hours per day. This may be extended to 10 hours per day, but not more than twice a week. Once a driver has completed six consecutive daily driving periods, they must take a weekly rest (see below).

- Weekly driving: the weekly driving limit is 56 hours (this is comprised of 4 × 9 hours plus 2 × 10 hours, the maximum possible within six successive 24-hour periods).

- Fortnightly driving: within any two consecutive weeks, the maximum permitted driving is 90 hours (this means that a driver driving for 48 hours in any week may only drive for 42 hours the following week and must have only driven for 42 hours the previous week).

- Breaks from driving: a total of 45 minutes' break must be taken at or before the end of 4.5 hours of continuous or cumulative driving. The 45-minute break may be split into two breaks, the first at least 15 minutes long, the second at least 30 minutes long. If split they must be taken as 15 minutes then 30 minutes. It is illegal to take them as 30 minutes then 15 minutes.

- Daily rest: a driver must take 11 hours' consecutive rest in any 24-hour period. This may be reduced to nine hours no more than three times between any two individual weekly rest periods.

- Split daily rest: the daily rest required in any 24-hour period may be split into two periods. The first period must be at least three hours and the second period must be at least nine hours (again, these periods must be taken in this order).

- Weekly rest: a weekly rest must be 45 consecutive hours, but can be reduced to 24 hours either at base or away from base. If it is reduced then a full regular 45 hours' rest must be taken the following week, because one full 45-hour weekly rest must be taken in any two consecutive weeks. In the cases of reduced weekly rests, reductions must be compensated 'en bloc' (in one period of time that must be attached to a daily or weekly rest period). The compensation must be taken before the end of the third week, following the week in which the reduced weekly rest was taken. A weekly rest must also be taken after six successive periods of 24 hours following the last weekly rest period (this prevents the driver from working seven days a week). A weekly rest that spans two 'fixed weeks' can be allocated to either of those weeks.

- Ferry/train daily rest: where a driver accompanies a vehicle that is conveyed by a ferry or train, a regular (11 hours) daily rest may be interrupted, not more than twice, for embarkation and disembarkation activities not exceeding one hour in total. During such daily rest periods, the driver must have access to a bunk or couchette.

- 'Double manning': within 30 hours of the end of a daily or weekly rest period, any driver engaged in multi-manning must take a daily rest period of at least nine hours. (What the 30-hour rule means is that on 'double-manned' operations, both drivers can work for a total period of 21 hours before both having to take a daily rest with the vehicle stationary. However, the statutory breaks from driving can be taken with the vehicle on the move.)

Note 1: It is important that when referring to 'breaks' and 'rests' you use the correct terms, because in the examination if you refer to a 'break' as a 'rest' you may be marked incorrect as they have different definitions.

Note 2: If taken in a vehicle, daily and weekly rests must only be taken in a stationary vehicle that has 'suitable sleeping facilities'.

Note 3: The weekly, daily and 'ferry' rest provisions are really important. In spite of them being somewhat complex, you must understand them in detail.

Military reservists' rest periods

Concessions exist for military reservists who are also drivers who drive under EU drivers' hours regulations. These have been granted in order to enable them to attend training and other activities and to return to their civilian occupation without contravening any of the normal rest-requirement regulations. These are as follows:

- In relation to the weekly rest, the rules apply to 15 days' annual camp and up to 10 weekend training sessions per year (a total of 35 days per year). They allow the reservist to go on these training exercises providing that they do not go on training on consecutive weeks, other than when on annual camp.
- The reservist must take a full weekly rest period no later than the end of the sixth day after a period of weekend training.
- The reservist must take a period of 11 hours' daily rest before the start of work following a period of weekend training.

Exemptions and derogations from the EU rules

In relation to exemptions and derogations from the EU rules your GV262 lists these. But the main exemptions are for vehicles not exceeding 3,500-kilogramme gross vehicle weight (GVW) – GVW means exactly the same as the terms maximum permitted weight (MPW) and maximum authorized mass (MAM); drivers in the armed forces or emergency services and drivers on journeys that are made entirely off road or on an island of less than 2,300 square kilometres are out of the scope of the EU rules.

Within the EU rules, derogations are not the same as exemptions. A derogation is where the UK has decided it needs to opt out of some of the requirements of the rules to ensure that domestic operations and essential services can be maintained. This means that derogations apply to the UK only (clearly each EU member state also has their own derogations for the same reasons). Whilst declaring derogations to be UK-wide, there are some separate arrangements for Northern Ireland.

Most of the derogations apply to local (within 100 kilometres of base) operations, service providers, driving instruction, farm milk collections and drivers of vehicles not exceeding 7,500 kilogramme GVW operating for Royal Mail or carrying materials, equipment or machinery for the driver's use in the course of their work (examples might be fencing contractors, plumbers, builders and similar tradespersons).

The working time rules for drivers under EU drivers' hours (RTD)

Whilst we have looked at the rules and the exemptions and derogations we have not, as yet, looked at the working time rules for EU drivers, which were introduced in 2005. This is often referred to as the Working Time Directive, although as we will see this term is not strictly correct as there are two sets of working time rules. We covered the working time rules for non-mobile workers and 'British domestic' drivers earlier in this section, so now we look at the working time rules that apply to drivers driving under the 'EU' drivers' hours regulations. These are generally referred to as RTD rules.

If you operate a vehicle within the scope of the EU drivers' hours regulations, then you are also bound by the Road Transport (Working Time) Regulations 2005 (as amended), unless you are an occasional mobile worker (see below). These regulations also apply to self-employed drivers driving under EU drivers' hours regulations.

The 2005 regulations include rules covering:

- Weekly working time, which must not exceed an average of 48 hours per week over the reference period: the reference period for calculating the 48-hour week is normally 17 weeks, but it can be extended to 26 weeks if this is permitted under a collective or workforce agreement. There is no 'opt-out' for individuals wishing to work longer than an average 48-hour week, but breaks and 'periods of availability' do not count as working time. A maximum working time of 60 hours can be performed in any single week providing the average 48-hour limit is not exceeded.

- Night work: if night work is performed, working time must not exceed one 10-hour period in any 24-hour period. Night time is the period between midnight and 4 am for goods vehicles. The 10-hour limit may be exceeded if this is permitted under a collective or workforce agreement.

- Breaks: mobile workers must not work more than six consecutive hours without taking a break. If working hours total between six and nine hours, working time should be interrupted by a break, or breaks, totalling at least 30 minutes. If your working hours total more than nine hours, working time should be interrupted by a break or breaks totalling at least 45 minutes. All breaks should be of at least 15 minutes' duration.

- Rest: the regulations are the same as the rest requirements laid out in the EU drivers' hours rules.

- Record keeping: records need to be kept for two years after the period in question. This means that if tachograph records are used to record working time compliance, they need to be kept for two years.

For clarity, if a driver is recording a period of availability (POA) such as waiting for a ferry or waiting for a delivery or collection point to open, providing the time when work can recommence is known in advance, the POA can be recorded as rest for working time purposes.

Drivers are also bound by two earlier provisions under the Working Time Regulations 1998 (as amended). These state that a worker is entitled to 5.6 weeks' paid annual leave and that night workers are entitled to health checks.

Whilst it is the DVSA that enforces the provisions of the 2005 Regulations and the requirement for health checks for night workers (under the 1998 Regulations), it is ACAS that gives advice relating to annual leave entitlements.

We have now covered drivers driving under the EU drivers' hours regulations but, if you drive outside of the EU, there is a different set of rules that you need to comply with; although they are exactly the same as the EU rules they are titled differently.

The European Agreement on International Road Transport (AETR)

The countries where you need to comply with these rules are mainly Russia, Central Asian countries and many Balkan states. Where journeys are made to other countries in Europe outside the EU or AETR, the domestic laws of those countries should be observed. If unsure about whether or not a country is covered by AETR or domestic rules, then advice can be found in the GV262 or from trade associations or the DVSA.

In addition to being exactly the same drivers' hours rules as the EU rules, AETR tachograph rules are also exactly the same as the EU tachograph rules (see below).

Having now covered two identical sets of international driving hours' rules and the working time regulations for most UK 'mobile workers' we can now look at the British domestic drivers' hours rules.

British domestic drivers' hours rules and Working Time Regulations (HAD)

These rules stem from the 1968 Transport Act and are now somewhat dated but they do still apply and they are enforced as rigidly as the EU rules. The domestic rules generally apply to vehicles not exceeding 3.5 tonnes GVW, certain specialized vehicles, and certain public authority and essential service providers' vehicles, and only apply to journeys that are entirely completed within the UK.

The British domestic rules categorize drivers into two distinct groups in relation to the rules that need to be obeyed. First there are drivers who drive for less than four hours in any 24-consecutive-hour period (Group One drivers) and then there are drivers who drive for more than four hours in any consecutive 24-hour period (Group Two drivers).

There are also definitions that clarify issues, as there were with the EU rules. For domestic drivers' hours purposes the following definitions apply:

- A 'day' is any period of 24 consecutive hours.
- A 'week' is a period beginning at midnight Sunday until midnight the following Sunday.
- An 'emergency' is any event that causes or is likely to cause a serious interruption to the maintenance of public services; a serious

interruption to the use of roads, railways, ports or airports; danger to the life or health of persons or animals; or serious damage to property.

You will see that these 'emergencies' are not the same as the EU 'unforeseen events'; they are more focused on maintaining essential services and public safety, although domestic drivers can also depart from the rules under such domestic emergency situations.

The rules for Group One drivers

- Daily driving: not exceeding four hours in any 24-consecutive-hour period within a week.
- Daily duty: not specified, although rules under the Working Time Regulations for domestic drivers do apply (see below).

The rules for Group Two drivers

- Daily driving: not exceeding 10 hours.
- Daily duty: not exceeding 11 hours in any 24-consecutive-hour period within a week.

The distinction here is quite clear but it is the fact that the driver drives for less or more than four hours on any day of the week that makes compliance and monitoring of drivers' hours a little more complicated, because a Group One driver cannot change to be a Group Two driver if they have completed more than 11 hours' duty on any day that week or if they plan to complete more than 11 hours' duty later in the same week, otherwise they will have broken the 11-hour duty limit for Group Two drivers as their 'Group One' status once they have exceeded 11 hours' duty is valid for a whole week.

In reality, this means that any driver who completes, or is scheduled to complete, more than 11 hours' duty within a fixed week cannot become a Group Two driver. In this respect, duty will also include any work for a second employer. This makes monitoring quite difficult in many cases, especially where agency staff may be used who may have driven for more than four hours under the EU rules and worked perhaps 13 hours on that day, because when this type of 'mixed driving' occurs neither set of regulations can be broken. In addition, if you employed an agency driver under domestic rules and they drove for more than four hours they could not work for more than 11 hours any day that week even if they had, or were to, drive under the EU rules (further details are below).

The working time rules for drivers under domestic drivers' hours (HAD)

The Working Time Directive (WTD) is referred to as the Horizontal Amending Directive (HAD). Whilst it mainly covers non-mobile workers it does also apply to drivers who drive under 'domestic' rules and not EU drivers' hours rules.

The Horizontal Amending Directive states that:

- An average working week must not exceed 48 hours (an average working week is normally calculated by using a 17-week qualifying period to arrive at a weekly average).

- The qualifying period may be changed by a collective agreement with a trade union or employee representative body to a maximum of 52 weeks.

- Staff who complete a total of six consecutive hours' work must have a 20-minute break.

- Staff must have 11 consecutive hours' rest during each 24-hour period. This period must be 'consecutive' and must not be interrupted.

- Staff must have a minimum of 24 hours' weekly rest for every period of seven days.

- 'Night work' is defined as any period of seven hours which includes any of the hours from midnight to 5 am.

- A 'night worker' is someone who normally works at least three hours at night (as defined above).

- Night workers must only work a maximum of eight hours in any 24-hour period. The eight-hour maximum is also an 'average' time and is also calculated over whatever qualifying period is used to calculate an average working week.

- All workers who have completed at least 12 months' service are entitled to 5.6 weeks' (28 days') paid holiday each year.

- Employees with less than 12 months' service are entitled to holidays on a pro rata basis.

If you drive a vehicle subject to the GB domestic drivers' hours rules or are an occasional mobile worker, you are also affected by four provisions under the 1998 Working Time Regulations. Note that a mobile worker would be exempt from the 2005 Regulations if they work 10 days or fewer within the scope of the European drivers' hours rules, in a reference period that is shorter than 26 weeks; or they work 15 days or less within the scope of the European drivers' hours rules, in a reference period that is 26 weeks or longer.

The rules under the directive include the following:

- a weekly working time, which must not exceed an average of 48 hours per week over the reference period (although individuals can 'opt out' of this requirement if they want to);
- an entitlement to 5.6 weeks' paid annual leave;
- health checks for night workers;
- an entitlement to adequate rest.

These four rules share similarities with the RTD, although 'adequate rest' means that workers should have regular rest periods. These rest periods should be sufficiently long and continuous to ensure that workers do not harm themselves, their fellow workers or others and that they do not damage their health in the short or long term. In practice this makes 'adequate' very difficult for a manager to determine.

The reference period for calculating the 48-hour average week is normally a rolling 17-week period. However, this reference period can be extended up to 52 weeks, if this is permitted under a collective or workforce agreement. However, the 1998 Regulations do not, as yet, apply to 'self-employed drivers' (a topic that will be looked at next) driving under British domestic rules.

As with the RTD, DVSA enforces working time limits and the requirement for health checks for night workers under the 1998 Regulations for drivers operating under the GB domestic drivers' hours rules (and occasional mobile workers), whilst ACAS can help with issues relating to rest or annual leave.

Definition of self-employed under the 1998 Regulations

You are self-employed if you are running your own business and are free to work for different clients and customers. However, you are not classed as 'self-employed' if you only have a single client or customer.

Note: HAD also has a definition of a part-time driver but it is basically the same as the one above for the 1998 Regulations, although somewhat more 'complex and lengthy'.

Mixed EU/AETR and GB domestic driving

Many drivers spend some of their time driving under one set of rules and some under another set, perhaps even on the same day. If you work partly under EU/AETR rules and partly under GB domestic rules during a day or a week, the following points must be considered:

- The time you spend driving or on duty under EU/AETR rules cannot count as a break or rest period under GB domestic rules.

- Driving and other duty under GB domestic rules (including non-driving work in another employment) count as other work, but not as a break or rest period under EU/AETR rules.

- Driving and other duty under EU/AETR rules count towards the driving and duty limits under the GB domestic rules.

- When driving under each set of rules, you must comply with the requirements of the rules being driven under, for example, the daily rest provisions for domestic and daily and weekly rest requirements for EU/AETR driving.

Driving limits

The GB domestic limit (a maximum of 10 hours' driving per day) must always be obeyed. But at any time when a driver is actually driving under the EU/AETR rules, they must obey all the rules on EU/AETR driving limits and breaks.

Rest periods and breaks

A driver must always obey the EU/AETR rules on rest periods and breaks on days and weeks when driving within the scope of EU/AETR rules is carried out.

Where a driver works under GB domestic rules in one week and the EU/AETR rules in the second week, the weekly rest required in week two must start no later than 144 hours (6 consecutive days) following the commencement of duty on or after midnight on Sunday/Monday.

Please try to make sure you understand the issue of Group One and Group Two drivers and the problems when EU and domestic driving are mixed and both are carried out by a driver during a single week.

Key points you need to know

- Detailed understanding of the EU drivers' hours regulations.
- Detailed knowledge of the RTD.
- Countries of the EU and rules and application of AETR.
- Detailed understanding of British domestic drivers' hours regulations.
- Detailed knowledge of the HAD.
- Mixed driving problems and restrictions.

Notes

It is really important that you gain sufficient knowledge and understanding of this section relating to drivers' hours and working time and that you are able to either produce a legal schedule using these rules or scrutinize a schedule for non-compliance relating to these rules. Also note that the exam questions set will almost certainly include a ferry journey of some sort or a 'night out' scenario.

Please also note that you really should obtain a GV262, or download a copy, because it contains details and examples that will help you with your studies.

In order to complete this section relating to drivers' hours and working time we will now move on to look at the different records and record keeping that relate to the rules and other issues stemming from the layout and order of the set syllabus. Once again, your GV262 contains important information relating to drivers' hours records and needs to be used as an important point of reference.

Tachographs

Tachograph rules

Under EU regulations, there is a general requirement to use either an analogue or a digital tachograph. This requirement and most of the rules relating to tachographs are contained within EU Regulation 165/2014, which, when introduced, exempted some drivers from using tachographs and some vehicles from requiring tachographs to be fitted.

Whilst not an exact statement it is fair to say that where drivers are exempted from the EU and AETR drivers' hours regulations they will also be exempted from compulsory tachograph fitment to their vehicles – although they can use a tachograph if they choose to. Should they use a tachograph, even though not compulsory, it must be in full working order and in date for inspection and calibration.

Typically, the following activities are exempted from tachograph use throughout the EU:

- emergency service vehicles;
- vehicles not exceeding 7,500 kg GVW used for private movements of goods;
- specialized breakdown vehicles operating within 100 km of base;
- within the UK we also exempt:
  - vehicles used for door-to-door domestic refuse collection;
  - vehicles carrying live animals between farms and markets within 100 km;
  - vehicles used by utility services (gas, electricity, water).

Analogue tachographs

Analogue tachographs are the old type of tachograph where a record is produced on a circular waxed chart (Figure 3.1). They were fitted to vehicles registered before 2006 and use a stylus to make imprints into the wax-coated surface of the chart.

There are three styli used to separately record:

- speed;
- distance travelled;
- the driver's activity (known as the 'mode').

FIGURE 3.1 Analogue tachograph

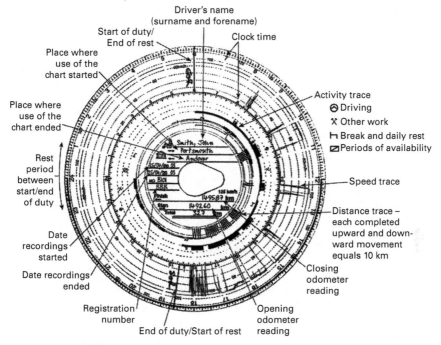

SOURCE: DVSA publication GV262

Most analogue tachographs are classed as 'automatic'. This means that the instrument will automatically record driving when the vehicle begins to move off. There will be no need for the driver to put the mode switch to a 'Driving' position. The machine will then default to 'Duty' mode when the vehicles comes to rest.

Driver obligations and responsibilities

The 'centrefield' (inner part) of the chart is used by the driver to write their name, the vehicle registration number, the location of the start and end of the journey, the date, and odometer readings. The reverse of a tachograph chart normally contains an area for recording manual entries and details of other vehicles driven during the period covered.

A driver is required to enter the following information on the centrefield of a tachograph chart that he or she is using in order to record their activities:

- Surname and first name (the law does not stipulate which order the names are put in as this was tested in the European Court).

- The date and place where the use of the chart begins and ends (if the locations of start and finish are the same they must still be recorded in full because 'as above' or 'same' are not actual locations).

- The registration number(s) of the vehicle(s) driven (where multiple vehicles are driven there are additional spaces to record this, either on the front or on the front and rear of the chart).

- The time at which any change of vehicle takes place (there is also room for this in the additional spaces provided).

- The odometer readings:
  - at the start of the first journey using the chart;
  - at the end of the last journey using the same chart;
  - at the time of any change of vehicle, whilst also recording the odometer readings from both vehicles.

On the face of the chart in the centrefield there is also a space for the driver to record the total distance (in kilometres) travelled whilst using the chart, but this calculation does not have to be completed by the driver in order to satisfy the actual regulations, although it may well be a company policy or instruction.

It is not acceptable for written entries to extend outside the centrefield area in case they hide or corrupt any recording made by the styli. For instance, if the driver's name is something like 'Maxamillion Cartwright-Hammersmith' (apologies if there is a driver with that name) or a place name is so long that it must be abbreviated (as in Llanfairpg. on Anglesey) in order to be accommodated in the space provided, then the full name should be noted on the reverse of the chart.

The reverse side of the chart can also be used by the driver to manually record any other additional information that may be required, as in cases where the driver may be working away from the vehicle, in the case of an unforeseen event, or to record their activities in cases where the tachograph breaks down.

Employers may also ask drivers to indicate on a chart where their duty (or rest) begins and ends so that they can ensure a full record has been made. In these cases the driver may mark the face of the chart with start and finish of duty times but they must never make a mark on the face of the chart that obliterates any machine-made (styli) recordings.

Each tachograph has a 12-hour clock face to enable the driver to monitor times against break requirements and other benchmarks. The clock must be correct for either am or pm as the chart is a 24-hour chart and so the time recorded can be 12 hours out if the clock is not set correctly. This is the driver's responsibility, as is the need to adjust the clock when the clocks are put forward or back during the year for daylight saving.

It is also the driver's responsibility to ensure that they can produce their current chart and charts for the previous 28 days to enforcement officers and that, on international journeys, the clock continues to record the original time (UK time) in order for enforcement officers to monitor duty, driving, break and rest requirements and to ensure that the recordings made are 'continuous'.

Charts and records

As a further issue, drivers are fully responsible for operating the tachograph and making records correctly. These responsibilities are outlined below:

- Drivers must carry enough charts for the whole journey, including spare charts in case any become damaged or enforcement officers seize any.

- Drivers must not use a chart to cover any period in excess of 24 hours.

- Drivers must ensure that the correct type of chart is being used for the specific model of tachograph.

- Drivers must verify that the tachograph is correctly calibrated by checking the attached plaques inside the tachograph head.

- Drivers must enter centrefield details at the first use of the chart, when changing vehicles and when completing the use of the chart.

- Drivers must ensure that the time displayed is set to the official time of the country in which the vehicle is registered.

- Drivers must use a second chart if a chart is damaged while in use and attach this one to the first chart on completion. When doing this the driver needs to make sure they do not 'deface' any recordings on either chart.

- Drivers who change to a vehicle with an incompatible tachograph to the chart in use, or who change vehicles so many times that all the details cannot be accommodated on one chart, must use a second chart.

- Drivers must operate the mode switch correctly in order to record their activities, breaks and rests accurately.

- Drivers must make manual entries on the chart in respect of duty, work or breaks away from the vehicle.

- Drivers must record unforeseen circumstances where the rules have been breached, or to correct an incorrect recording.

- Drivers must make manual entries when the tachograph ceases to work correctly and report any such incidents to the operator.
- Drivers must produce a chart, or charts, upon request by a DVSA examiner or police officer.
- Drivers must not remove the chart from the tachograph before the end of their duty period unless authorized to do so. Where this is done for enforcement purposes the driver needs to get the chart endorsed by the official/officer concerned.
- Drivers may only remove a chart when changing vehicles or to make manual entries in the event of an unforeseen circumstance or equipment malfunction or other notifiable incident or occurrence.
- Drivers must be able to produce charts and statutory manual records for the current day and the previous 28 calendar days at the roadside, if so requested.
- Drivers must return used charts to the operator or employer within 42 days.
- Drivers who have been issued with a digital tachograph driver's card must also produce that card upon request even when driving a vehicle with an analogue tachograph.

Analogue tachographs are slowly being replaced by more modern digital tachographs, which in spite of being relatively new are planned to change in 2018 or 2019 when a second-generation tachograph is scheduled to be introduced that will use satellite technology. This will help (amongst other things) enforcement bodies to locate vehicles, meaning that drivers are not required to record any start/finish locations; allow visiting foreign drivers to use temporary driver cards; and allow more focused targeting of offences being recorded by the vehicle units. Further developments in the future may include applications such as remote monitoring and tracking of suspect drivers, vehicles or operators, and incorporating load weight sensors to prevent gross and axle overloads.

Digital tachographs

Digital tachographs record the activities of both the driver and the vehicle. In the case of the driver the machine makes a record on the driver's digital tachograph card whilst also recording the same details on the vehicle unit (VU) itself. The VU is capable of holding information relating to all drivers and all vehicle activity for a period of up to 12 months (Figure 3.2).

FIGURE 3.2 Digital tachograph

SOURCE: Continental

Operators must download the driver information from the VU within a maximum time limit of 90 days, but must also ensure that they download the information from the individual drivers' cards within a maximum period of 28 days.

Unlike the analogue tachograph, digital tachographs default to recording 'other work' (duty) for the driver (and any second driver) when the vehicle stops. Because of this, drivers and crew members must use the mode switch correctly to record their legally required break and rest periods.

Also unlike the analogue tachograph, the digital tachograph VU and drivers' cards record all time entries in Universal Time Coordinated (UTC). This simplifies enforcement issues but the driver needs to consider this when inputting any information into the VU manually.

The driver can set the internal clock to any local time if they wish to do so, but this will not change the actual record from recording UTC. In addition, all times on any printouts are also shown in UTC time, irrespective of any local time being recorded by the driver.

There are proposals for 'smart digital tachographs' to be introduced in 2019. These will enable 'control authorities', who have the driver's consent, to access a driver's personal data (with the driver's permission) and to 'track' vehicles using 3 hourly satellite fixes.

Driver cards and records

Driver cards are available from the Driver and Vehicle Licensing Agency (DVLA). Application forms can be either downloaded from the DVLA website or collected from DVSA testing stations. It is deemed a serious offence for any driver to be in possession of more than one driver's card or for drivers to use anyone else's card or allow another driver to use their card.

Because it is a legal requirement for the driver of a digital tachograph-equipped vehicle driving under EU drivers' hours rules to use a driver card, the VU will record any instances where a driver's card is not used.

Where a driver's card is either lost or malfunctions the driver may drive without the card for a maximum of 15 calendar days, providing that he or she produces two printouts – one at the start of the journey/daily duty and another at the end. Both printouts must be marked with the following:

- the driver's name or driver card or licence number and signature, so the driver can be identified;
- any manual entries* needed to show periods of other work, availability and rest or break.

The driver must also report the problem to the DVLA and apply for a new card within seven calendar days of the loss or malfunction. The DVLA then have eight days in which to issue a replacement card.

---

* A true manual record, which the driver can enter under certain circumstances, should only be necessary in cases where the driver breaches the rules due to an unforeseen event, the driver needs to correct a record or if the instrument malfunctions. In these circumstances, if the machine cannot accept driver manual input, the driver should record their activities or reasons on the reverse of a portion of print roll or use a blank analogue tachograph chart, if they have one.

When driving a vehicle that is equipped with a digital tachograph, drivers have many responsibilities in a similar fashion to the responsibilities relating to analogue tachographs. In the case of digital tachographs, drivers must:

- Ensure that their driver card is inserted into the correct slot (slot 1) from the moment they take over the vehicle, and that the VU and card are ready to be used before the vehicle is moved.
- Record the country in which they begin and end their duty. This must always be carried out even if the card is left in overnight.
- Ensure that any work undertaken since the driver card was last removed from a tachograph is manually recorded using the manual entry facility on the tachograph.
- Ensure that the instrument is calibrated by inspecting the calibration plaque or using the VU menu.
- Ensure that the tachograph is working correctly. This can be difficult at times for drivers, but some errors and incorrect working are recorded by the VU as error codes or pictograms.
- Carry sufficient spare print rolls on board the vehicle so that a printout can be produced, if required.
- Ensure that the mode switch is used correctly to record other work, periods of availability, rest and breaks.

- Take reasonable steps to protect their driver card from dirt or damage.
- Use only their own driver card to make recordings and manual entries.
- Ensure that the card is not removed from the tachograph during the working day unless otherwise authorized (removal for changes of vehicles and removal for enforcement purposes are allowed).
- On multi-manning operations the drivers must ensure that the drivers' cards are placed in the correct slot (slot 1 for actual driving and slot 2 when co-driver).
- Produce their cards for downloading by their employer within 28 days of use.
- Produce their driver card, records and manual records for the current day and the previous 28 calendar days to enforcement officers at the roadside.

General/common rules

We can see that the responsibilities are often very similar between the analogue and digital versions of tachographs and there are other similarities including:

- Common use of the mode-switch symbols to be used to record driving (wheel), other work (crossed hammers), availability (known as the sandwich) and breaks and rest (bed) – see Figure 3.3.
- The common requirement that the driver must make a manual entry where any of the symbols have been used incorrectly.
- In cases where a vehicle that comes within the scope of EU rules is at a location that is neither the driver's home nor the place where the driver is normally based, the time the driver spends travelling to or from that location must be classed as driving/duty unless the driver is in a ferry or train and has access to a bunk or couchette.

FIGURE 3.3 Mode-switch symbols

SOURCE: GV262 DVSA Guide to Drivers' Hours and Tachographs

- Drivers must record all other work and periods of availability (including work for any other employers) on all driving and non-driving days within a week where they have come within the scope of the EU drivers' hours rules.

- Any driver who works for more than one operator must provide each operator with sufficient information to allow each operator to make sure that the rules relating to drivers' hours and records are being complied with.

- Some analogue and digital tachographs automatically record all time spent as a 'second driver' when the vehicle is in motion as a period of availability, and do not allow the mode to be changed by a crew member. The enforcement authorities will accept the first 45 minutes of this time as a break from driving, providing that the VU and driver cards do not show any driving by the 'second driver'.

- Drivers who may need to drive a vehicle fitted with an analogue tachograph and a vehicle fitted with a digital tachograph on the same day must use a chart and a driver card to record activities covering both vehicles.

- Drivers using either type of tachograph must produce simple records (start/finish) for any non-driving days if they drive a vehicle covered by the EU regulations on drivers' hours and record keeping in order to produce an accurate record of the activities performed during the entire fixed week. This can be done by manually filling out a tachograph chart or by entering details manually into a digital tachograph VU.

- The requirement for a formal layout of Letters of Attestation* to explain breaks in a full 28-day tachograph record – where a driver may have been sick or on holiday – was lifted with the introduction of EU Regulation 165/2014. However, even though no replacement format has been agreed, on international journeys it is recommended that Letters of Attestation* from the employer are provided for drivers travelling through other countries to cover any sick leave, annual leave and time spent driving a vehicle that is out of the scope of EU/AETR rules during the preceding 28 days.

---

* Operators are advised to carry on using the old formal Letter of Attestation to avoid problems with the enforcement authorities because drivers are still required to produce charts for the previous 28 days on request. Where the old Letter of Attestation is used, it should provide contact details at the company of someone who can explain and vouch for the driver. The letter should then be signed by a senior member of the staff.

Up to now we have discussed issues that mainly affect the driver in relation to the rules relating to tachographs. However, operators are also bound by statutory rules in relation to drivers' records and so we will now look at the other side of this 'joint' responsibility.

Operators' roles and responsibilities

Transport operators have legal responsibilities and liabilities for their own compliance with the regulations and that of the drivers under their control.
To fulfil these obligations, operators:

- must properly instruct drivers on the rules relating to tachographs;
- must properly schedule work so the rules on drivers' hours can be met;
- must take all reasonable steps to prevent breaches of the rules;
- must make regular checks of charts and digital data to ensure compliance;
- must ensure that tachographs have been properly calibrated, inspected and recalibrated, as required;
- must supply sufficient type-approved charts and printer rolls to drivers;
- must ensure the return of used analogue tachograph charts from drivers within 42 days;
- must download data from the VU at least every 90 days and from drivers' cards at least every 28 days;
- must not make payments to drivers related to distances travelled and/ or the amount of goods carried if by so doing it would encourage breaches of the rules;
- must be able to produce records to enforcement officers for 12 months.

Operator digital tachograph cards

In addition to drivers' digital tachograph cards (mentioned above), organizations and holders of operator licences are issued, upon request, with 'company cards'. Operators apply for company cards by contacting the DVLA to obtain an application (form ST2A). These cards allow the operator to download data from the VU, as is required, at least once every

90 days. In respect of holding data they do not store data but simply allow the operator to download data for display and printout on company card readers or computer programs.

Company cards also allow the operator to 'lock in' information and to 'lock out' unauthorized access to the driver information held on the VU. This can be necessary for 'commercial confidence' and security reasons when the vehicle is going for service or test, having the tachograph recalibrated or if the vehicle is to be 'hired out'. The 'locking out' feature is also especially useful when the vehicle is going 'off fleet' or being sold.

Because of the 'lock in – lock out' facility it may be necessary for operators who use hired vehicles to instruct their drivers on how to use the company card to download VU data if the vehicle is to go 'off hire' or be sold away from the normal base.

Breakdown of equipment

If a VU (digital) or analogue tachograph breaks down the repair must be carried out as soon as possible and, in any case, within seven days of the breakdown. If the vehicle is not going to return to base within seven days then the repair must be carried out 'en route'. This requirement is covered by EU legislation.

Note: Many EU member states do not allow vehicles with defective tachographs to enter or transit their territory and so any operator planning an international journey should not use a vehicle with a defective tachograph even if the driver is recording their activities using a manual record.

Within the UK operators and drivers are not deemed to have committed an offence when the tachograph breaks down providing:

- they can prove to a court that the vehicle was on its way to a place where the recording equipment could be repaired;
- they can prove it was not immediately practicable for the equipment to be repaired and the driver was keeping a manual record;
- where a seal is broken and the breaking of the seal was unavoidable and could not be immediately repaired.

These three provisions are only accepted in cases where there are no other breaches of the regulations associated with the failure of the equipment.

In relation to the breakdown of a VU, operators may need to ask the authorized repair centre to download any data held on the VU. Repair organizations do this by using a 'workshop card', which allows them to calibrate, recalibrate, adjust and change settings. These cards are only issued to authorized tachograph repair centres.

If the breakdown means that the repair centre cannot retrieve the information the operator requires then the centre should issue the operator with a 'Certificate of Undownloadability', which the operator must retain for at least 12 months, in the same way that they would retain other tachograph records.

Note: In addition to a driver card, a company card and a workshop card there is a fourth card, an enforcement card, which is used by the enforcement authorities to interrogate a VU and enable them to download up to 12 months' information from it.

Inspection and calibration

Whilst tachographs do break down occasionally they are usually reliable and are subject to statutory rules that mean they must be correctly installed, correctly sealed, and inspected and calibrated at set times. Any work performed on tachographs can only be performed by the vehicle manufacturer or an approved tachograph calibration centre.

Upon installation, an 'installation plaque' is fixed either to the tachograph itself or somewhere near to the tachograph. The plaque gives the date by which any following inspection and/or recalibration must take place. These subsequent inspections and calibrations will be recorded by the inspection facility who will issue certificates showing details of any inspection/calibration work carried out.

The rules for inspection and recalibration are statutory rules and must be complied with. However, they are slightly different for each type of tachograph. For instance, analogue tachographs must be inspected every two years and recalibrated every six years.

However, digital tachographs must be recalibrated every two years, or after any repair, or if the operator changes the registration number. In addition they need recalibration if the recorded UTC time is incorrect by more than 20 minutes and in situations where the operator changes the tyre circumference or the 'characteristic coefficient' of the tyres, perhaps by fitting 'low profile' tyres or new, smaller tyres following 'down-plating'.

Drivers' record books and record keeping

The remaining method of recording a driver's activities is by keeping a record book. Record books are required by drivers driving under the British domestic drivers' hours regulations that we discussed earlier. The book itself currently has to be of a set layout and design, although this is due to change in the near future. However, at the present time the record book must:

- be designed to produce an original and a copy of each record sheet;
- enable the driver to record both duty and driving times;
- contain guidance notes relating to how the driver should fill out the record book;
- contain guidance on when the driver needs to return the record book to the operator.

In relation to the checking of record books, the driver must take the book to the operator for countersignature within seven days of the end of the previous week. After countersigning, the employer must retain the duplicate copies of the sheets and return the book to the driver.

When the book is finally full, the driver has to return the book to the operator within 14 days of it becoming full and the operator then needs to retain the completed book for a minimum period of 12 months, or two years if it is to be used to record working time.

Record books are not required for drivers driving for the police, fire brigade or armed services, drivers who do not drive on public roads or for private (non-commercial) driving.

Record keeping for mixed driving

During any week where a driver drives under different sets of rules, if they are driving under EU drivers' hours rules they need to record any driving and other work carried out under either AETR or British domestic rules either on a tachograph, or, as in the case of British domestic rules, as a manual entry on either a blank tachograph chart or as a printout from a digital tachograph.

Key points you need to know

- Detailed understanding of the tachograph regulations.
- Detailed knowledge of drivers' roles and responsibilities.
- Detailed knowledge of an operators' roles and responsibilities.

- Driver and company card use.

- Tachograph breakdown, repair, inspection and recalibration procedures.

- Driver record book procedures and mixed-driving requirements.

Notes

....

....

....

....

....

....

....

....

....

....

As with drivers' hours, tachographs and drivers' records are a statutory issue in relation to operator licensing and a key section of the syllabus and you will be examined on them in detail so you will need to be thoroughly familiar with the topic.

Related offences, penalties and DVSA powers

In relation to drivers' hours and records, operators and drivers can both be found liable for breaches of the regulations. For this reason, drivers need to understand and comply with the rules and operators need to regularly check that there are no problems.

Typically, operators need to check for items such as insufficient breaks and rests being taken and/or driving and duty times being exceeded, as well as that any records produced by drivers are correct in their format and the correct activities have been recorded.

Where offences are detected, including deliberate attempts at falsifying records, the operator is bound by the terms of the Operator Licence to inform the driver and to take actions to prevent any recurrence. This requirement usually means that initially drivers need to be warned and the warning recorded and acknowledged by the driver concerned. Should no improvement be made then further actions, up to and including dismissal, may be required. In cases of deliberate deception, dismissal is normally the only acceptable action available to the operator if they are to protect the licence.

Whilst there are clear means of taking action against drivers and operators, where an infringement of drivers' hours rules occurs the law protects drivers who can prove that, because of unforeseen circumstances, they were unavoidably delayed and subsequently breached the rules.

In the case of infringements concerning records, the law protects an operator from conviction if they can prove that they took all reasonable steps to make sure that the driver kept proper records.

However, there is one minor difference in relation to liability between the EU rules and British domestic rules. This is the fact that the EU rules make transport undertakings liable for any infringements committed by their drivers, whereas domestic rules also protect operators if a driver was involved in other driving activities that the operator could not possibly have known about.

Penalties and deposits

Graduated fixed penalties and deposits were introduced into the UK in 2009. This meant that drivers who commit offences and who have a UK address (that can be verified as valid) are normally dealt with by means of a fixed penalty notice, where the 'graduated' penalty means that the level of the fine is linked to the severity of the offence.

Drivers without a valid address (normally foreign drivers) are asked to pay a deposit equal to the fixed penalty, and further driving will be prohibited until such payment is made.

The fixed penalty and deposit systems do not in any way prevent the DVSA or police being able to bring more serious charges, if this is appropriate.

Note: In October 2015 the UK introduced a system allowing the enforcement authorities to issue fixed penalties for offences detected on a driver's record at any time over the last 28 days. However, awarding fixed penalties for historic offences is only done in cases where the DVSA conduct a roadside check and find, at the time of the check, that there is a current offence being committed that is in itself prosecutable. This 'historic offence' provision allows the DVSA to issue fixed penalties against foreign drivers who, so far, have been unable to be charged in spite of recent past offences having been recorded whilst the vehicle was in the UK.

Powers

To enforce the regulations, authorized DVSA vehicle examiners have the power to:

- inspect vehicles;
- prohibit and direct vehicles;
- investigate possible breaches of regulations;
- instigate, conduct and appear in proceedings at a Magistrates' Court or Sheriff Court.

Sanctions

Authorized examiners have the ability to take actions against offending drivers and operators depending upon the severity or nature of the offence. These actions include:

- Verbal warnings for minor, isolated infringements that appear to have been committed either accidentally or due to the inexperience of the driver or operator.
- Issuing offence rectification notices which may be issued to operators for infringements that are not related to safety. The notice gives operators 21 days to carry out any remedial action. Failure to take action by the operator means that prosecution may follow.
- Prosecution is considered where it is in the public interest. This means that more serious infringements are those that lead to actual prosecution. The driver, the operator or even the operating organization can all be prosecuted.
- Prohibition is an enforcement action taken to reduce or remove a threat to road safety.
- A prohibition notice normally means that the driving of a vehicle is prohibited until the conditions stated on the prohibition notice are satisfied. However, prohibitions can be immediate or 'delayed'. Where a condition 'delays' the prohibition it is normally done to enable the vehicle to get to a place of safety or repair.
- Referral to the Traffic Commissioner (TC). Referral means that where the driver is the holder of a vocational licence and/or the operator is the holder of an operator's licence, enforcement staff may report any infringements for consideration by the TC. This can be done whether or not any prosecution is to be brought.

Co-liability

The EU drivers' hours rules make organizations such as some freight forwarders, some contractors and subcontractors, and some driver employment agencies responsible for ensuring that any 'contractually agreed' transport time schedules comply with drivers' hours rules.

That concludes the somewhat 'thorny' issue of penalties and offences relating to drivers' hours and records, and the syllabus now requires us to briefly look at the Driver Certificate of Professional Competence (DCPC). In so doing it is to be noted that the syllabus also includes DCPC later in the final chapter. This duplication is as a direct result of the layout of the EU Directive.

Driver Certificate of Professional Competence (DCPC)

EU Directive 2003/59 requires all vocational (C1, C and CE category) drivers to hold a Driver Certificate of Professional Competence (DCPC) in addition to their vocational driving licence. This requirement means that since 10 September 2009 newly qualified vocational drivers have had to undergo initial DCPC training as a part of gaining their vocational driving licence. Vocational drivers who passed their tests before that date also had to complete 35 hours of periodic DCPC by 9 September 2014.

In either case, completion of 'initial' or 'periodic' training means that the driver concerned is issued with a Driver Qualification Card (DQC), which must be carried at all times and produced upon request.

Once the DQC is issued the driver effectively enters a new five-year period where they are subject to 'periodic' DCPC training, which means that they must complete 35 hours of DCPC training within five years of the issue of the DQC, if they wish the card to be renewed and to continue driving professionally. This five-year process will continue for as long as the driver wishes to drive professionally.

Private driving not related to a business or profession (perhaps hiring a 7.5-tonne vehicle to move house) is excluded from the DCPC requirement.

The initial DCPC qualification is a part of the overall driving test process and the full process is outlined below. As you can see, the DCPC elements constitute Modules 2 and 4:

- Module 1: Theory and Hazard Perception Test. This consists of 100 multiple-choice theory questions (85 pass mark) and 19 hazard video clips (100 marks with 67 pass mark). Because a pass of Module 1 only remains valid for a period of two years, the full programme needs to be completed within that time or the module will need to be retaken.

- Module 2: Driver CPC Case Studies. This is taken as a computer test taking around 1.5 hours with seven case studies. Each of the case studies is based on real-life scenarios with six to eight questions on each.

- Module 3: The Practical Driving Test.

- Module 4: Driver CPC Practical Demonstration Test. This is undertaken using an actual vehicle to assess the candidate's practical skill and knowledge on a 'show me, tell me' basis, where the examiner covers issues such as safety, emergency situations, and vehicle safety checks and load security.

Module 1 must be passed before taking module 3, and module 2 must be passed before taking module 4.

The periodic training courses for the required 35 hours of training every five years are only available through approved training providers. The approved providers must use approved trainers to deliver approved training, and the whole process is overseen, administered and monitored by the Joint Approvals Unit for Periodic Training (JAUPT).

Whilst there is no requirement for a course to include a test or pass/fail element, there is a requirement that the minimum length of each training session must be at least seven hours, over and above delegate registration and any breaks. Note that a course of seven hours may be split into two 3.5-hour sessions for operational reasons, but the second session must start within 24 hours of completion of the first session.

Note: In April 2015, JAUPT announced that drivers who passed their vocational test in the past but who have not used their entitlements to date may now either undertake the full 35 hours of periodic training or take modules 2 and 4 of the initial DCPC qualification to enable them to gain their first DQC only.

Drivers who drive lorries, and who also drive buses or coaches, are only required to complete one set of 35 hours' training every five years. They do not need to undertake any 'passenger'-specific DCPC training.

There are several groups of drivers exempted from the requirement for DCPC, including the following:

- nationals of EU member states or employees of a company based in a member state (providing they DO NOT drive a vehicle requiring C1, C1E, C or CE category licence);

- vehicles that are not allowed to exceed 45 kilometres per hour (kph);
- vehicles being used by or under the control of the armed forces, police, a local authority, or fire and rescue authority;
- vehicles being road-tested or new or rebuilt vehicles that have not been put into service;
- vehicles driven to and from pre-booked appointments at official testing centres;
- vehicles being used in emergencies or rescue missions;
- vehicles being used for driving lessons or driving tests;
- non-commercial carriage of passengers or goods for personal use;
- vehicles carrying material or equipment to be used in the course of the driver's work;
- vehicles driven within 100 km of the driver's base and not carrying passengers or goods.

DCPC is now becoming more widely known about and is becoming a part of many drivers' everyday professional life, but it is in the syllabus and it is examined. In the next chapter we examine fiscal law.

Key points you need to know

- General understanding of offences.
- General understanding of powers and sanctions.
- Initial and periodic DCPC, structure, formats and requirements.

Notes

....
....
....
....
....
....
....
....
....
....

Self-test example questions

OCR-type questions (multi-choice)

1 Under what circumstances would an HSE inspector issue: i) a Prohibition Notice; ii) an Improvement Notice?

a A Prohibition Notice will be issued if an HSE inspector has reason to believe that whatever activities are being carried out could be illegal and not in the public interest, and an Improvement Notice would be issued by HSI inspectors to instruct a business that they need additional safety training before they can continue to operate.

b A Prohibition Notice will be issued if an HSE inspector has reason to believe that the company concerned does not take health and safety seriously and does not issue all staff with PPE, and an Improvement Notice would be issued by HSE inspectors to record that the improvements required had been made and the company was now free to carry on trading.

c A Prohibition Notice will be issued if an HSE inspector has reason to believe that whatever activities are being carried out may result in either a serious danger to health or a serious risk of injury, and an Improvement Notice would be issued by HSE inspectors to correct situations where they can clearly see that some sort of lesser breach of the regulations is occurring, and is likely to continue to occur.

d A Prohibition Notice will be issued if an HSE inspector has reason to suspect that the company is trying to provide false details in relation to accidents and health and safety issues at work, and an Improvement Notice would be issued by HSE inspectors to provide an agreed timescale for improvement activity to be carried out before the company is reinspected and certified as being a safe place of work.

2 Which of the following are the three steps of a disciplinary procedure that will ensure the employer does not have to attend an employment tribunal?

a

Step 1: The employer must invite the employee to attend a disciplinary hearing, where the employee is able to be represented, so that matters can be discussed.

Step 2: Following the meeting the employee must be told of any decision made by the employer and disciplinary action can begin.

Step 3: The employee must be permitted to have the right to seek help from a trade union.

b

Step 1: The employer must send a written statement outlining the reason for the intended action and invite the employee to attend a meeting, where the employee is able to be represented, so that matters can be discussed.

Step 2: Following the meeting the employee must be told of any decision made by the employer, before any disciplinary action can actually begin.

Step 3: The employee must be permitted to have the right to appeal the decision made.

c

Step 1: The employer must suspend the employee but continue payment whilst the full details are investigated and appropriate action can be developed.

Step 2: Following the suspension the employee must be told of any decision made by the employer, with reasons for the decision being clearly explained.

Step 3: The employee must agree with the decision and either leave the company or seek financial compensation through an employment appeals tribunal.

d

Step 1: The employer must inform the employee's recognized trade union representative and explain, in writing, the reasons behind the intended disciplinary action.

Step 2: The employer and employee concerned must meet and discuss the issues raised and any likely actions that the employer may be considering taking against the employee.

Step 3: The employee must be permitted sufficient time to produce a response to the issues raised at the previous meeting or ask the recognized trade union to contact ACAS in order to adjudicate.

3 What are the three different business circumstances that can lead to an employee(s) being made redundant?

a The three business circumstances include: where a business no longer trades as a limited company and needs to downsize; where the business no longer has sufficient customers to warrant keeping higher than required staff numbers; and where a business is affected by changes in working conditions and technological standards and needs to recruit younger employees.

b The three business circumstances include: where a business no longer carries out the type of work or business the employee was employed for; where the business no longer carries out business in the place or location where the employee is employed; and where a business no longer requires the employee to carry out a particular type of work.

c The three business circumstances include: where a business goes into liquidation; where the business no longer carries out business in the place or location where the employee is employed; and where a business is taken over by another business.

d The three business circumstances include: where a business needs to retrain staff in order to reskill; where the business no longer feels able to carry on in traditional markets; and where a business no longer requires all the employees it used to need.

4 Which of the following answers are all actions that a driver must take if he/she loses his/her digital tachograph card whilst out on the road?

a The driver may drive without the card for a maximum of seven calendar days, produce two-hourly printouts right throughout the working day and report the problem to DVLA and apply for a new card within 10 calendar days of the loss.

b The driver may drive without the card for a maximum of 21 calendar days, produce a daily printout at the end of the journey/duty and report the problem to DVLA and apply for a new card within 15 calendar days of the loss.

c The driver may drive without the card for a maximum of 14 calendar days, produce a daily printout at the start of the journey/daily duty and report the problem to DVLA and apply for a new card within three calendar days of the loss.

d The driver may drive without the card for a maximum of 15 calendar days, produce two printouts – one at the start of the journey/daily duty and another at the end – and report the problem to DVLA and apply for a new card within seven calendar days of the loss.

OCR case study-type question

See past papers referred to in Chapter 1, but note that there will be at least one case study question relating to drivers' hours and records and so you should work through the CILT long-answer example question below, because both examination bodies write similar questions on this topic.

CILT-type questions (short answer)

1 Briefly explain the circumstances that would lead a HSE inspector to issue:

a a Prohibition Notice;

b an Improvement Notice.

2 Briefly describe the three steps that go together to form an acceptable disciplinary procedure that will avoid the employer having to attend an employment tribunal.

3 Briefly describe the three business circumstances that can lead to an employee(s) being made redundant.

4 What actions must a driver take if he/she loses his/her digital tachograph card whilst out on the road?

CILT-type question (long answer)

A driver operating under Drivers' Hours Regulation EC561/2006 and the Working Time Directive (RTD) is about to leave on a journey from Manchester to Milan. The following facts apply to the journey:

- The distance from Manchester to Dover is 540 km.

- The vehicle will use the Dover to Calais ferry.

- The vehicle will deliver to Paris and Marseille before making the final delivery in Milan.

- The distance from Calais to Paris is 260 km.

- The distance from Paris to Marseille is 960 km.

- The distance from Marseille to Milan is 480 km.

- The vehicle will travel at an average speed of 80 kph.

- The driver has all available driving hours' concessions (extended driving days and reduced daily rests) available.

- The driver must spend 15 minutes checking the vehicle at the start of each daily duty period.

- The driver must take all breaks and rests as late as legally possible.

- The driver must assist with unloading at Paris and Marseille, which will take three hours each time.

- The ferry leaves at 14.30 UTC. French local time of UTC +1 hour will apply after disembarkation.

- The time on the ferry is to be recorded as POA.

- Embarkation and disembarkation on and off the ferry takes 15 minutes before the ferry departs and after it arrives, which is recorded as driving time.

- You must use local times throughout the journey.

Using Table 3.1, calculate the earliest possible local time that the vehicle can arrive in Milan (all distances and details are for test purposes only and the number of available lines in the table is not significant).

TABLE 3.1 Calculation table

Time	Activity	Notes
06.00	Start Work	
06.00 – 06.15	Check Vehicle	

These types of questions are ALWAYS included as 'long questions' by both OCR and CILT and often involve ferries, nights out and different time zones. You must read the set questions carefully to ensure that you get all the facts and answer exactly what is required.

Once you are happy that you can answer questions such as those above then, as before, please feel free to move on to the next chapter, which examines fiscal law. However, if you are unsure or not certain about any of the content, or any of the 'key points you need to know' then please revisit until you feel that you have a full grasp of the material and what is required. Please also remember that these were only sample questions and both OCR and CILT can provide actual examples.

Fiscal law

04

This chapter will give you the required understanding of the relevant types of taxation that apply to freight transport operations and other forms of business and personal taxation.

The syllabus requires that you need to be familiar with:

- the rules governing value-added tax (VAT) on transport services;

- the rules governing motor vehicle tax (VED);

- the rules governing the taxes on certain road haulage vehicles and be familiar with tolls and infrastructure user charges;

- the rules governing income tax.

In order to follow the syllabus layout of this somewhat 'wide-ranging' section, we begin by looking at VAT.

Value-added tax (VAT)

There are three levels of VAT that apply to goods or services within the UK. These are:

- Standard rate: currently 20 per cent, which applies to most goods and services, including most transport services and provision.

- Reduced rate: currently 5 per cent, which is applied to fuel and power used in the home and is applied to charities.

- Zero-rated: the zero rate* applies to items such as food and drink not bought in cafes or restaurants, books and newspapers and children's clothes.

---

* For clarity, zero-rated goods and services are those items to which the UK Government 'may' one day apply VAT, whilst exempted goods and services (see below) are those that HM Government sees as never being liable for VAT.

Whilst there are three levels of VAT there are also some goods that are totally exempt from VAT. These include items such as selling, leasing and letting houses; insurance; and doctors' and dentists' services.

Registration

Companies expecting to have, or having, annual sales exceeding a predetermined value (£85,000 in 2017) need to register for VAT with Her Majesty's Revenue and Customs (HMRC). This registration process is required as soon as a company realizes that their sales figure will exceed the threshold. Companies with a lower figure of annual sales can still register for VAT voluntarily, should they wish to do so. When the company registers, which is normally done online, it will be issued with an individual VAT number that must be used on all VAT-related invoices and for payment or refunds of VAT to and from HMRC.

Where an actual online application is not feasible, all VAT registration forms are available on the HMRC website and can then be printed, completed by hand and submitted by post. Most businesses are only required to submit a single form when making their application, but businesses trading internationally and partnerships will need to complete an additional form explaining further details.

In addition to a VAT number, successful registration also leads to HMRC issuing a VAT registration certificate (VAT 4) that includes details of the business and the date of registration.

Application

When a company is registered for VAT and buys goods or services from another supplier, VAT is charged. The current rate is 20 per cent, which is added to the initial cost. This charge is known as an input tax. Similarly, when the company sells its own goods or services, it charges its customers VAT, and this is known as an output tax.

Normally, a VAT-registered company has to complete the VAT return every three months. This 'quarterly' return gives details of its input tax and output tax. The difference in input tax and output tax is a sum that is payable to HMRC. However, if the input tax is greater than the output tax, the company can claim money back from HMRC.

Whilst most small and medium-sized companies pay VAT quarterly, any company is able to agree to alternative payment schedules with HMRC. This enables some companies to pay VAT annually. This is termed 'annual accounting'.

In addition, some companies are able to avoid paying VAT until they themselves have been paid (cash accounting) and other companies pay a single reduced rate for VAT on sales only but are unable to recover VAT on purchases (flat-rate accounting).

Once a company is registered and applying VAT, it is a legal requirement that records must be kept for a minimum period of six years. This means a full six years, and any records from the current year must also be produced, if required.

Invoicing

A properly formatted VAT invoice must be issued by every VAT-registered company for each transaction. The invoice must contain certain information if it is to be accepted by the tax authorities. Because of this every VAT invoice must show:

- a specific invoice number;
- the date of supply of the goods or services (known as the tax point);
- the name and address of the business supplying the goods or services;
- the supplier's VAT registration number;
- the customer's name and address;
- the type of supply that was made (such as the carriage of a consignment and/or a specific description of the goods);
- the quantity of any goods or the details of the services;
- the rate of tax levied and the amount payable (excluding VAT) for each item listed;
- the total amount payable (excluding VAT);
- any cash discount offered;
- the total amount of VAT charged.

VAT in other EU countries

The VAT system is only relevant within the EU. Outside of the EU, similar systems operate but they are not a system of VAT, as we know it. In spite of VAT being an EU-wide tax, the levels of VAT do vary in each member state, appearing to give advantages to businesses in countries charging lower VAT rates on goods and services. Nevertheless, the principles of VAT are the same across all EU countries.

In the UK, any company that is VAT registered is able to claim back VAT from another EU country. This is done by HMRC issuing the company with a Certificate of Status, which is valid for a period of 12 months. The claim is then made online using the HMRC website and the foreign VAT reclaim portal. HMRC then forwards the claim to the relevant country for the payment to be made. All claims must be submitted within nine months of the tax year in which the relevant expense was incurred.

In cases where cabotage is being undertaken (where an operator from one country establishes itself in another in order to undertake local work), the operator is normally required to register for VAT in the country where the work is being undertaken and not in their home country, as the VAT is payable to the country where the operations were carried out.

In addition, the VAT status of the customer (business customer or private individual) also determines what VAT is to be charged and in which country a UK-based operator may need to register for VAT.

For example, on a journey from the UK to Spain for a UK-based business customer, the UK VAT rate would be charged. For a journey back to the UK from Spain for a private customer, then the UK operator would need to register for VAT in Spain and charge the Spanish rate. This general principle clearly demonstrates how the 'status' of business or private acts to influence what VAT is paid.

As a final point in relation to VAT, it is worthy of note that, in spite of a perfectly good system being in place with HMRC in the UK, some EU countries still require companies to be VAT registered in that country in order for any claim to be paid.

Motor vehicle taxation (VED)

Large goods vehicles are subject to Vehicle Excise Duty (VED) based upon the gross weight of the vehicle and the number of axles. In addition there are tax concessions for vehicles with low emissions, such as Euro VI emission standards, and there is additional tax for some rigid vehicles that tow heavy draw-bar trailers. Since the introduction of the 'Heavy Goods Vehicle User Levy' (see later) the total VED paid for UK-registered vehicles also includes payment of the levy.

The DVLA in Swansea is the overseeing body for VED and every vehicle registered in the UK is kept on file at the DVLA's central database.

This way of controlling VED now means that owners cannot pass on a vehicle to a new owner with any existing VED that is still valid. Owners who sell vehicles and notify the DVLA of the sale now automatically receive a refund and new owners now need to apply for VED in their own right.

Another development has been that the DVLA now allows VED to be paid monthly or six-monthly – either by a normal payment or by establishing a direct debit, or annually by a single payment. However, if the VED is paid monthly or biannually, a 5 per cent surcharge is applied.

Under EU standardization, goods vehicles and trailers fall into broad categories for VED and construction and use purposes. These are defined and categorized:

- A goods vehicle is defined as a motor vehicle with at least four wheels designed and constructed for the carriage of freight.

  Goods vehicles are then categorized as category N vehicles:

  - Category N1: vehicles designed and constructed for the carriage of goods and having a maximum mass not exceeding 3.5 tonnes.

  - Category N2: vehicles designed and constructed for the carriage of goods and having a maximum mass exceeding 3.5 tonnes but not exceeding 12 tonnes.

  - Category N3: vehicles designed and constructed for the carriage of goods and having a maximum mass exceeding 12 tonnes.

- Trailers are also defined and categorized: a trailer is defined as a goods vehicle drawn by a motor vehicle. There are two main types of trailer:

  - A drawbar trailer, which is a trailer pulled by a rigid prime mover, where the trailer supports the load independently of the drawing vehicle. (The term 'drawbar' refers to the fact that these trailers are 'pulled' or 'drawn' by the prime mover).

  - A semi-trailer, which is a trailer that forms part of an articulated combination, where more than 20 per cent of the weight of the trailer and load are borne by the tractor unit.

  Trailers are also then categorized as category O vehicles:

  - Category O1: trailers with a maximum mass not exceeding 0.75 tonnes.

  - Category O2: trailers with a maximum mass exceeding 0.75 tonnes but not exceeding 3.5 tonnes.

- Category O3: trailers with a maximum mass exceeding 3.5 tonnes but not exceeding 10 tonnes.
- Category O4: trailers with a maximum mass exceeding 10 tonnes.

Note: For VED purposes, cars, dual-purpose vehicles (estate cars and some 4×4s), car-derived vans (small vans that have a car equivalent) and small goods vehicles up to 3,500 kg maximum authorized mass (MAM), such as Ford Transits, are all taxed at the same general rate although there are variations depending upon emissions and engine type/size.

Rates of VED

Since the time of introduction of the HGV Road User Levy (see below) some of the existing A–G VED bands have been divided into subsections based on configuration and emission standards, and larger vehicles, those exceeding 12,000 kg, are categorized into rigid vehicles, rigid vehicles drawing trailers, and articulated vehicles. In addition, lower-rate band charges are applied if the vehicle qualifies for a reduced pollution discount or grant, as mentioned earlier.

However, some rigid vehicles also attract 'trailer duty'. This duty needs to be paid when a rigid vehicle exceeding 12,000 kg GVW draws a trailer exceeding 4,000 kg. This only applies to rigid vehicles drawing trailers and is not applied to semi-trailers of articulated combinations.

Note: The acronym GVW has the same meaning as maximum authorized mass (MAM) and maximum permitted weight (MPW), all of which are used by the enforcement authorities, vehicle manufacturers and in the trade press and teaching material.

Initial registration

Often it is the vehicle dealer who will apply for first registration and for the first taxation period but, in cases where the operator applies, the following documents must be produced by post to the DVLA in Swansea:

- a completed application form (V55/1 or V55/2);
- the initial registration fee;
- the appropriate vehicle excise duty fee;
- the vehicle suppliers' invoice with Certificate of Conformity (CoC);
- proof of identity (usually by producing a passport or photocard driving licence).

Renewals

A similar process applies to VED renewals at the DVLA although some vehicle VED renewals are able to be done completely online. This is made possible by the DVLA holding records relating to test certificates and vehicle insurance validity. However, it is also still possible to renew VED at selected post offices.

For renewals at post offices you must provide:

- the V11 renewal form sent by the DVLA;
- a valid certificate of insurance;
- a current test certificate;
- a reduced pollution certificate, if applicable;
- the appropriate vehicle excise duty fee.

VED for all vehicles can be purchased monthly or six-monthly by a normal payment or by direct debit at a 5 per cent surcharge, or for 12 months by a single payment, and runs from the first day of each month (only full months can be purchased). This process is the same as that applied to private cars.

Reduced levels of VED

To qualify for a reduced pollution discounted rate of VED, which applies to some vehicles exceeding 12,000 kg MAM, through the HGV Road User Levy charging system, a vehicle must be able to meet emission standards 'better than the levels required by law for that type of vehicle at the time of registration, based on the "Euro" emission levels of Euro I–Euro VI'. This definition means that all newly registered large goods vehicles in the UK must now conform to Euro VI emission standards.

In the case of older vehicles, emissions can be reduced by retro-fitting items such as particulate traps, systems that recirculate the exhaust gases or by fitting new, more efficient engines.

Upgrading the emissions standards of vehicles is particularly relevant at the present time because, since April 2015, vehicles fitted with early Euro II and III engines were issued with a final reduced pollution certificate. In turn, reduced pollution certificates ceased to be issued for these vehicles after 31 March 2016, and all reduced pollution certificates for these vehicles expired in February 2017. The whole scheme, including certificates for Euro IV and V engines finished in December 2017 and the reductions for reduced emissions are now included in bands of the HGV Road User Levy (see below).

Returns and Statutory Off Road Notification (SORN)

Many operators need to remove vehicles from service at certain times of the year, and/or when work contracts are subject to change or alteration. In these types of circumstances the VED can be terminated and any refund made by the DVLA. However, the vehicle needs to be kept on record by the DVLA and to do this the operator must declare the vehicle is 'out of service' and currently not paying VED by declaring this to the DVLA using a Statutory Off Road Notification (SORN). Each SORN is valid until the vehicle is either retaxed, sold, scrapped or permanently exported from the UK.

Whilst failure to renew the VED is subject to the issue of an automatic fine notification, a false declaration of a SORN can lead to a fine of up to £5,000 or two years' imprisonment.

Exemptions from VED

The following vehicle classes are exempt from VED:

- vehicles used by the armed forces or the Crown;
- police, fire, ambulance and mine rescue vehicles;
- vehicles manufactured before 1 January 1976;
- a vehicle travelling to and from a test station, providing this is the only purpose of the journey, and the test appointment has been pre-booked;
- agricultural tractors;
- certain vehicles used for the carriage of people with disabilities, which are not ambulances, but need to be identified as ambulances.

HGV Road User Levy

The HGV Road User Levy was introduced to ensure that, as in many other EU member states, visiting foreign vehicles pay a proportion for the upkeep of the road network and infrastructure. UK operators also pay the levy but it was incorporated into the rate of VED (as discussed earlier), which was reduced to ensure that, overall, the total road taxation (Road User Levy and VED) did not rise for domestic operators when the levy was introduced.

It should be noted that the UK levy does not apply to passenger vehicles or goods vehicles not exceeding 12,000 kg GVW. The 12,000-kg threshold is set by the overarching EU 'Eurovignette Directive', which only allows these types of levies to be set at weight not exceeding 3,500 kg or 12,000 kg.

For UK operators, the levy charges are 'banded' into bands that are based on the weight of the vehicle, the number of axles and periods of 6 or 12 months. The levy band charges also relate to the use of heavy trailers (exceeding 4,000 kg) and abnormal indivisible load (AIL) operations, with AILs having to pay the maximum fees that can be charged. As a part of the levy, it was decided that, in order to encourage the use of low-emission vehicles, after 2017 the Euro II and Euro III engine vehicles will no longer be entitled to concessions based on low emissions.

UK operators pay the levy as part of the initial vehicle registration process and at the same time as any subsequent VED renewals, with charges for UK-registered vehicles being between £100 and £1,000 per year.

For UK operators applying to renew VED, the levy rate includes a reduced pollution discount for vehicles with Euro IV to Euro VI engines. These discounts replaced the Reduced Pollution Certificates (RPC), which were previously issued for 'low emission' vehicles exceeding 12,000 kg GVW and which originally included Euro II and Euro III engines.

Foreign operators need to pay before their entry to the UK. Payment by foreign operators can be made online, at payment facilities at truck stops close to the channel ports, at the channel ports in mainland Europe, and at pay facilities on the ferries or at the Channel Tunnel European terminal. These charges vary from around £10 a day up to £1,000 per year. They may also purchase daily, weekly or monthly vignettes, but a surcharge applies when 'short-term' applications are made.

Non-payment is normally subject to a fixed penalty, but it can lead to immobilization of the vehicle in cases where the driver cannot pay the fixed penalty deposit or provide a suitable UK address. As a final sanction, fines of up to £5,000 can be imposed and, in the most serious cases, operators can be banned from using vehicles within the UK at any time in the future.

Detection of non-payment or avoidance of payment is usually made by the system of automatic number-plate recognition (ANPR) installed on the principal routes throughout the UK.

Other charges

Whilst we will all usually need to pay VED in one way or another, we also need to recognize that there are other payments and charges that need to be made for using different parts of the road network both at home and abroad. We will begin by considering UK-based charges and then go on to look at the picture in Europe.

Congestion charging

Congestion charges, also known as road user charges or as a zonal toll, cover a defined area including the congestion charge area of London or Durham, where the charges are aimed solely at reducing traffic congestion at certain times. The most well-known charge is probably the London Congestion Charge, which is administered by Transport for London (TfL) within the capital. This charge is a daily charge for vehicles entering the defined charge area, with discounts being given for operators who register with TfL for prepayment or auto payment.

Low emission zones / clean air zones

Another form of road charging is made for vehicles entering a low emission zone (LEZ), now more frequently referred to as a clean air zone (CAZ), initially introduced in London in 2008. These zones operate 24 hours a day, seven days a week (including bank holidays). Other LEZ/CAZs, based on the London model, are planned for several other major cities including Birmingham, Derby, Leeds, Nottingham and Southampton in England and Aberdeen, Dundee, Edinburgh and Glasgow in Scotland by 2018/2019.

The original standards have changed since that date and operators are advised to confirm compliance or non-compliance through the TfL website. In general terms (but only as a guide), vehicles registered after 1 October 2006 and any that have a Reduced Pollution Certificate or are subject to a Reduced Pollution Grant are 'normally' deemed to comply.

Non-compliant vehicles are treated in different ways. For example:

- The first time a non-compliant LGV is detected within the LEZ/CAZ, the operator is issued with just a warning letter.

- If a non-compliant LGV is used again, then it attracts a daily penalty charge of £200 for an LGV. This charge can be paid up to 64 days before travel into the zone, on the day of travel into the zone or up to midnight on the day after travel into the zone.

- Non-payment of this initial daily penalty charge leads to a further daily penalty charge of £1,000. This will be reduced by 50 per cent if paid within 14 calendar days, but increased by 50 per cent if not paid within 28 calendar days.

Note: London is also planning to introduce an ultra-low emission zone (ULEZ) in 2019. This zone is planned to operate 24 hours a day, seven days a week, and will restrict access for large goods vehicles and 'large vans'. To be compliant, vehicles will need Euro VI emission standard engines to travel to, or through, an area extending from the North and South Circular Roads. If vehicles without

Euro VI engines wish to enter or transit the zone it is expected that they will have to pay a 'sliding scale' fee of between £12.50 and £100 per day. Penalties for non-compliance will be the same as for the current LEZ/CAZ (above).

In addition to the ULEZ, since October 2017, there is now an additional charge of £10.00 (known as the T-Charge) levied on what are termed 'most polluting vehicles' operating within the current London Congestion Zone.

In preparation for the ULEZ, there is a Transport for London (TfL) 5-year programme known as 'LoCITY'. LoCITY helps operators, including the London boroughs, to understand the alternative low carbon and clean fuel technologies prior to the requirement for Euro VI vehicles within the planned ULEZ.

Tolls

Highways England (HE), Transport Scotland, the Welsh Assembly Government, or the Local Highway Authorities either own, or own and operate, most of the roads within the UK and so these roads are subject to the current VED scheme. However, where private investment has been used, such as for the M6 Toll Road, then tolls are charged to enable the investor to recover the initial investment, maintain the road and make a profit. This is also the case with many of the toll bridges within the UK.

Most systems of tolling used on major toll areas such as the M6 Toll Road, the Dartford Crossing and the Severn Crossings, operate systems of vehicle recognition, using electronic tags carried in the vehicle and a customer account that requires prepayment. It is also worth noting that all bridge toll charges have been scrapped in Scotland and that some toll charges are only levied in a single direction.

For examination purposes you can be asked to identify routes with, or without, tolls and so a list of some of the UK principal toll charge points, in addition to the M6 Toll Road, already discussed, is set out below:

- The Tyne Tunnel on the A19 at Wallsend.
- The Mersey Tunnel on the M53 between Liverpool and Birkenhead.
- The Humber Bridge on the A15 near Hull.
- The Thames Crossing* on the M25 at Dartford.
- The Severn Bridges** on the M4 and M48 between Bristol and Newport.
- The Tamar Bridge on the A38 between Plymouth and Saltash.

---

* There is no charge for using the Thames Crossing between 10 pm and 6 am. However, any payments that are due must be paid either in advance or by midnight the day after crossing. Payment cannot be made at the time of crossing.

** The tolls on the Severn Bridges are expected to be greatly reduced or even scrapped some time in 2018 as the two bridges are transferred into public ownership.

Clearly, there are many other minor toll crossing points, such as the Dunham Bridge over the River Trent and the Cleddau Bridge in South Wales, but the charges are generally quite low and it is a fact that toll crossing points and toll roads are much more commonly encountered when travelling in Europe. For that purpose, and because the syllabus requires you to have an outline appreciation of the European road network, we will now look at country-wide charging in Europe.

European tolls

Whilst the EU standardizes many things, the systems of tolling and infra-structure charges differ from member state to member state. An overview of some of the different systems (in alphabetical order) is below:

- Austria: Austria operates the Go-Box system, a small box that has to be purchased close to the border and fixed in the window of a vehicle. Overhead gantries then monitor the movements of the vehicle with charges levied on the number of axles and distance travelled by vehicles exceeding 3,500 kg MAM. Currently foreign drivers carrying out cabotage operations within Austria also need to carry proof that they are being paid a wage that is at least equal to the Austrian minimum wage rate.

- Belgium: From 1 April 2016 all goods vehicles over 3500 kg GVW travelling in Belgium need to have an on-board unit (OBU). The system will be enforced by automatic number-plate recognition (ANPR) cameras and mobile enforcement. The toll charges are based on the gross weight of the vehicle, the vehicle's emissions and the road type and will vary from region to region. Because of this change, Belgium withdrew from the Eurovignette system that it used to operate. Within Belgium there is also a charge for using the Liefkenshoek Tunnel in Antwerp.

- Bulgaria: Bulgaria has a vignette system for all foreign goods vehicles using national roads, similar to the Eurovignette. The vignettes need to be purchased at border points and are available for periods of a week, month or year.

- Croatia: There are two toll collection systems in Croatia – the open and the closed systems. The open system is used on some bridges and tunnels and short stretches of tolled roads where there is only one toll plaza and drivers immediately pay the toll upon arriving. The closed system is a system where every driver passes through two toll booths. It works by drivers being given a ticket at the first toll booth and then presenting it at the second toll booth. The toll is based on distance travelled and the size of vehicle.

- Czech Republic: The Czech Republic applies a distance-based charge, using a small electronic device fitted to the vehicle, for all vehicles over 12,000 kg using the highway and expressway network.

- Denmark: Denmark operates the Eurovignette toll system. The other countries operating this system include Luxembourg, the Netherlands and Sweden. Heavy goods vehicles and vehicle combinations with a GVW of 12 tonnes must have a valid Eurovignette when driving in the countries named above.

- France: France operates several local tolling systems but the main tolls are levied for using motorways and trunk roads, and tolls are applied for using different 'sections' of the network. The French system is coordinated through the use of a registered account and an electronic device fitted to the vehicle which automatically records the journey and debits the account, although many roads still have toll booths for cash payments at the time of use. France is another country that has introduced a requirement for foreign drivers to prove that they are paid at a rate of at least equivalent to the French minimum wage. This requirement is for both cabotage and delivery/collection activities.

- Germany: Germany has a Motorway User Charge (LKW-Maut) where a prepayment is made or post-payment is collected through a GPS-based system requiring an electronic device to be fitted to the vehicle. In 2015, Germany introduced additional tolls for vehicles exceeding 7.5 tonnes GVW by extending the toll charges to include additional major roads on the federal road network. Because of these changes, Germany left the Eurovignette toll scheme. Currently, foreign drivers collecting or delivering loads (but not just in transit) in Germany also need to carry proof that they are being paid a wage that is at least equal to the German minimum wage rate.

- Greece: Tolls are applied on the main Greek motorways. There is also a toll related to a 'road development tax' for using the E75 road border crossing.

- Hungary: Tolls, which are based on the gross weight of the vehicle, are levied on the main Hungarian motorways.

- Ireland (Republic of): Most motorways and tunnels do have some tolls and charges but ordinary roads are generally toll free.

- Italy: Tolls are applied on the main Italian autostrade and also at the Fréjus and Mont Blanc tunnels. Tolls are based on distance travelled and the gross weight of the vehicle and can be paid in cash, by purchasing prepayment cards or by using the automatic 'Telepass' system, which uses an on-board sensor and overhead gantries.

- Luxembourg: Luxembourg operates the same Eurovignette toll system as Denmark, the Netherlands and Sweden. This requires LGVs with a GVW exceeding 12,000 kg to have a valid Eurovignette when driving in the countries named above.

- Netherlands: The Netherlands operates the Eurovignette toll system (as above), and also levies tolls for some tunnels and some major bridge crossings.

- Norway: Although not in the EU, Norway does levy tolls on many Norwegian main roads, often through the distance-based AutoPASS system, which requires the fitting of an on-board unit known as a 'bar tag' to all goods vehicles exceeding 3,500 kg GVW. Norway also has a maximum limit of 600 litres of fuel being carried on vehicles entering its borders.

- Poland: Poland's toll system requires foreign vehicles to use an electronic in-vehicle device known as viaBOX. Toll gantries fitted with antennas are located above the toll roads. The toll charges are based on distance travelled, vehicle size and vehicle emissions.

- Portugal: Tolls are levied on most Portuguese motorways. Payment can be made by credit, debit or DKV cards, or by using a prepayment electronic card known as 'Via Verde'.

- Romania: Romania has its own Ro-vignette system. The vignette is available to foreign vehicles for periods of 1, 7 and 30 days, as well as 6 and 12 months.

- Slovakia: Slovakia requires foreign vehicles to pay a road tax levy when entering the country and requires a vignette for some sections of the motorway and trunk road network.

- Slovenia: Slovenia levies tolls on some sections of the motorway and trunk road network.

- Spain: Tolls are applied on most Spanish motorways. The distance-based tolls can be paid in cash or through an electronic system that uses an on-board unit and overhead gantries.

- Sweden: Sweden operates the Eurovignette toll system, but there are also tolls for vehicles crossing over to Denmark using the Øresund Bridge.

- Switzerland: Again, although not an EU member state, Switzerland operates a heavy vehicle charge (LSVA) for vehicles exceeding 3,500 kg GVW. The LSVA is based on gross vehicle weight, distance travelled and engine emissions.

- Turkey: Also clearly not an EU member but Turkey levies what is called a 'road transit tax'.

From the details above, it is clear that operators sending vehicles abroad need to investigate the charges they will be expected to pay over and above normal operating costs when quoting for any work. In addition, some of these tolls are higher during public holidays and at weekends and many cities in Europe also operate 'lorry ban' schemes that, if ignored or contravened, carry substantial fines. It should also be noted that the 'minimum wage requirements' for some countries are currently under scrutiny by the European Commission.

Key points you need to know

- The rules relating to VAT in the UK and Europe.

- The rules relating to VED and SORN at all stages.

- How the HGV Road User Levy fits into VED and how it operates.

- The outline of congestion charging and LEZ/CAZ schemes.

- The principal UK toll routes.

- An outline of EU toll schemes, especially the Eurovignette, MAUT and LSVA.

Notes

Once again we have covered a required section of the syllabus and we now need to look at taxation as it relates to self-employment, employment and business undertakings.

Income tax for the self-employed

Sole traders and partners in unlimited liability partnerships pay income tax. This is based on their earnings and any benefits they may receive from their business. This system is referred to as 'pay as you earn' (PAYE). This form of PAYE is paid by individuals who are classed as 'self-employed', whereas company employees pay employee PAYE, which as we will see below is different.

Self-employed workers have two main ways of paying income tax. They must either submit their income tax declaration forms to HMRC no later than 31 October each year using self-assessment forms, which they can have completed for them or fill out themselves. Based on the self-assessed details HMRC will then establish what tax needs to be paid.

Alternatively, they may choose to use 'online' self-assessment, in which case they have until 31 January to submit their forms. In either case, if the forms are not submitted by these due dates HMRC will issue a fine of £100 to the individual concerned even if the return is submitted just one day late. This fine rises the longer the return remains 'not submitted'.

HMRC sets the 'tax year' as the period from 6 April to 5 April the following year, with actual payments having to be made twice a year on 31 January and 31 July, respectively. The self-employed are also required to pay National Insurance (NI) contributions and to retain records of their business activities and tax records for at least five years.

Employed staff income tax and NI

HMRC uses a code number to assess the amount of income tax to be paid by individual employees. Because all employees have their own code number, which is set by HMRC according to the level of income received and tax allowances, depending upon circumstances, the code numbers can be 'high' or 'low'. In reality, what this means is that an employee with a high tax code number has more allowances before they need to pay tax, and so pays less than an employee with a low tax code number, who will need to pay tax at a lower value of allowances.

As an example, an employee with a tax code of 825 would begin to pay tax on income and allowances once they reach a total value of £8,250, but a person with a tax code of 605 would begin to pay tax sooner, once their income and allowances reach a value of £6,050.

Where staff are employed, it is the absolute duty of the employer to ensure that income tax and NI contributions are paid by all staff classed as 'employed'. The employer does this by making monthly (or even weekly) tax deductions from the gross pay of the workers and sending it to HMRC to arrive by a specific day of the following month.

In addition to paying the employees' income tax, employers also have to pay employer's NI contributions for the staff they employ.

Note: Employees who benefit from having 'perks' such as a company car or discounted purchases are also required to pay tax on the 'benefit in kind' as a form of unearned income.

Business taxation – corporation tax

Whilst individuals pay income tax to HMRC, companies pay what is known as 'corporation tax' to HMRC. Every company has to complete a tax return based upon its profit for its own financial year, which can be any period of 12 months – unlike the set year used by HMRC. Corporation tax is paid on all company net profits (profit before tax) at a current standard rate of 20 per cent. This is planned to be reduced down to 18 per cent for the beginning of the 2020 financial year; payment being due no later than nine months and one day after the end of the company's stated financial year.

To conclude this chapter's 'wide-ranging' section of the syllabus, in the next section we consider the implications of operating recovery vehicles and using trade licences.

Recovery vehicles

A recovery vehicle is a vehicle that is defined as being 'constructed or permanently adapted for lifting, towing or transporting disabled vehicles'. For examination purposes you require factual knowledge only relating to these vehicles; the required points are as follows:

- Recovery vehicles must not lift, tow or recover more than two vehicles.
- Recovery vehicles cannot be operated under trade licences (trade plates – see below).
- Recovery vehicles are subject to type approval at first registration.

- Recovery vehicles are classed into two groups for reduced VED purposes: vehicles between 3,500 and 25,000 kg, and vehicles over 25,000 kg.

Operations

Recovery vehicles are only allowed to:

- recover a disabled vehicle(s);
- move vehicles from a place where they became disabled to places of repair or disposal;
- move vehicles between repair locations or from a place of repair for disposal;
- carry tools, equipment and fuel to be used solely for the repair or recovery of a disabled vehicle;
- carry passengers and their personal effects providing that they were previously carried on the disabled vehicle.

Any other activities, including delivering vehicles following repairs or taking repaired vehicles to auctions for sale, would be illegal if a recovery vehicle was to undertake them.

The permitted speed limits for recovery vehicles carrying out the actual recovery of vehicles are split into three groups depending upon the size of the recovery vehicle:

- Recovery vehicles up to 7,500 kg are not subject to any special speed limits, and the national limits apply.
- Recovery vehicles over 7,500 kg but not exceeding 44,000 kg, are subject to reduced speed limits:
  - 60 mph on a motorway;
  - 50 mph on a dual carriageway;
  - 40 mph on any other road.
- Recovery vehicles operating under a Special Types General Order (STGO) and operating in excess of a maximum of 44 tonnes are subject to even lower speed limits:
  - 40 mph on a motorway;
  - 30 mph on a dual carriageway;
  - 30 mph on any other road.

Note: In emergency situations, the police and local authorities can instruct recovery vehicles to remove disabled vehicles that are either causing an obstruction, presenting a danger of some kind or preventing access.

Trade licences

For examination purposes, the issue of trade licences (commonly known as trade plates) requires mostly factual points:

- Trade licences can only be held by:
  - vehicle dealers and distributors;
  - vehicle manufacturers, testers, converters and valeting businesses;
  - operators with workshops carrying out their own repairs.
- Trade licences are issued by the DVLA.
- Trade licences are valid for either 6 or 12 months.
- Trade licences are only available to start from either 1 January or 1 July (if you purchase between these dates it is allowed but you 'lose' any months that have become 'spent').
- The trade licence takes the form of a pair of licence plates showing the number in red lettering on a white background.
- The plates must be clearly displayed on the front and rear of the vehicle to which the licence is being applied.
- There is no specified limit on the number of trade licences that a business can hold.
- If the application for a trade licence is refused the applicant can appeal to the Secretary of State for Transport, providing this is done within 28 days of the refusal.

Trade licences may only be used to:

- move vehicles between premises for repair, weighing or testing;
- collect or deliver vehicles for repair;
- deliver vehicles to or from a place of sale, storage, transport, disposal or operator's premises;
- demonstrate vehicles;
- test equipment after fitting or repair.

When operating a vehicle under a trade licence:

- No goods are to be carried unless the load is being carried for demonstration or test purposes, unless they are tools and equipment necessary for the vehicle in question, or unless the load comprises another vehicle or trailer being carried for a permitted purpose.

- The only passengers allowed to travel in a vehicle operating under a trade licence are:

  - a prospective purchaser;

  - a person conducting any test or trial (perhaps a fitter);

  - a person required in connection with permitted use (perhaps a statutory attendant).

Key points you need to know

- How the self-employed pay income tax.

- How companies pay PAYE.

- How the tax code numbers operate.

- How companies pay corporation tax.

- Facts on recovery vehicles.

- Facts on trade licences.

Notes

Self-test example questions

OCR-type questions (multi-choice)

1 A UK company that is VAT registered is able to claim VAT back from another EU country by:

  a Using a Certificate of Conformity, issued by HMRC. This certificate is valid for a period of 12 months. The claim is then made online using the HMRC website and the foreign VAT reclaim portal. All claims must be submitted within six months of the tax year in which the relevant expense was incurred.

  b Using a Certificate of Guarantee, issued by HMRC. This certificate is valid for a period of six months. The claim is then made online using the HMRC website and the foreign VAT reclaim portal. All claims must be submitted within 12 months of the tax year in which the relevant expense was incurred.

  c Using a Certificate of Origin, issued by HMRC. This certificate is valid for a period of two years. The claim is then made online using the HMRC website and the foreign VAT reclaim portal. All claims must be submitted within three months of the tax year in which the relevant expense was incurred.

  d Using a Certificate of Status, issued by HMRC. This certificate is valid for a period of 12 months. The claim is then made online using the HMRC website and the foreign VAT reclaim portal. All claims must be submitted within nine months of the tax year in which the relevant expense was incurred.

2 The system of road tolling in Germany can be described as:

  a A system where additional tolls are levied on vehicles exceeding 3.5 tonnes GVW, either by a prepayment or by post-payment, which is collected through a GPS-based system using roadside sensors.

  b A system where additional tolls are levied on vehicles exceeding 7.5 tonnes GVW, either by a prepayment or by post-payment, which is collected through a GPS-based system requiring an electronic device to be fitted to the vehicle.

  c A system where additional tolls are levied on vehicles exceeding 12 tonnes GVW, either by a prepayment or by post-payment, which is collected through a GPS-based system using roadside sensors.

    d A system where additional tolls are levied on vehicles exceeding 18 tonnes GVW, either by a prepayment or by post-payment, which is collected through a GPS-based system requiring an electronic device to be fitted to the vehicle.

3 Self-employed people must pay their income tax to HMRC in one of two ways by certain dates or suffer a fine. What are these methods of payment, the dates and what is the level of fine for submitting a return one day late?

    a Using self-assessment the payment must be made no later than 31 October each year; alternatively they may use online self-assessment, in which case they have until 31 January to submit their forms. In either case, if the forms are not submitted by these due dates HMRC will issue a fine of £100 to the individual concerned.

    b Using online self-assessment the payment must be made no later than 31 October each year; alternatively they may use self-assessment, in which case they have until 31 January to submit their forms. In either case, if the forms are not submitted by these due dates HMRC will issue a fine of £1,000 to the individual concerned.

    c Using self-assessment the payment must be made no later than 31 December each year; alternatively they may use online self-assessment, in which case they have until 31 January to submit their forms. In either case, if the forms are not submitted by these due dates HMRC will issue a fine of £500 to the individual concerned.

    d Using online self-assessment the payment must be made no later than 31 December each year; alternatively they may use online self-assessment, in which case they have until 1 April to submit their forms. In either case, if the forms are not submitted by these due dates HMRC will issue a fine of £1,000 to the individual concerned.

4 i) The speed limits for recovery vehicles over 7,500 kg but not exceeding 44,000 kg are 50 mph on a motorway, 40 mph on a dual carriageway and 30 mph on a single carriageway. ii) The speed limits for recovery vehicles operating in excess of 44 tonnes are 40 mph on a motorway, 30 mph on a dual carriageway and 30 mph on a single carriageway. These statements are:

    a (i) true (ii) false;

    b (i) true (ii) true;

    c (i) false (ii) true;

    d (i) false (ii) false.

CILT-type questions (short answer)

1 Briefly explain how a UK company that is VAT registered is able to claim back VAT from another EU country.

2 Briefly explain the system of road tolling in Germany.

3 Briefly discuss the two ways in which self-employed workers can pay income tax to HMRC and the penalty for late payment.

4 What are the speed limits on the three main classes of roads (single carriageway, dual carriageway, motorway) for recovery vehicles over 7,500 kg but less than 44,000 kg and recovery vehicles operating at 60,000 kg?

CILT-type question (long answer)

Discuss the ways in which an operator may first register a vehicle with the DVLA, renew the VED, gain a reduced pollution discounted rate of VED or claim total exemption from VED.

Once you are happy that you can answer questions such as those above then, as before, please feel free to move on to the next chapter, which examines business and financial management of the undertaking. However, if you are unsure or not certain about any of the content, or any of the 'key points you need to know', then please revisit until you feel that you have a full grasp of the material and what is required. Please also remember that these were only sample questions and both OCR and the CILT can provide actual examples.

Business and financial management

05

This is a large section of the course that includes many important and sometimes seemingly difficult subjects, which need to be fully understood. In particular you will need to understand the subjects relating to finance and costings. You will be examined on these areas in depth in order to ensure that you are able to understand company accounts, costs and budgets and also produce a fully costed proposal.

Specifically, the syllabus requires that you should:

- be familiar with the laws and practices regarding the use of cheques, bills of exchange, promissory notes, credit cards and other means or methods of payment;

- be familiar with the various forms of credit (eg bank credit, documentary credit, guarantee deposits, mortgages, leasing, renting, factoring) and the charges and obligations arising therefrom;

- know what a balance sheet is, how it is set out, and how to interpret it;

- be able to read and interpret a trading account, profit and loss account, and balance sheet;

- be able to assess the undertaking's profitability and financial position, in particular on the basis of financial ratios;

- be able to prepare and interpret a budget;

- be familiar with the cost elements of the undertaking (eg fixed costs, variable costs, working capital, depreciation) and be able to calculate costs per vehicle, per kilometre, per journey or per tonne;

- be familiar with discipline and grievance procedures;
- be able to draw up an organizational chart relating to the undertaking's personnel as a whole and to organize work plans;
- be familiar with the principles of marketing, publicity and public relations, including transport services, sales promotion and the preparation of customer files;
- be familiar with the different types of insurance relating to road transport (liability, accidental injury/life, non-life insurance) and the guarantees and obligations arising therefrom;
- be familiar with the applications of electronic data transmission in road transport;
- be able to apply the rules governing the invoicing of road haulage services and know the meaning and implications of Incoterms.

Before we look at the documentation relating to business transactions, we must briefly note that there are two types of banks we may have to deal with. First, there are high-street banks, who act as clearing banks or 'joint stock banks'. These are the banks we normally use within our daily lives, offering us current accounts (where there is little or no interest paid on the account) and deposit accounts (which do attract a certain level of interest). Second, there are merchant banks. These are banks that serve the business community and we do not normally use them for personal banking; they generally act to sell and buy shares and raise finance for major business ventures and investments.

We begin by producing a sequential list of the different documents that form most simple business transactions and that also often act to form a legally binding contract.

Business transaction documents

In order the documents are:

1 An estimate: an estimate gives an outline or 'general' assessment of the work to be done and an approximate price. Estimates can be verbal or written.

2 A quotation: a quotation clearly lays out the details of any proposed service or work to be provided, an exact price for what is offered, and any terms and conditions that may be applicable, providing the

customer is happy with the original estimate. Quotations often have a set time period for which they are valid and, if accepted, may be deemed to be 'acceptance' under the law of contract.

3 An order: this would normally be the next document. The order for the work to go ahead will often include a purchase order number so that it can be identified easily.

4 A pro-forma invoice: if a company is to do business with a new customer then a pro-forma invoice would normally be issued. A pro-forma invoice asks for some, or all, of the fee to be paid in advance. They are not always issued but, for large transactions with new customers, they can be.

5 An invoice: in general business, an invoice would be the next document. A standard invoice is issued once the job has been completed and will usually include details of all the goods or services provided, the parties involved and the terms of payment.

6 A debit note or credit note: following the issue of the invoice, if any adjustments are needed to the account these are made by the supplier issuing either a debit note or a credit note. Debit notes are issued to correct any undercharge, whilst credit notes are issued to correct any overcharge.

7 A statement: finally, once an account is established it is monitored through the issue of statements. These are usually issued monthly or quarterly and have a summary of all work completed during the period whilst also itemizing what invoices have been settled and what might be outstanding. They are issued periodically to inform customers of the status of the account, what transactions have been settled, and what are outstanding.

Payment of accounts

Payment of accounts can be made by many means including paying cash, paying by cheque, by travellers cheques, or by using a debit or credit card (although credit cards often require a small charge for making the payment). However, company credit cards are often used to enable drivers to purchase spares and fuel or to pay tolls and similar expenses. Because credit and debit card companies provide statements, this enables operators and employers to see exactly what has been spent, what it was spent on and when it was spent. A derivation of a debit or credit card is a 'charge card', which allows customers to purchase items from a specific business (usually the card issuer), up to a certain value.

Note: International Fuel Agency cards can also be used to make payments for fuel and sundries, in the same ways as debit or credit cards, but these cards carry a standing charge for the issue and use of them, and normally need full settlement on a monthly basis. The main benefit for many operators of using these cards is that the account statements issued by the card provider are seen as sufficient by HMRC for operators wishing to reclaim VAT paid on fuel purchases whilst abroad.

Business payments may also be made using automated systems such as direct debits or standing orders, where payments are made under instruction from the account holder. The main difference between a direct debit and a standing order is that, when paying by direct debit, the bank will release variable amounts each month to fully 'settle' what is outstanding, whereas with a standing order the bank will release a fixed sum each month.

Larger business payments are often made by some automated, or electronic, credit transfer system such as the Bankers' Automated Clearing System (BACS), which provides a secure method of payment and normally sees payment made within three working days. Alternatively there is the much quicker system of the Clearing House Automated Payment System (CHAPS), which makes 'same-day' payments but at a premium charge.

Increasingly, alternative electronic options for payments are being used by businesses. Not least systems such as PayPal, which enable payments to be made online for items such as tyres or spare parts and consumables, and many major banks now have electronic business banking allowing online payments to be made by the account holder to customers and staff.

Bank drafts are an alternative payment method when a business is dealing with new customers, or customers with poor credit history. A bank draft requires the customer to pay in advance in the same way as a pro-forma invoice. A bank draft requires the customer to go to the bank and pay in the required sum before the actual bank draft – which guarantees that payment will be made – will be issued by the bank concerned. However, banks charge for the issue of these drafts.

The syllabus specifically requires you to understand three further methods of payment, which are:

- Bills of exchange: a bill of exchange is a written order demanding payment by one person to another either at the present time (termed payment 'at-sight') or at a set time in the future. There are three parties to a bill of exchange. These are:
  - The drawer: the party that issues the bill (usually the seller).
  - The drawee: the recipient of the bill (usually the buyer).
  - The payee: the party paying (usually the seller's bank).
- Letters of credit: a letter of credit gives a nominated bank authorization to make a payment upon 'satisfactory completion' of some work or service provision. Where problems arise, the bank will not make any payment until everything has been resolved.
- A promissory note is the final payment method we need to include. A promissory note simply guarantees payment by the customer to the supplier at an agreed time or upon completion of some work or service provision.

If we now understand the sequence of a business transaction and the various ways of making payments, next we need to begin to come to terms with how businesses are actually financed, how they use their funding and how they keep accounts and records.

First, we will look at how we finance a business. We will look at how, in the same way that we borrow money in the short term, with a high interest rate (for things such as the purchase of a new TV), we also borrow money in the longer term, with a low rate of interest, when taking out a mortgage to buy property. This short-term/long-term dilemma is the same for businesses as it is for individuals.

In relation to business there are some differences, however, because businesses have more options to delay payments and use internal funding. Because of this we will be using some financial terminology that you may not be familiar with, but we will try to clarify as we go along.

Short-term financing

For business purposes, the term 'short term' means any loans taken out over a period not exceeding 12 months. These include:

- Overdrafts, which are reviewed and renewed annually.
- Delaying payments to creditors such as suppliers.*
- Using money collected to pay tax such as VAT.*

- Debt factoring, which is a system where a business 'sells' a debt to a 'factoring house' in order for the factoring house to make payment on behalf of the customer. The factoring house takes a proportion of the debt and then pursues the debtor and, whilst the business does not receive the full outstanding amount, they are able to continue in business, or expand, as required.

---

* Whilst these are methods of delaying payment, the payments will have to be met either as agreed, or later than agreed with a surcharge normally being added.

Long-term financing

For business purposes, the term 'long term' means any loans taken out over a period exceeding 12 months. These include:

- Mortgages, leasing property and assets or long-term rental of property and assets.
- Using 'share capital', which is where the money invested by the shareholders is used by the business for major projects and expansion.
- Issuing 'debentures', which are long-term loans by an investor that have a fixed rate of return.
- Using 'revenue reserve', which is money that has been 'ploughed back' into the business by the shareholders. Because of this it is a 'loan', because if a shareholder leaves a business then monies retained (or 'reserved') by the business to that shareholder must be repaid.

In the following sections we will be using some financial terms, including the terms 'sources' and 'uses'. 'Sources' refer to money that is used to finance the company (as above); what we use the money for is termed 'use'. These are normally referred to as 'assets' and, as with short-term and long-term sources, the same time periods apply to 'current assets' (short term – less than 12 months) and 'fixed assets' (long term – more than 12 months).

Financial accounts and financial ratios

Companies have to produce accounts every year and declare them to Companies House. In cases of limited companies the accounts need to be retained for a period of three years and for plcs the period is six years.

The main accounts we will concentrate on are the trading and profit and loss account (usually referred to as the profit and loss account), which covers financial records covering a period of one year, and the balance sheet, which provides a 'snapshot' of the financial health of a company at a set date within the financial year. These are also accompanied by a directors' report, declaring that they are a true record of company activity and profitability.

Note: The figures used in all the following examples and illustrations are not meant to be actual figures; they are for demonstration purposes only.

The balance sheet

The balance sheet is a 'snapshot' of the company on a certain day of the year. Unlike the profit and loss account (P&L), it is not a record of performance, merely a financial statement. Both the balance sheet and the P&L are required to be produced in a set format.

It is the balance sheet that uses the terms 'sources' and 'uses' of funding in order to show where our long- and short-term funding comes from and where we used it to purchase fixed and current assets. The balance sheet is aimed at supplying information that is sufficient for the reader to ascertain the 'financial health' of the company by clearly identifying the assets owned by the company and the 'liabilities' (debts) faced by the company.

The term 'liabilities' is used here as it is a balance sheet term that applies to both short-term debts (current liabilities) and long-term debts (long-term liabilities).

As a management tool or as a guide to a potential investor it allows the reader to assess such things as whether or not borrowings provided any planned increase in the value of the company assets, or the ability of the company to meet its current liabilities and to properly assess possible effects in any changes to credit terms. These pointers will become clearer as we progress.

You will see 'working capital' and 'capital employed' on the balance sheet. These are there as part of the required format, and will become relevant later:

- Working capital is calculated as current assets minus current liabilities.
- Capital employed is calculated as the fixed assets plus the working capital. It can also be described as the fixed and current assets minus the current liabilities.

TABLE 5.1 Balance Sheet as of 1 September 2015

FIXED ASSETS		
Freehold property	£1,910,000	
Freehold land	£675,000	
Company vehicles	£975,000	
Plant and equipment	£229,500	
Furniture and fittings	£52,500	
		£3,842,000
CURRENT ASSETS		
Stock	£57,400	
Debtors	£296,000	
Cash	£20,700	
		£374,100
MINUS		
CURRENT LIABILITIES		
Creditors	£143,700	
Overdraft	£35,000	
Taxation Due	£149,100	
		£327,800
WORKING CAPITAL		**£46,300**
CAPITAL EMPLOYED		**£3,888,300**
MINUS		
LONG-TERM LIABILITIES		
10-year bank loan	£400,000	
NET ASSETS		**£3,488,300**

(Continued)

TABLE 5.1 Balance Sheet as of 1 September 2015 (*Continued*)

	Authorized Capital	Issued Capital
FINANCED BY:		
Ordinary shares	£3,500,000	£2,500,000
Revenue reserve		£988,300
		£3,488,300

Notes:

1 In the balance sheet found in Table 5.1 you can see that although the authorized share capital is £3,500,000, meaning the company can sell shares up to that value, the company has only issued (sold) shares to shareholders to a value of £2,500,000, meaning that they could sell another £1 million worth of shares if they wanted to finance some sort of expansion.

2 You will need to remember the formula for calculating working capital (above) for your examination.

3 You will need to remember the formula for capital employed (above) for your examination (please also note that capital employed is often described as 'total capital employed'). In real terms it is actually the total amount of money tied up in the business.

You can also be asked to look at a balance sheet to calculate some financial ratios that are used to assess the ability of a company to meets its current liabilities. The details are set out below.

Working capital ratio

The working capital ratio is also known as the current ratio. This is actually used to assess how companies can meet their current debts (liabilities) by using their current assets. As such it is known as a 'liquidity ratio'.

In an ideal situation it is felt that a working capital ratio of 2:1 is the ideal. This would mean that, for every £1 owed as current liabilities there would be £2 of current assets to pay for them. Any ratio with less than 1:1 would mean that the company could not meet its current liabilities and, as such, it is no longer deemed 'liquid'.

The formula used is:

$$\frac{\text{Current Assets} : 1}{\text{Current Liabilities}}$$

If we again use our figures we will arrive at a worki

$$\frac{£374,100:1}{£327,800} = 1.14:1$$

This means that there is currently £1.14 to meet every £
is a little below the ideal ratio of 2:1, but it is still above

Acid test ratio (quick assets ratio)

The second liquidity ratio we need to calculate is the quick assets ratio, also known as the acid test ratio. In this ratio the value of any stock (a current asset) is taken out of the calculation (this is done because stock values fluctuate and specialized stock may have incurred significant cost but may be almost worthless if a contract where it was needed was lost).

The ideal for a quick asset ratio is a ratio of 1:1, which would indicate the company could meet all its current liabilities without having to sell any stock to do so as it would still have at least £1 of current assets for every £1 of current liabilities.

The formula used is:

$$\frac{\text{Current Assets (Minus Stock)}:1}{\text{Current Liabilities}}$$

If we again use our figures we will arrive at a working capital ratio of:

$$\frac{£374,100 - £57,400}{£327,800} = \frac{£316,700:1}{£327,800} = 0.97:1$$

This means that the company (in our example balance sheet) would be unable, just, to meet its current liabilities without needing to sell some stock or, alternatively, reduce the very large debtors sum to bring in some hard cash. This is exactly the type of situation that might lead a company to use a debt factoring house to bring in any bad debts, if the situation required it.

Total capital employed is also important because, for your examinations, you will also need to remember the formula for calculating the return on capital employed (ROCE) (an explanation of this is given below).

The total capital employed, which is recorded within the balance sheet, allows interested parties, especially potential investors, to record the figure and then assess it with information relating to costs that are contained within the P&L. By so doing they can better assess any actual return on any investment they may make by calculating the net profit before tax as a percentage of the total capital employed.

this, the percentage return on capital employed is calculated by the following formula:

$$\frac{\text{Net Profit before Tax} \times 100}{\text{Total Capital Employed}} = \%$$

In our case, if we had a net profit before tax of £558,100 (see below) this would be:

$$\frac{£558,000 \times 100}{£3,888,300} = \frac{£55,800,000}{£3,888,300} = 14.35\%$$

In essence, this demonstrates that the balance sheet and the P&L contain information that, whilst relating to different aspects of the business, can be combined to provide vital information about the financial 'health' of a business for various interested parties. In this case, the P&L must be the next account that we need to consider in detail.

The trading and profit and loss (P&L) account

The principal account is the trading and P&L account. It is called the trading and P&L account because it has the trading account at the top and the P&L account below, in relation to how it is structured (see below):

- The 'trading account' shows turnover minus the direct costs (also called 'costs of sales'). This results in a figure that is the gross profit.

- The P&L account shows the gross profit minus the indirect costs (also called overheads) to give us a figure that is the net profit before tax. It is this net profit that is declared to HMRC.

Having mentioned the elements of the P&L let's consider them in a little more detail:

1 The turnover of a company is the sum of all monies received from the sales or provision of services.

2 Direct costs are the costs directly associated with the actual direct provision of sales or services. These will include such things as vehicle fuel, tyres, insurance and maintenance, VED and drivers' wages.

3 Gross profit is the figure obtained by deducting the direct costs from the turnover. This is often calculated into percentage terms to monitor how these direct costs are either increasing or decreasing in relation to turnover.

4 The gross profit figure from the trading account is then transferred to become the opening figure in the P&L account.

5 From this opening figure the indirect costs (overheads) such as the costs of advertising, telephones, office salaries, heating and lighting, and other 'general' costs are then also deducted, to give us our 'bottom line' figure, which is the net profit before tax.

6 Net profit before tax is the figure declared as the real profit and is calculated by deducting the indirect costs from the gross profit. However, this figure can also be recorded as a loss in cases where a company spends more than it earns.

An example of a trading and P&L account is shown in Table 5.2. It should be noted that it is in the format required by the tax authorities.

TABLE 5.2 Trading and P&L accounts

Trading account to 1 September 2015

Haulage		£1,950,000
Warehousing		£1,290,000
Workshop services		£285,000
	TURNOVER	**£3,525,000**
Less direct costs		
Vehicle fuel		£915,000
Tyres		£78,000
Maintenance		£223,000
Vehicle insurance		£74,000
Vehicle excise duty (VED/levy)		£53,000
Vehicle depreciation		£110,000
Operator licensing fees		£12,000
Drivers' wages or salaries		£835,000
	TOTAL DIRECT COSTS	**£2,300,000**
Turnover		£3,525,000
		Minus £2,300,000

(Continued)

TABLE 5.2 Trading and P&L accounts (*Continued*)

	GROSS PROFIT	£1,225,000
Percentage of gross profit to turnover		= 34.75%

P&L account to 1 September 2015

Gross profit carried down from trading account		**£1,225,000**
Less indirect costs		
Rent and rates		£98,000
Building and site insurances		£38,700
Office staff salaries		£89,600
Directors' salaries		£145,000
Employers' liability insurance		£12,500
Office cleaning		£12,000
Office consumables		£14,200
Advertising		£65,200
Telephone		£84,600
Computer support		£18,900
Legal and accountancy fees		£55,100
Heating and lighting		£18,200
Public relations		£15,000
	TOTAL INDIRECT COSTS	**£667,000**
	GROSS PROFIT	**£1,225,000**
		Minus £667,000
	NET PROFIT (before tax)	**£558,000**
Percentage of net profit to turnover		= 15.83%

Once we have these figures we are then able to make use of the P&L by comparing the costs and levels of turnover 'year on year' so that we can see if the business is growing, shrinking or remaining constant; we can also compare costs year on year in order to see if certain costs are rising disproportionately. For instance, if turnover remains the same but drivers' costs rise by 20 per cent then we need to investigate what is happening. Comparisons like these also enable us to see if our proposed business plans are actually working so that we can perhaps see whether we are either expanding the business in line with our plans or reducing costs in line with our plans.

These sorts of comparisons are vital if we are to control our costs in line with business activity and will be made in detail by the accounts department, who will then advise management accordingly. Any trends (both good and bad) will then probably be announced at the AGM.

Whilst the P&L is an important management tool it does have the limitation that it is all historic information. This means that if things are not happening as planned it can be up to a year before we learn about it. This fact alone now means that many organizations produce P&Ls for their own management purposes several times a year in order to be made aware of any unplanned changes and to enable them to take any remedial action much quicker.

Once the P&L has been accepted at Companies House it is published and available to be read by anyone. This means that, in addition to providing HMRC with a figure on which to tax the company, it is also a useful document for any prospective investors, for organizations who may be approached for loans, for other companies (perhaps planning a takeover) and for competing companies to assess the competition.

Key points you need to know

- Transaction documents.
- The types of funding.
- P&L in detail (including uses and application).
- Balance sheet in detail (including uses and application).
- The purpose of, and how to calculate, financial ratios.

Notes

We have now looked at the balance sheet and the P&L and the required calculations and ratios, but we still have other areas of finance to cover, including budgets, cash flow, costings and depreciation. We will start with budgets and cash flow.

Budgets and cash flow

Budgets are a mechanism used to control expenditure and to act as a planned way of working; they set spending targets and limits and enable companies to monitor their actual financial performance against their 'planned' financial performance. They are often referred to as 'plans defined in financial terms'.

They come in different types. For instance, there are cash flow budgets (also referred to as cash flow analyses) and there are operational budgets. Operational budgets can be developed in two different ways:

- Historic budgets, where information from previous years is used to predict what the budget should be for the following year.

- Zero-based budgets, which do not assume any prior performance or targets but are developed completely from information that predicts what will be required in the future.

Whilst historic budgets are easier to develop, zero-based budgets tend to be more accurate but do take more time to produce.

Cash flow budget (cash flow analysis)

Cash flow budgets generally rely upon historic information and 'what is expected to happen'. They cannot really be developed from a zero-base position.

It is often argued that a budget that looks into the future is an actual budget but, in relation to cash flowing into, and out of, a company, cash flow analysis should be the term used to forecast when the money will actually flow into, and out of, the company. This is somewhat a matter of semantics and we can use either term providing we understand the activities and issues concerned.

The main point of any cash flow analysis/budget is to accurately predict when money flows into and out of the business so that we can establish if we will need any short-term borrowings, such as an overdraft, or if we need to offer discounts for prompt payment, or even if we need to renegotiate our credit terms with our suppliers or change our ordering cycles and order sizes.

All the above possibilities will allow us to get money in and/or pay money out at different times so that we can align money in to money out and, as much as possible, avoid having to borrow at a short-term (high-interest) rate. For example, if our customers pay us earlier than normal we may have sufficient cash to pay our suppliers on time without needing additional funds. Cash flow budgets/analysis also allow us to establish if it is better for our business to settle accounts differently so that we can avoid big fluctuations of 'cash in versus cash out' over our financial year.

Note: You will see in the example given in Table 5.3 that in a cash flow budget/analysis, the 'closing balance' of each month becomes the 'opening balance' for the following month and that negative figures are enclosed in brackets.

Clearly, this budget shows that the impact of paying tax and for buildings insurance in the same month (October) has had a serious effect, especially as receipts are low in October. In addition, both receipts and payments do fluctuate month on month as do the miscellaneous expenses. It is these sorts of major fluctuations that need to be reduced as far as possible by perhaps asking customers for early payment, renegotiating the terms of insurance (perhaps by paying monthly) and even negotiating with the tax authorities to stagger payments instead of paying a large sum all at once.

It is these sorts of issues that will be part of your examination questions when budgeting is included. Next, we examine a different type of budget.

TABLE 5.3   Cash flow budget/analysis

Month	September	October	November	December
Opening balance	*£43,600*	*£32,100*	*(£9,740)*	*(£10,870)*
Receipts cleared	£28,900	£16,800	£23,750	£38,200
Receipts clearing	£14,200	£8,400	£7,480	£18,930
Total receipts	*£86,700*	*£57,300*	*£21,490*	*£46,260*
Payments cleared	£21,900	£14,660	£14,620	£10,980
Payments clearing	£11,300	£12,450	£7,650	£7,990
Agency fees	£4,600	£8,600	£9,480	£11,610
Misc expenses	£780	£1,930	£610	£1,880
Christmas payments	Nil	Nil	Nil	£5,000
Taxation due	Nil	£18,400	Nil	Nil
Buildings insurance	Nil	£11,000	Nil	Nil
Total payments	*£38,580*	*£67,040*	*£32,360*	*£37,460*
Closing balance	£32,100	(£9,740)	(£10,870)	£8,800

Operational budgets

These are budgets that most operational managers will use during their working lives. They are generally produced by senior management and are often 'non-negotiable' in relation to any variance being permitted.

The layouts of budgets vary but the general pattern will be something like the example shown in Table 5.4. You will note that where there is an

TABLE 5.4 Sample operational budget

Related item	Actual spend	Budget figure	Variance figure	Variance percentage
Fuel	£302,000	£320,000	(£18,000)	(5.62%)
Maintenance	£19,600	£19,000	+£600	+3.16%
Tyres	£27,000	£22,000	+£5,000	+22.73%
Accident damage	£15,000	£17,500	(£2,500)	(14.29%)
Drivers' wages	£188,000	£192,000	(£4,000)	(2.08%)
Agency staff	£11,600	£13,500	+£1,900	(14.07%)
Driver CPC	£600	£600	Nil	Nil
Staff training	£9,600	£8,800	+£800	+9.09%
Insurance	£4,300	£4,450	(£150)	(3.37%)
Consumables	£2,500	£2,380	+£120	+5.04%

'underspend' the figures are put in brackets; where there is an overspend the figures are preceded by a '+' symbol. This is a general format/style when budgets are produced.

From the figures in Table 5.4 we can see that, for some reason, there was a big overspend on tyres. This is exactly the sort of issue that you, as a transport manager, would be expected to investigate and provide an answer for.

In relation to both cash flow and operational budgeting it is the managers who will be expected to act in the best way possible for the company concerned, by smoothing cash flow and by investigating major variances. It is also true to say that it is a manager's role to spend money wisely and not to purchase 'nice to have' items just to use up any underspend for fear of having a budget cut the next year!

One method of supporting effective budgeting is to manage the stocks that a company holds. By managing when to order stock and how much to order, we can smooth cash flow. However, we do need to monitor 'lead times' to ensure that the stocks we require arrive before we run out of the stock item(s) concerned.

In managing stock we need to undertake stock checks (including bulk fuel tank reconciling) in order to ensure we actually do hold the stocks we believe we hold; and we need to monitor stock levels to identify any obsolete stock items that can perhaps be sold, or returned in order to ensure that we do not have 'dead money' within the business.

Our final two financial topics are operational costings and depreciation, examined below.

Operational costing

The ability to cost for goods or services and for a business to make a profit are absolute requirements for any business owner or manager. Far too many transport businesses have opened, only to go into receivership in a very short time because the owner(s) did not understand where all the costs come from or that profit is required in order to be able to renew assets and meet all the liabilities they are faced with. Costs have been a focus for this examination in the past and, to this end, we begin by looking at the four main types of costs and two key definitions. The main types of costs are:

- Fixed costs: fixed costs are also known as 'standing costs'; they are costs that do not alter in relation to the amount of work carried out. For example we need to pay vehicle insurance and VED irrespective of whether the vehicle is on the road for one day per week or seven days per week.

- Variable costs: variable costs are also known as 'running costs'; they are costs that vary according to the amount of work carried out. For example, the more miles you travel the more fuel you will use and the more wear there will be on the tyres.

- Direct costs: as we learned earlier, direct costs are also known as 'costs of sales'; they are those costs that can be directly linked to some sort of operational unit. For example, the direct costs relating to a vehicle would be fuel, tyres and maintenance.

- Indirect costs: also covered earlier, indirect costs are also known as 'overheads'; they are those costs that cannot easily be allocated to any single operational unit. In relation to vehicle operation, they would include things such as operator licences, advertising, and office and directors' salaries.

The two key definitions are:

- Cost units: cost units are expressions of costs such as 'pence per mile' or 'kilometres per litre'.

- Cost centres: cost centres are parts of a business (including vehicles) where costs need to be allocated in order for them to function.

Note: Both direct and indirect costs can be either 'fixed' or 'variable'. For example, a direct fixed cost would be VED and a direct variable cost would be fuel; whereas an indirect fixed cost would be a director's salary but an indirect variable cost could be the office heating bill.

Let's now look at how costs are calculated.

Fixed (standing) costs

Because fixed costs are based on time and need to be paid irrespective of the level of work activity it is vital that they are monitored closely and that we try to get good utilization of our assets. For example, if our fixed costs are £1,200 per week and we operate four days a week then they are £300 per day and we need to recover that every day from our customers, just to meet costs before we start to operate or make a profit. However, if our vehicle operates six days a week, then our daily fixed costs are only £200 per day. This means that when quoting for work we can already be much more competitive.

The point above means that the money we need to pay our fixed costs is only generated when the vehicle is actually working and no vehicle works 365 day a year. They do not work when being tested, serviced, repaired and they don't usually work on bank holidays and at all sorts of different times. This means that our total annual fixed costs need to be recovered over about 250–255 days' yearly operation and not over 365 days of a full year.

For example: an operator has a fleet of eight vehicles, they each operate 252 days a year and work for 9.5 hours a day. The fixed costs include:

Drivers' wages (8 × £22,000)	= £176,000
Vehicle insurance	= £23,000
VED (8 × £1,250)	= £10,000
Vehicle depreciation	= £62,000
Total fixed costs	= **£271,000**

This would mean that the annual fixed cost for each vehicle would be:

£271,000 divided by 8 = £33,875

To produce that annual sum we would have to divide £33,875 by 252 for a daily fixed cost, which would be £134.42 per day. It would also mean that to calculate the hourly fixed cost of a vehicle the operator would then need to divide £134.42 by 9.5, which equals £14.15 per hour.

Variable (running) costs

Most operators calculate their variable costs on a 'per mile' or 'per kilometre' basis. However, to arrive at a total variable cost you do need to add all the individual elements together using simple calculations. Let's look at this now.

For example, using the three main variable costs of fuel, tyres and maintenance where:

- Fuel is £1.20 per litre and the vehicle travels 5 km:

$$\text{Calculation is}: \frac{\text{Cost per litre}}{\text{Fuel consumption}} = \frac{£1.20}{5} = £0.24 \,^* \text{per km}$$

- Tyres cost £180 each, there are 14 tyres on the vehicle and a set of tyres lasts for 90,000 km:

$$\text{Calculation is}: \frac{\text{Cost of ALL tyres}}{\text{Expected life}} = 14 \times £180 = \frac{£2,520}{90,000} = £0.028 \,^* \text{per km}$$

- Maintenance is carried out under contract for an annual fee of £9,000 and the vehicle covers 102,000 km per year:

$$\text{Calculation is}: \frac{\text{Total annual cost}}{\text{Annual km}} = \frac{£9,000}{102,000} = £0.088 \,^* \text{per km}$$

- We now need to add £0.24 + £0.028 + £0.088 = £0.356.
- This means that it costs 35.6 pence for every kilometre the vehicle travels.

---

* In your examination, please be careful to get the decimal point in the right place when doing running costs, as any error will make your calculations completely incorrect.

Total costs

Having now calculated our time (fixed costs) and our distance (running costs) we can calculate the total costs of doing work.

For instance, using our figures above: if we are asked to do a job covering 260 kilometres that will take seven hours we can calculate that our costs will be:

$$(7 \times £14.15) + (260 \times £0.356) = £99.05 + £92.56 = £191.61$$

However, we have not added any profit yet, so if we wanted to charge a 12.5 per cent profit surcharge we would then add that to the £191.61 to arrive at a 'charge out' rate of:

$$£191.61 + £23.95 = £215.56$$

This is a fairly easy example and in the exam you will be asked to consider additional factors such as:

- pounds sterling into euros (exchange rates);
- distances in miles and kilometres;
- nights out (note: a three-day job = two nights out);
- ferry costs (single crossing or return);
- ferry costs by metre length of vehicle;
- adding VAT (or not).

Now that we can see where the types of costs come from and how they fit together to get a charge-out rate we need to think about a further issue in relation to indirect costs. Whilst these are time based (annual) and need to be factored in, they are also difficult to apply to individual vehicles in a fair manner because a 25-tonne payload vehicle can generate more revenue than a 5-tonne payload vehicle and so we need a fair method of apportioning our indirect costs. This is done in the following ways:

- For a fleet of same-size vehicles we simply divide our annual indirect costs by the number of vehicles on a daily basis. For example, if our overheads are £60,000 per year and we have our eight vehicles operating 252 days per year we would divide £60,000 by 252 = £238.10 per day and then divide £238.10 by 8 = £29.76 per day, per vehicle (this could then be done hourly if required).

- When operating fleets of mixed vehicles it is a little more complicated. For example, using the information above, if our eight-vehicle fleet was comprised of 3 × 15-tonne payload vehicles plus 4 × 12-tonne payload vehicles and 1 × 22-tonne payload vehicle our total fleet payload would be 45 + 48 + 22 = 115 tonnes.

  To find the annual cost of overheads per tonne payload we would then need to divide our £60,000 by 115 = £521.74 per tonne payload.

  To apportion this to the vehicles we would then multiply £521.74 by 15, 12 and 22 respectively to arrive at:

  - an annual overhead cost for a 15-tonne payload vehicle of £7,826.10.
  - an annual overhead cost for a 12-tonne payload vehicle of £6,260.88.
  - an annual overhead cost for a 22-tonne payload vehicle of £11,478.28.

Now we have 'scaled' costs based on individual payloads we simply divide the annual cost by 252 and/or then again for the hourly cost.

Note: These can be checked in the exam by multiplying the annual costs by the number of vehicles of each size to work it back to a total of £60,000. For example:

$$3 \times £7,826.10 = £23,478.30$$
$$4 \times £6,260.88 = £25,043.52$$
$$\text{plus } £11,478.28$$

Added together = £60,000.10

As most fleets are 'mixed', by calculating the costs of overheads in this way the larger vehicles need to recover additional costs based on their ability to generate higher revenue than the smaller vehicles.

Some (but very few) companies calculate the cost of overheads on a combined 'per vehicle and per payload' basis. In this case we simply halve the total indirect costs and calculate one half 'per vehicle' and one half 'per payload' and then add the two resulting figures to give us our total. In essence, it means doing each of the calculations identified above on a 50 per cent basis and adding them together.

Note: You need to be sure that you understand the points above because, whilst it looks like overheads are treated differently, or are a separate cost in some way, they are not. All you need to remember is that once you have a daily or hourly overhead cost it is simply added in as one of the components of a daily or hourly fixed cost.

Configuration of costs

Costs can also be calculated depending upon what information a customer may require. For instance, if you calculate the cost of a job (including profit) to be £1,800 and the customer wants 26 pallets delivering it will be £1,800 divided by 26 = £69.23 per pallet. This method can also be used to calculate costs and charge-out rates per tonne or even per litre.

In addition, if the £1,800 job was to cover 300 miles the cost would be £6 per mile. Using the figure above, the £1,800 could also be calculated as an overall hourly charge if the customer required it. This general technique can also be used by operators to calculate the hourly standing costs of vehicles, providing they know the annual standing costs and the days per year that the vehicle operates. It can also be used to calculate the minimum daily distance that a vehicle needs to travel in order to recover its costs.

For example, if the total annual standing costs for a vehicle are £6,900.00 and the vehicle works 230 days per year, the calculation would be:

$$\frac{69,000}{230} = 300 \text{ km per day}$$

This means that the vehicle will need to travel (work) 300 kilometres every day in order to cover its standing costs.

Before moving on to depreciation we should just take a moment to consider what are known as 'marginal costing' and 'open book' costing.

'Marginal costing' can be used by operators to offer discounts to customers for services such as a 'back-haul', where the fixed (and/or some of the running) costs were covered by the customer paying for the outward leg of the journey. In short, a low price can be quoted because the main costs are already covered.

'Open book' costing is a system where the haulier calculates the costs (without any profit surcharge) and shows these to the customer. If the customer is happy then the customer will offer a fixed 'management fee', on top of the declared and agreed costs, to the haulier to complete the work.

Depreciation

The term 'depreciation' applies to the loss of value of an asset over its lifetime. Calculating depreciation when we either finish with an asset, wish to sell it or value it for accountancy purposes, such as recording asset values on the balance sheet, gives us a realistic value of an asset at any point in during its lifetime, and a realistic amount for which the asset could be sold.

When depreciating vehicles we always need to ensure that the tyre equipment is not included in the calculations (see below) because tyres are classed as a variable (running) cost and depreciation is classed as a fixed (standing) cost and the two costs cannot normally be mixed together or it will produce errors in the calculations.

There are two main methods of calculating vehicle depreciation:

- Straight-line depreciation, where a set amount is taken off the value of the vehicle each year. This is not a very accurate method as it does not really reflect the fact that the value of vehicles reduces more rapidly when they are new than it does as they get older. However, it is acceptable for accountancy purposes.

- Reducing-balance depreciation, where a percentage of the value of the vehicle is taken off the value of the vehicle each year, which more accurately reflects the 'true' value of the vehicle as it gets older.

Let's now look at each method and an example of each.

Straight-line method

Let's say we plan to buy a new vehicle for £115,000 and we plan to keep it in service for six years, when the dealer has estimated that the vehicle will still be worth £37,500. (This value of £37,500 is known as the residual value of the vehicle.)

The vehicle cost is: £115,000
The tyre equipment is valued at: £ 3,000
Purchase price (less tyres) is: £112,000
Minus the estimated residual value: £ 37,500
Sum to depreciate is: £ 74,500

Vehicle life is six years, so annual depreciation is:

$$\frac{£74,500}{6} = £12,416.67 \text{ per annum}$$

A straight-line depreciation calculation is usually laid out in column form showing the expected value at the end of each year, as shown in Table 5.5 below.

TABLE 5.5 Straight-line depreciation

	Annual depreciation	Accumulated depreciation	Written-down value
Initial cost (less tyres)	–	–	£112,000
Year 1 end	£12,416.67	£12,416.67	£99,583.33
Year 2 end	£12,416.67	£24,833.34	£87,166.66
Year 3 end	£12,416.67	£37,250.01	£74,749.99
Year 4 end	£12,416.67	£49,666.68	£62,333.32
Year 5 end	£12,416.67	£62,083.35	£49,916.65
Year 6 end	£12,416.67	£74,500.02	£37,499.98

Table 5.5 shows the £75,000 total depreciation 'writing down' the value to the expected £37,500. The slight variances are due to rounding up or down and are insignificant for the values concerned. Please also note that depreciation of major assets is usually calculated to the nearest £1 but this table has been produced as a demonstration of the process.

The next form of depreciation is the method known as 'reducing-balance' depreciation.

Reducing-balance method

The reducing-balance method is a method that recognizes that vehicles devalue more rapidly when they are new. The reducing balance removes a set percentage from the value of the vehicle each year. Whilst the set percentage is not a fixed percentage, HMRC accept that a percentage of between 15 per cent and 25 per cent is acceptable for taxation purposes.

In the reducing-balance method we do not use a residual value but we depreciate the vehicle at a percentage rate that will ensure that the value at the 'end of life' will reflect a realistic value close to what we would expect it to be. For our example we use a rate of 17 per cent.

The format is similar to the straight-line format, as shown below in Table 5.6.

TABLE 5.6 Reducing-balance depreciation

	Annual depreciation	Accumulated depreciation	Written down value
Initial cost (less tyres)	–	–	£112,000.00
Year 1 at 17% of £112,000	£19,040	£19,040	£92,960.00
Year 2 at 17% of £92,960	£15,803.20	£34,843.20	£77,156.80
Year 3 at 17% of £77,156.80	£13,116.66	£47,959.86	£64,040.14
Year 4 at 17% of £64,040.14	£10,886.83	£58,846.68	£53,153.32
Year 5 at 17% of £53,153.32	£9,036.06	£67,882.74	£44,117.26
Year 6 at 17% of £44,117.26	£7,500.00	£75,382.74	£36,617.26

Again we can see that the figures do not exactly reduce the value of the vehicle to a value of £37,500 but the variation is acceptable as it is 'close'. Please also note that the calculations were rounded up and down in order to work with two decimal places (as most calculations will be for your examinations).

The main point is that Table 5.6 shows quite clearly how the annual depreciation reduces as the vehicle gets older. The difficulty with depreciation comes when we need to depreciate trailers, as we normally operate more trailers than articulate tractors and because trailers do not in themselves generate any revenue but they do incur costs over periods of time. With trailers we need to calculate the total annual depreciation figure for all the trailers and divide it into the number of tractor units within the fleet.

For example, if we had 12 trailers each incurring £800 depreciation per annum we would have a total trailer depreciation cost of £9,600.

If we had eight tractor units we would then divide £9,600 by 8 = £1,200. This £1,200 would then be added to the depreciation cost of each of the tractor units in order to ensure that we were costing in sufficiently to ensure we had the funds to replace the trailers at the end of their working lives.

Key points you need to know

- The purpose and use of cash flow budgeting.
- How to construct and analyse a cash flow budget.
- The purpose and use of operational budgets.
- How to analyse an operational budget.
- Types of costs.
- How to calculate and apportion costs.
- How to produce total costs and charge-out rates.
- The different methods of depreciation.
- How to construct a table of depreciation for each method.

Notes

....

....

....

....

....

....
....
....
....
....

Once again we have reached the end of a very important subsection and it cannot be stressed enough how important it is that you ensure that you understand the content that relates to finance, accounting, costings, budgets and depreciation as you will be examined on these in some detail.

We are now able to shift the emphasis on to other issues that relate to business. We begin by looking at organizations and then go on to look at staff management and some legal requirements.

How organizations are structured

There are four main types of organizational structure, all of which are designed to provide benefits to the organization concerned. The main benefits, however, are that clearly defined structures enable all staff and management to:

- clearly identify every staff position (job) within the organization;
- clearly lay out clear lines of responsibility;
- clearly illustrate spans of control;
- clearly identify reporting lines.

The four main structures are:

- Tall structures: where there are many levels of management such as in the armed forces or in large organizations such as the Royal Mail or major banks. These structures tend to be fairly inflexible and are structures where control is evident at each of the many levels.

- Flat structures: these are the opposite of tall structures, where there are very few levels of management, where staff can have more wide-ranging responsibilities and the structures are fairly flexible. These structures would typically be found in smaller businesses and at depot level within larger organizations.

- Hierarchical structures: organizational structures where responsibility and control are set depending upon the 'seniority' or levels of management. These are the structures that you will most commonly encounter in the transport sector where, typically:
  - drivers report to supervisors;
  - supervisors report to junior managers;
  - junior managers report to senior managers;
  - senior managers report to directors;
  - directors report to the managing director.
- Matrix structures: these differ from hierarchal structures in that they are structures found in large organizations where staff work across more than one function or more than one location within the organization. This type of structure is widely used for work on specific projects, where staff from many disciplines may need to work together or where staff may need to travel between different sites and locations.

Note: The standards in the syllabus do require you to 'be able to draw up an organizational chart relating to the undertaking's personnel as a whole and to organize work plans, etc'. To be able to do this you may want to draw up a hierarchal chart for your own organization or one that you may have experienced previously.

Management definitions

Whilst the syllabus requires that you be able to draw up an organizational chart relating to the undertaking's personnel as a whole and to organize work plans, the examinations may need you to explain the plans you draw up and how staff within the plans will be managed. In order to do that you need to understand a few key definitions such as:

- Objectives: an objective identifies the overall aims of a role or function. An objective such as 'gaining a CPC within six months' is fine because it relates to our next definition, which is the acronym SMART.
- SMART stands for 'Simple' – 'Measurable' – 'Achievable' – 'Realistic' – 'Time-based'. All objectives need to be written using SMART.

In relation to work measurement there are further terms that you may need to understand such as:

- Responsibility: relating to the fact that all staff are responsible for doing certain jobs.

- Delegation: the process used in hierarchal structures to pass tasks to more junior staff. It is important to note that delegating does not include passing responsibility to any junior staff. The manager delegating always remains responsible.

- Authority: the authority of a job holder, or the authority that goes with a specific level of job, is really a limit or restricting factor on the extent of actions and responsibilities that can be taken by different staff members.

- Coordination: the term used to identify when different functions or departments work together for the benefit of the whole organization.

- Key performance indicators (KPIs): performance targets that are seen as key to the effective operation of a business. They identify the most important activities and measure how well they are being performed. They often relate to customer service and operational excellence.

- Performance management: this term refers to a system of staff appraisals where performance is measured and reviewed, improvement issues agreed, any training needs identified and SMART objectives agreed and set.

- Staff development: this is often included as a part of performance management and is where the company identifies employees it considers could act in different, or more senior, roles if they needed to. Training and development are provided accordingly and ensure that staff are better equipped to step into another role should the need arise on a temporary or permanent basis. It also helps staff to recognize other roles and responsibilities. It may be possible to rotate staff between job roles to give a more comprehensive set of skills.

Our final area for organizational terms and definitions relates to effective communications within an organization, because effective communication is the main way that organizations are able to ensure that all staff are properly informed and aware of situations, thus enabling them to support the organization in its objectives.

Effective communication means using different means of communicating to ensure the message is delivered – and all methods of communication must be appropriate for any given situation. The main ways of communicating include:

- Verbal communication: this can either be face to face or via a communication method such as radio, phone or even Skype.

- Written communication: this can be carried out in a number of ways such as notices, texts, letters, memos, e-mails and even tweets.

- Visual communication: such as using signs or pictures on videos or on-screen.

In all cases it is vital that communication should be designed in a way that is clear, unambiguous and suitable for the audience it is aimed at. It is also vital that communication within organizations is 'two-way' and not always simply 'top-down'; there are times when it needs to be 'bottom-up'.

Having covered terms, definitions and explanations that you may need we can now look at staffing when things may not go exactly to plan.

Grievance and discipline

By law, all disciplinary and grievance procedures need to be fair, structured and proceed in a number of set stages. At least three stages are required or the company may risk being taken to an industrial tribunal and being fined.

In relation to making an official statement of grievance, it must be understood that a grievance is deemed to be 'an official complaint by an employee regarding an occurrence at work'. In addition, grievances should only be made when other, less formal, attempts to find a solution have been exhausted.

To make a grievance, the employee should set out the grievance in writing and submit it to the employer. The employer should then arrange a meeting to discuss the issue, at which the employee is entitled to be accompanied (often by a union official or worker representative). Following this meeting the employer needs to investigate the issue and inform the employee of any decision, whilst advising them of their right to appeal.

The employee must then inform the employer as to whether or not they intend to appeal and another meeting has to be organized where the employee may also be accompanied. Following any second (appeal) meeting the employer informs the employee of their decision.

In relation to discipline, the employer must give a written statement to the employee setting out the allegations being made against them. Following that, a meeting has to be arranged where the case is put to the employee and the employee is entitled to respond. The employee may be accompanied to this meeting.

Following this meeting the employer will make a decision and must inform the employee accordingly and inform them of their right to appeal, should they wish to do so. Should the employee wish to appeal, a second (appeal) meeting has to be arranged where a different (usually more senior) manager will hear the appeal and will then inform the employee of the appeal decision.

Disciplinary action would also normally follow a staged process with verbal, written and final written warnings being in place before dismissal. Serious breaches of conduct, such as theft, arson, assault or fraud could result in the employee being subject to instant dismissal and earlier stages of the disciplinary process being ignored.

Note: There are some examination questions relating to organizational structures and staffing issues. It would help you if you could think about the logical nature of reporting lines and also any performance review or disciplinary procedures within an organization that you might be familiar with.

That concludes the specific staffing-related issues required for the course, and we can go on to look at marketing and public relations.

Market research and marketing

Marketing activity is generally only delivered after market research has been carried out in order to establish whether or not any planned marketing of goods and services is likely to succeed and to establish the market segment(s) where the marketing may be most effective.

Market research is carried out by assessing what are known as 'primary data' and 'secondary data'.

Primary data is used after the market research has focused on specific questions that require specific answers. The questions used to obtain primary data must be clear and not in any way misleading if a good 'response rate' is to be achieved.

Primary data can be obtained:

- By asking people to complete postal questionnaires. This is a relatively cheap method of market research but it does suffer from low response rates.

- By carrying out telephone interviews, which also suffers from a relatively low response rate.

- Conducting one-to-one personal interviews (often in the high street). This is an expensive method of market research but one that does get good response rates.

Response rates are clearly a big issue in relation to obtaining primary data, not least because of cost, but also in relation to what are known as 'conversion rates'. Conversion rates relate to the number of people that the market research finds are likely to be 'converted' (or convinced) that they will respond positively to any subsequent marketing activity.

Secondary data for market research is used to obtain more general data in relation to a market, or markets. It is often referred to as 'non-reactive' surveying as it does not involve activities by customers. Secondary data can be gained from both internal and external sources because it is data that already exists. For instance, there are internal sources of secondary data such as customer records, sales data and supplier information. There are also external sources of secondary data including sources such as news reports, government statistics, the internet and trade journals.

All market research, whether aimed at developing specific primary data or more general secondary data, must be aimed at the correct sections of the market in question. Market sections are known as market 'segments' and market segments are the components that form a whole market. For example, livestock haulage is a segment of the entire transport market, as is the carriage of dangerous goods, and international haulage is a segment of the entire transport market in the same way as 'national only' operations.

In any case, once we have conducted market research and focused on the required market segments we can now actually begin to conduct marketing itself.

Marketing

Marketing is based on the fact that products have a life cycle. The stages of a product's life cycle are known as: development – growth – maturity – saturation – decline.

The life-cycle stage that the product is in will determine the type of marketing activity required. For example, marketing is much more evident during the development and growth stages.

Marketing is also based on what is known as the marketing mix. The 'marketing mix' is known as the 'four Ps'. These are product, price, place and promotion. These four factors determine the marketing strategy of a product because:

- The 'product' needs to be suitable and appropriate for the intended market.
- The 'price' needs to reflect the product's quality and characteristics.

- The 'place' of sale needs to be suitable for the product.
- The way the product is 'promoted' needs to attract suitable buyers.

In general terms, marketing is usually associated with some sort of promotional activity in order to make potential customers and current customers more aware of the goods or services on offer. It can be done in many different ways and we will look at the different types of marketing activity below. What is important to note is that:

1 The method of marketing must be appropriate for the goods and services on offer.

2 The method of marketing must be suitable for the intended audience.

3 Marketing activity needs to be measured to assess success or failure or percentage response.

4 Marketing activities often form KPIs for many organizations.

Examples of different methods (types) of marketing are given below:

- Internet selling is probably the best example of direct marketing activity. It is relatively cheap to create and gives almost total 'global' access to customers.

- Social media such as smartphone applications that are primarily used for people to interact, of which Facebook and Twitter are two examples, can also be used for advertising and customer contact. Social media applications are also relatively cheap to operate and are a good way of providing 'live' information to customers.

- Telephone sales have something of an 'image problem' as they have become almost 'nuisance' calls for many recipients, especially when the call is a 'cold call'. In addition, they are relatively expensive. However, in the business to business (B2B) sector they are more commonly used and accepted.

- Advertising can be done through TV, radio, books, magazines, newspapers, posters, billboards and any number of different ways. Whilst it can also be a part of internet selling and social media applications it is the choice of the right form of advertisement that is important. For example, opening a new store in a town would be much better advertised in a local newspaper than on national TV.

- Direct mail ('junk mail') is both cheap and can be focused on individual areas or sections of the community where the products and services offered are thought likely to be needed or wanted.

- Marketing is also done at exhibitions and at trade fairs where particular trades or business sectors can come together to focus on the promotion of goods and services within those sectors. Examples include motor shows, boat shows, fashion shows and any number of exhibitions put on at the National Exhibition Centre (NEC) Birmingham.

What we have seen so far is that market research, and marketing itself, will lead to the company gaining information and data relating to current and potential customers. This data may be general business data such as accounts, but where it is more specific, or personal, and we intend to store it, it may be subject to controls under the Data Protection Act and/or the Freedom of Information Act and we now need to examine briefly each of these.

Data protection

The Data Protection Act applies to computerized personal data and personal data held in structured manual files held by all data controllers within organizations. The overall authority for the Act is the Information Commissioner's Office (ICO), which is a part of the Department for Constitutional Affairs.

The ICO enforces the requirements of the Act, promotes compliance and good practice, and manages the notification scheme. Under the terms of the Act, individuals have the right to 'opt out' of having their data used for direct marketing, and 'opt out' of fully automated decision making about them. They also have the right to have access to their data, to prevent it being processed and to seek compensation where their rights are infringed.

Individuals wishing to view data held about them can request to do so by submitting a 'subject access request'. Upon receiving such a request, the organization concerned must act with 'due diligence' to fulfil the request.

Where data is held, the organization holding the data must appoint data controllers who must comply with rules, including ensuring that the data is:

- accurate, relevant and not excessive;
- kept securely and for no longer than necessary;
- fairly and lawfully processed, for limited purposes in accordance with individuals' rights;
- only transferred to other countries with adequate protection.

Controllers must also meet conditions when processing sensitive data relating to things such as their political opinions, ethnic origin, health or sexual orientation and ensure that the individual is fully aware that the data has been collected.

Should a controller process information relating to individuals, they must inform the ICO of their activities unless they are exempt. Exemptions exist when processing manual records, when processing core business activities and when processing charities' membership records.

Freedom of Information Act

In addition, the Freedom of Information Act effectively extended the earlier Data Protection Act by making all recorded personal data held by data controllers in public authorities (including that in manual files) subject to controls.

The public bodies concerned include central and local government, the police, schools, colleges, universities and the health service and most public and advisory bodies. The Freedom of Information Act does allow these public bodies to withhold certain information from an individual but the individual concerned must be informed of why it is being withheld. Public authorities must comply with requests by individuals to see the information relating to them within 20 working days or explain to the individual why additional time is needed.

Note: Scotland has its own, very similar, Freedom of Information Act, covering public authorities operating solely within Scotland.

Having reviewed marketing and how marketing data must be controlled we now move on to public relations.

Public relations

Public relations (PR) is often viewed as simply being a different form of marketing but this is not true. PR has clearly defined roles and responsibilities, not least to ensure that the organization is presented in the most positive or correct/favourable way to the outside world and, to some extent, to employees and staff.

In order to achieve this, many organizations employ PR professionals to make statements to the media or business world and strictly forbid other employees and staff from talking to the media or making any sorts of policy statements on behalf of the organization concerned.

PR professionals also act to keep the image of the company in a favourable light by interacting with local communities, arranging events, organizing customer-focused events and working with charities; all of which are clearly aimed at maintaining positive customer and business relationships.

Key points you need to know

- The four different management structures.
- The definitions and terms used in business management.
- Grievance and discipline procedures.
- Primary and secondary data definitions and aims.
- Types of marketing activities.
- How data needs to be controlled.
- Data legislation (the two Acts).
- The role of PR.

Notes

....

....

....

....

....

....

....

....

....

....

Continuing with business management issues, we now move on to look at insurance.

Insurance

Insurance policies are available either by paying annually or in instalments, and are the method that business uses to convert an unknown risk into a known cost. We begin with motor insurance and then other forms of insurance covered by the syllabus.

Note: In recent years the term 'accident' appears to have been largely replaced by the words 'incident' or 'collision'. However, we will use the term 'accident' as incidents and collisions are not clearly defined in law whereas a 'road traffic accident' is clearly defined.

Motor vehicle insurance

With very few exceptions, the law requires all motor vehicles in the UK to have a minimum level of 'third-party' insurance cover. Third-party cover effectively protects other vehicles (third parties), third-party drivers and passengers if injured, and damage to, or loss of, the third party's property resulting from an accident involving the insured vehicle.

Third-party cover is also extended to include all employees whilst travelling on company vehicles. All third-party policies must provide unlimited cover for personal injury claims, payments for emergency medical treatment and payments for damage to a third-party vehicle or property.

Third-party cover can also be extended to include things such as 'fire and theft' provision or even further extended to fully comprehensive policies, where all risks are covered.

If insurance is taken out with an insurance company, for the policy to be valid there are a number of conditions that need to be met:

- The company providing the insurance must be a member of the Motor Insurers' Bureau (MIB).
- The correct information about the vehicle(s) and driver(s) must be given.
- The driver must have a current driving licence for the vehicle concerned.
- The vehicle(s) must be roadworthy.
- If applicable, the vehicle must have a current test certificate.
- The vehicle must be subject to current VED.

In the UK it is the Certificate of Insurance (or a Cover Note) that provides proof of valid insurance. There are certain facts that relate to them:

- The certificates must be issued within four days of renewal.
- The certificates must be returned within seven days of cancellation.
- Certificates can be requested to be produced by a police officer or a DVSA examiner.

- If the certificate cannot be produced at the time of request, it must be taken to a police station within seven days of the request.
- Any attempt to alter an Insurance Certificate is classed by the courts as 'forgery'.

Note: Today, the police are also able to establish whether or not a vehicle is insured by using Automatic Number Plate Recognition (ANPR). Large fleet operators (or anyone else with sufficient funds) have an alternative to paying for insurance in the conventional way. They simply need to deposit £500,000 with the Accountant General of the Supreme Court as a bond. Doing this permits them to cover their third-party risks themselves. However, as this is a UK concession they still need to purchase third-party cover for vehicles operating abroad. If a deposit has been made with the Accountant General, a Certificate of Deposit will be used in place of the Certificate of Insurance.

The Green Card scheme and EAS

The MIB provides 'Green Card' insurance for international operations. However, the actual 'Green Cards', which offer proof of third-party cover to UK drivers driving in mainland Europe, are not issued by the MIB itself – they are obtainable from most motor insurance providers.

The Green Card simply acts as proof of third-party cover to enforcement authorities, the police and insurance providers abroad. Whilst carrying a Green Card is not a legal requirement, the cards are readily accepted as proof of insurance in over 40 countries, thereby reducing problems with presenting unfamiliar paperwork to these groups of people.

The European Accident Statement (EAS), which can be obtained from most UK insurers, is a form, in several languages, which satisfies the requirements of European insurers in relation to providing details of a road accident. It also acts to provide a common understanding of the facts in relation to road accidents. An EAS is a duplicate form to be filled out by each driver. It requires each driver to enter their name and address, details of insurance, details of the accident and details of any injuries. Each driver must then sign the form and exchange one copy, which is then submitted to the insurance provider to act as an agreed statement of fact that contains all the details the insurance providers require.

Compulsory business insurance

Employers' liability insurance

Most employers are required by law to take out employers' liability insurance. There are a few exceptions to this as in the cases of the police, local authorities, close family relatives working in a business and servants in domestic service for a private household.

The insurance provides cover for employees in the event of death, injury, or any disease contracted during the course of their employment, and ensures that the employee will receive any due payments or compensation should the business in question be unable to pay itself. The policy must include cover of up to £5 million for each incident.

Failure to display a certificate of employers' liability insurance can result in fines based on a rate for each day the certificate has not been displayed.

Maritime insurance

Maritime insurance is normally compulsory when some goods on vehicles, or in containers, are not covered by CMR but do travel by sea. As we know, if the goods under CMR are not unloaded then CMR remains in force. However, if the goods are unloaded to travel by sea then maritime insurance (sometimes referred to as 'marine insurance') will be required.

Discretionary business insurances

Public liability insurance

This provides cover for people who are not company employees, such as visitors, guests or members of the public who may suffer injuries, loss or have an accident whilst on company premises. These policies are also designed to provide insurance in cases where the accident or loss may have been caused by a company employee. The cover should also be formed in such a way that it insures against damage and any subsequent repairs to adjoining or adjacent properties in the case of a fire or some other cause.

Professional negligence insurance

This acts to safeguard some businesses from claims from members of the public that, as a professional business, they should have acted in a more professional way to prevent an accident. For example, this type of insurance is commonly taken out by professional haulage operators to protect themselves from charges that they have failed in their duty of care to a customer, in one way or another.

Goods-in-transit insurance

Unfortunately for many unsuspecting customers, goods-in-transit insurance is not legally required in the UK and it is up to the customer to ensure that their haulier has this non-compulsory insurance before any business is conducted, although, as we saw earlier, most hauliers do declare their conditions of carriage, which normally include operating to RHA or FTA levels of insurance in relation to the goods carried.

Goods-in-transit insurance can be extended to cash-in-transit insurance where a driver may need to collect monies from customers or whilst money is being transferred by the company to a bank.

European health insurance card (EHIC)

The EHIC entitles the holder from the UK to emergency medical treatment whilst in any EU country, or any European Free Trade Area (EFTA) country (Iceland, Liechtenstein, Norway and Switzerland). EHICs are free of charge and can be downloaded from the NHS website.

The EHIC only provides emergency treatment at the same cost in any country as the charge may be for nationals of that country. This may be 'free' but there are also many countries where some sorts of charges are levied.

Property insurance

Whilst property insurance is normally required under the terms of a mortgage or lease, it is not legally required in other cases. However, as property is so expensive and damage to business premises can be so disruptive, property insurance is very commonly purchased in one form or another. For example, property insurance can cover damage by fire and flood and damage and loss caused by any theft.

It can also be formed to provide compensation for any 'consequential loss' to the business resulting from these sorts of incidents. Consequential loss insurance means that the company will be able to recover any losses associated with the normal running of the business whilst repairs or other actions are being taken.

Fidelity guarantee

A fidelity guarantee acts to protect the company against any dishonest acts committed by any individual employee or all of its employees. However, insurance companies will need to know that the company concerned actually made 'reasonable checks' prior to offering a person employment before any guarantee will be issued. Where dishonest acts do occur the insurance provider does not make any payment until the employee(s) concerned have been prosecuted.

Public highway damage insurance

This is insurance used by hauliers moving abnormal indivisible loads (AILs) to provide cover for any damage to the highway or bridges caused by the movement. If damage is recorded, the authority concerned has up to 12 months, from the day of the movement, in order to report it and file a claim. Our next area of consideration moves us on to what is known as 'information and communication technology' (ICT).

Information and communication technology (ICT)

Whilst the internet, or world wide web, is now seen as an everyday work tool, web-based resources are also used extensively to gather information, collect data and communicate. However, ICT does not always need to be 'ultra-high tech'. It can involve many applications that we consider as routine. In addition to the everyday use of emails, these include:

- Communication systems where operators may issue smartphones to drivers, have vehicles fitted with radios, mobile phones and fax machines.

  Note: Vocational driving licence holders using a mobile phone whilst driving attract a fine of £200 and six penalty points, whereas being caught a second time means the driver will need to face a Magistrates' Court, and risks disqualification and a fine of £1,000.

- Closed-circuit television (CCTV) systems using digital cameras either fitted to vehicles to aid reversing or to view the front of the vehicle in case of an accident or, perhaps most commonly, to act as a deterrent by recording activities on business premises. Where CCTV is used on-site the business must produce signs stating that it is in use in order to avoid any human rights or data protection issues.

- Routing and scheduling software packages now generally include not only the route and a schedule for the route but information relating to drivers' hours, costs and budgets.

- Global positioning systems (GPSs) and satellite navigation (satnav) are now commonly used to track vehicles and goods along their route so that customers can be informed of an expected arrival time and the business can plan when a vehicle may return to base in order to be used again. The data that is stored by these systems (usually on a 'cloud' system) can also be used by the operator on a historic basis to identify patterns of delay for vehicles so that schedules can be adapted in the future if necessary in order to ensure reliability.

- Telemetry is different to satnav or GPS. Telemetry is the electronic transfer of readings from instruments. It forms the basis of most engine management systems and is also used in vehicle load sensors and to record temperatures using thermographs. Telemetry is also used by the authorities to monitor traffic flow and then adjust variable speed limits accordingly.

- Automatic number plate recognition (ANPR) is not used by many operators but it is used to police operations and to check that vehicles are insured and taxed. It is also used in conjunction with other ICT applications such as 'weigh in motion' to detect axle and gross overloads on moving vehicles and to police compliance with the road user levy, congestion and LEZ/CAZ schemes.

- Other enforcement areas such as speed cameras, bus lane cameras, average speed monitors, parking compliance cameras and even Operator Compliance Risk Scores (OCRS – see the next section) are all ICT enforcement applications.

- Driver monitoring systems are used increasingly to monitor things such as speed, acceleration, braking and cornering activities to assess when drivers are acting harshly. The data can be sent as 'live' data back to the vehicle base and analysed in order to improve driver behaviour.

- Customer monitoring systems gather and record things such as orders placed, credit performance, returns and damages, which in addition to acting as a customer record can be used for marketing purposes.

- Fleet administration systems are used to record and plan vehicle maintenance, record repairs and costs, record tyre usage, renew VED, renew insurance, make changes to the operator's licence and record a whole range of fleet costs such as fuel, spare parts and leasing payments.

The list of applications above is not meant to be exhaustive but it is required to give you an overview of at least some of the typical ICT applications used within our industry.

Our final subsection relates to moving consignments under certain terms and conditions.

Incoterms

The Incoterms rules or International Commercial terms are a series of commercial terms published by the International Chamber of Commerce (ICC). The current set of these rules is referred to as Incoterms 2010.

Incoterms use three-letter abbreviations to identify the actual set of rules that apply to a consignment (in a similar way that airports use three-letter abbreviations – LGW being London Gatwick). Incoterms are designed to clarify the exact roles, responsibilities, costs and risks to both a buyer and a seller when goods are being moved. Most trading countries in the developed world use Incoterms and they are accepted by the authorities in all participating countries in a similar way to CMR (covered in Chapter 1) and TIR, ADR or ATP (covered in Chapters 6 and 7).

Incoterms are split into two groups: Group 1 applies to movements by all modes of transport; Group 2 relates to movements by sea and inland waterways.

The Group 1 Incoterms 2010 are detailed below as they apply to all modes of transport and multi-modal movements:

- **EXW** – ex works (named place)
  'Ex works' means that the seller's responsibilities end when they
  place the goods at the disposal of the buyer at the seller's premises, or
  another named place such as a factory or warehouse. It is the buyer
  who then has to bear all costs and risks involved in taking the goods
  from those premises. EXW represents the Incoterm that is the least
  onerous on the seller.

- **FCA** – free carrier (named place)
  'Free carrier' means that the seller delivers the goods, cleared for
  export, to the carrier nominated by the buyer at the named place. If
  delivery occurs at the seller's premises, the seller is responsible for
  loading. If delivery occurs at any other place, the seller is not
  responsible for unloading.

- **CPT** – carriage paid to (named place of destination)
  'Carriage paid to' means that the seller delivers the goods to a carrier
  nominated by the seller. The seller must also pay the cost of carriage
  necessary to bring the goods to the named place of destination. This
  means that the buyer bears all risks and any other costs occurring
  after the goods have been delivered. Under CPT the seller is also
  responsible to clear the goods for export.

- **CIP** – carriage and insurance paid to (named place of destination)
  'Carriage and insurance paid to' is similar to CPT but means that the
  seller delivers the goods to the nominated carrier, but the seller also
  has to produce insurance to cover any loss or damage to the goods
  during the transit. Like CPT, CIP also requires the seller to clear the
  goods for export.

- **DAP** – delivered at place (named place of destination)
  'Delivered at place' means that the seller pays for the carriage to the named place except for the costs related to import clearance. The seller also assumes all risks up to the point that the goods are ready for unloading by the buyer at the named place.

- **DAT** – delivered at terminal (named terminal at port or place of destination)
  DAT is a term that helps buyers and sellers using containerized consignments. It is the seller who pays for the carriage to a nominated terminal at the place of destination, except for any costs related to import clearance. It is also the seller who assumes all risks for loss or damage right up to the point that the goods are unloaded at the named terminal at the port or place of destination.

- **DDP** – delivered duty paid (named place of destination)
  'Delivered duty paid' means that the seller delivers the goods to the buyer, cleared for import, and not unloaded from any arriving means of transport at the named place of destination. The seller has to bear all the costs and risks involved in bringing the goods thereto including, where applicable, any 'duty' (which term includes the responsibility for and the risks of the carrying out of customs formalities, and the payment of formalities, customs duties, taxes and other charges) for import in the country of destination. DDP represents the most onerous to the seller.

Group 2 Incoterms are not included as they do not apply to consignments moved by road.

Key points you need to know

- Motor insurance, Green Card, EAS and EHIC.

- Employers' liability insurance.

- An overview of all other insurances.

- The difference between telemetry and other software.

- An overview of other ICT applications.

- EXW, DAT, DAP and DDP.
- An overview of the other Incoterms.

Notes

....

....

....

....

....

....

....

....

....

....

Self-test example questions

OCR-type questions (multi-choice)

1 i) Working capital is calculated as current liabilities minus current assets. ii) Capital employed is calculated as the fixed assets plus the working capital. These statements are:

   a (i) true (ii) true;

   b (i) false (ii) true;

   c (i) false (ii) false;

   d (i) true (ii) false.

2 Why is a P&L account limited in the information it supplies? How can companies act to minimize this limitation?

   a The P&L is limited because it only provides management information relating to current trading. Organizations can minimize this limitation by producing P&Ls in advance for their own management purposes.

   b The P&L is limited because it only provides projected financial forecasts. Organizations can minimize this limitation by producing P&Ls for their own management purposes, several times a year.

   c The P&L is limited because it only provides historic information. Organizations can minimize this limitation by producing P&Ls for their own management purposes, several times a year.

   d The P&L is limited because it only provides historic information. Organizations can minimize this limitation by having P&Ls produced by the accounts department before any AGM is planned to take place.

3 Which of the following are direct costs and which are indirect costs?

     1. directors' salaries;

     2. drivers' wages;

     3. vehicle maintenance;

     4. advertising;

     5. fuel;

     6. rent;

     7. heating and light;

     8. tyres.

  a Direct costs = 2, 3, 4 and 8; indirect costs = 1, 5, 6 and 7.

  b Direct costs = 1, 3, 5 and 8; indirect costs = 2, 4, 6 and 7.

  c Direct costs = 2, 3, 6 and 8; indirect costs = 1, 4, 5 and 7.

  d Direct costs = 2, 3, 5 and 8; indirect costs = 1, 4, 6 and 7.

4 How do the four Ps of the marketing mix determine the marketing strategy of a product? Because:

  a

     – The 'product' needs to be made available for the intended market.

     – The 'price' needs to reflect the product market where the product belongs.

     – The 'place' of sale needs to be suitable for the product.

     – The way the product is 'promoted' needs to attract suitable buyers.

  b

     – The 'product' needs to be suitable and appropriate for the intended market.

     – The 'price' needs to reflect the product's quality and characteristics.

- The 'place' of sale needs to be within cost-effective distances for distribution of the product.
- The way the product is 'promoted' needs to attract suitable buyers.

c

- The 'product' needs to be suitable and appropriate for the intended market.
- The 'price' needs to reflect the product's quality and characteristics.
- The 'place' of sale needs to be suitable for the product.
- The way the product is 'promoted' needs to have initial high investment and be properly researched.

d

- The 'product' needs to be suitable and appropriate for the intended market.
- The 'price' needs to reflect the product's quality and characteristics.
- The 'place' of sale needs to be suitable for the product.
- The way the product is 'promoted' needs to attract suitable buyers.

5 Which of the following explanations most accurately describes the Incoterm DAT?

a DAT helps buyers and sellers using containerized consignments. It is the seller who pays for the carriage to a nominated terminal at the place of destination, except for any costs related to import clearance. It is also the seller who assumes all risks for loss or damage right up to the point that the goods are unloaded at the named terminal at the port or place of destination.

b DAT helps buyers and sellers using bulk consignments. It is the seller who pays for the customs duties to a nominated port at the place of destination, except for any costs related to import clearance. It is also the seller who assumes all risks for loss or damage right up to the point that the goods are unloaded at the named terminal at the port or place of destination.

c DAT helps buyers and sellers using containerized consignments. It is the buyer who pays for the carriage to a nominated terminal at the place of destination, including any costs related to import clearance. It is also the buyer who assumes all risks for loss or damage right up to the point that the goods are unloaded at the named terminal at the port or place of destination, making it simple for the seller.

d DAT helps buyers and sellers using inter-modal consignments. It is the seller who pays for the carriage to a nominated terminal at the place of destination, including any costs related to import clearance. It is also the seller who assumes liabilities for customs charges and for loss or damage right up to the point that the goods are unloaded at the named port.

OCR case study-type question

See past papers referred to in Chapter 1.

CILT-type questions (short answer)

1 Briefly explain the formulas used to calculate working capital and capital employed.

2 Briefly discuss the major limitation of a profit and loss account and how companies can minimize this limitation.

3 Below are some company costs – which are direct costs and which are indirect costs?

 - directors' salaries;
 - drivers' wages;
 - vehicle maintenance;
 - advertising;
 - fuel;
 - rent;
 - heating and light;
 - tyres.

4 Briefly explain why the four Ps of the 'marketing mix' determine the marketing strategy of a product.

5 Briefly explain the meaning of the Incoterm DAT, clearly explaining the obligations of the buyer and seller.

CILT-type question (long answer)

Your company has been asked to produce a cost per pallet, in euros, for a one-way (no return trip) 26-pallet consignment to be delivered to a customer in Spain, using a maximum-length articulated combination.

Calculate cost plus profit charge per pallet in pounds sterling and then convert it to a cost per pallet in euros.

The following costs and details apply:

- The driver's costs are £75 per day plus a night-out allowance of £30.

- The distance is 1,860 km, the vehicle returns 3 km of fuel per litre and the fuel costs £1.05 per litre.

- Tyre costs (for all tyres) are £0.04 per kilometre.

- Maintenance costs are £0.05 per kilometre.

- The one-way trip will take two days.

- The ferry costs are £20.50 per metre of vehicle and trailer.

- Tolls and other costs for the single journey are £265.

- The company needs to add a 12 per cent profit surcharge.

- A euro is worth £0.74.

- Work to two decimal points and show all your working.

Access to the market

06

As with Chapter 3 (Social Law) that required you to download a GV262 for drivers' hours and tachograph information, this chapter requires you to download or contact the Central Licensing Office (CLO) in Leeds (see below) to obtain a GV74. This is the DVSA official Guide to Operator Licensing, and is also available through the gov.uk website. By obtaining one of these guides you will have all the relevant information you require in relation to operator licensing.

This in itself is important because this topic lies at the very heart of goods vehicle fleet operation and, consequently, you will be examined in depth on this subject.

Specifically, the syllabus requires that you should be familiar with:

- the occupational regulations governing road transport for hire or reward, industrial vehicle rental and subcontracting and (in particular) the rules governing the official organization of the occupation, admission to the occupation, authorizations for intra-community and extra-community road transport operations, inspections and penalties;

- the requirement for, and conditions applying to, the setting up and operation of a road transport company with respect to operator licensing;

- the various documents required for operating road transport services and the introduction of checking procedures to ensure that the approved documents relating to each transport operation and (in particular) those relating to the vehicle, the driver and the goods are kept both in the vehicle and on the premises of the undertaking;

- the rules on the organization of the market in road haulage services, as well as the rules on freight handling and logistics;

- border formalities, the role and scope of documents and TIR carnets, and the obligations and responsibilities arising from their use.

Operator licensing

Operator licensing, as we know it today, originated in 1968 and although the system has been updated and changed it is still a system based on quality of operation and not quantity of operation. By having this focus, operator licensing is clearly linked to improving road safety and compliance with legislation. It is controlled by the Department for Transport (DfT) and 'policed' by the Traffic Commissioner (TC) and DVSA.

Operator licensing applies to goods vehicles with a gross vehicle weight exceeding 3,500 kg and trailers exceeding 1,020 kg unladen weight, used in connection with a trade or business.

Non-business (private) use is not subject to operator licensing and goods vehicles deployed on other activities are also exempted, including:

- vehicles used under a trade licence;
- ambulance, fire brigade and police vehicles;
- gritters, snow ploughs and road sweepers;
- vehicles driven by steam or electricity;
- recovery vehicles providing they are used solely for that purpose.

Some other exempted vehicles are listed below but, at the time of writing, whilst these exemptions are still valid they are under review. Changes following the review must have been implemented by May 2018.

- road rollers;
- tower wagons;
- mobile cranes;
- showman's vehicles.

Licence requirements

Should you require an operator's licence ('O' licence), the following steps must be taken:

- Applications must be made to the DVSA Central Licensing Office (CLO) in Leeds.
- The application is made by completing a form GV79.
- Applicants need to allow at least nine weeks for the application to be processed.

- The applicant needs to advertise that they intend to open an operating centre.

- The advertisement must appear in a newspaper that is available in the area of the proposed operating centre.

- The full page of the newspaper containing the advertisement must be sent to the CLO with GV79.*

---

* Form GV79 has several annexes. Annexes A–D are a part of the initial application form whilst Annex E is a supplementary form which may, or may not, be required to be filled in. The annexes are:

Annex A – The advertisement (Form GV79A)

Annex B – Current financial levels (Form GV79B)

Annex C – Scale of fees (Form GV79C)

Annex D – Maintenance contract (Form GV79D)

Annex E – Supplementary environmental information (Form GV79E)

Note: Applicants who request a user name and password from the CLO can apply online. Online applications only take seven weeks and not the normal nine weeks for postal applications.

As there are three types of 'O' licence, the type of licence you wish to apply for also determines what skills you may have, your financial status, your past criminal record and other factors, which we discuss below.

First, let's look at the three types of 'O' licence and the criteria that must be met in order to be granted any one of them:

- First, there is a restricted licence: these are required by people who operate relevant vehicles and trailers (as detailed above) to carry their own goods. They cannot be used to carry for hire and reward (haulage) but they are valid for carrying goods in the UK and abroad.

- Next there is a standard national licence: these are required by people who operate relevant vehicles and trailers (as detailed above) to carry goods for hire and reward within the UK (haulage) and their own goods in the UK and abroad.

- Finally, there is the standard international licence: these are required by people who operate relevant vehicles and trailers (as detailed above) to carry goods for hire and reward (haulage) and their own goods throughout both the UK and abroad.

In order to be granted one of the three types of licence, certain criteria relating to the applicant and the business must be met. We now examine these criteria.

Criteria for a licence

- Any person applying for any type of 'O' licence has to be a 'fit and proper person'. To meet this criteria every applicant must declare any previous unspent convictions, including bankruptcy, and any transport related convictions.

- Every applicant must have a suitable 'operating centre'. This is defined as a place where the vehicle, or vehicles, will usually be kept, and it must be large enough to hold all the vehicles concerned and have safe access and egress. The centre must also be suitable in relation to the environment. In deciding this, the TC will consider the following:

  - the nature and use of land in the vicinity of the operating centre and the effect that granting the application would be likely to have on the environment;

  - the extent to which granting a licence, which will materially change the use of an existing (or previously used) operating centre, will harm the environment in the vicinity;

  - in cases where land has not previously been used as an operating centre, any planning application or planning permission relating to the operating centre or the land in the vicinity;

  - the number, type and size of the authorized vehicles that will use the centre;

  - the parking arrangements for the authorized vehicles that will use the operating centre;

  - the nature and times of use of the operating centre;

  - the nature and times of use of any equipment at the operating centre;

  - the number and frequency of vehicles that would be entering and leaving the operating centre.

Note 1: Should there be issues about the environmental 'suitability' of the proposed operating centre, the TC requests the completion of a form GV79E, which is used to provide additional environmental information.

Note 2: Upon application, the applicant needs to apply for a maximum authorized number of vehicles for the centre and to list the actual number of vehicles either in their possession or expected to be operated. The difference between the actual number and the total authorization is known as the 'margin' and it is the margin that allows the fleet to grow, providing that the total authorization is never exceeded.

- Applicants must demonstrate to the TC that they will maintain their vehicles correctly. In order to do that they must:
  - Declare who is to maintain the vehicles and, if it is an external maintenance provider, submit a maintenance contract.
  - Submit samples of the forms to be used both for vehicle safety inspections and for drivers' daily checks and defect reporting.
  - Declare the proposed periods between planned safety inspections.
  - Demonstrate that they have a planning system for all vehicle safety inspections that can show planned inspections for a minimum period of six months in advance.
  - Declare they will retain all the vehicle maintenance records for a minimum period of 15 months.

  Note: The DVSA has its own Guide to Maintaining Roadworthiness that gives further details. You are advised to download a copy (also on the gov.uk website) as it will help you here and later, in Chapter 7, when maintenance is covered in more detail.

- The applicant for any standard licence must be able to prove to the TC that they have sufficient 'financial standing' to operate any proposed fleet of vehicles. In order to do this they must demonstrate that they have, or can have access to figures of €9,000 for the first vehicle and €5,000 for each subsequent vehicle authorized. In 2017, these euro figures equated to £7,850 and £4,350.

  Note 1: For a restricted licence, in 2017 these figures were £3,100 and £1,700, respectively and at the time of writing had not changed. These levels are now reviewed annually and will change on 1 January every year.

  Note 2: Should there be issues about financial standing the TCs may seek the help of accountants or financial professionals in order to ascertain the true financial position.

  Note 3: Applicants must also declare any, and all, previous bankruptcy or financial failures.

- Applicants for standard licences (but not restricted licences) need to demonstrate that they are not only 'fit and proper', as defined above, but that they also have 'good repute'. To ascertain whether or not this is so, the TC will look at any 'relevant' (criminal) unspent convictions that either resulted in a fine more than £2,500 or 60 hours of community service (or equivalent), or any more serious offences. These offences do not need to be linked to transport.

Note: Good repute must be ascertained for any, and all, directors, partners or transport managers.

- Applicants for standard licences (but not restricted licences) must nominate a person who is deemed to be 'professionally competent' in road freight operations. In addition, this person must be able to prove that they have 'effective control' of the fleet on a day-to-day basis.

Note 1: In order to demonstrate 'effective control', the TC insists that the nominated person (usually the transport manager) must complete a set number of hours of work each week, depending upon the size of the fleet, and make a declaration to this effect. For example, for a fleet of:

- 2 or fewer vehicles = 2–4 hours per week;
- 3 to 5 vehicles = 4–8 hours per week;
- 6 to 10 vehicles = 8–12 hours per week;
- 11 to 14 vehicles = 12–20 hours per week;
- 15 to 29 vehicles = 20–30 hours per week;
- 30+ vehicles = 30 hours per week – full-time;
- 50+ vehicles = full-time plus additional assistance.

Note 2: Further hours may be required for fleets operating a number of trailers. The main point is that the nominated person needs to have 'effective and continuous control of the fleet on a day-to-day basis'.

Note 3: Where more than 30 vehicles are operated and a single transport manager is in charge the TC will need evidence of how 'effective control' will be achieved and monitored.

Note 4: If the 'transport manager' is not a company employee, but an external specialist, they can work for no more than four operators and oversee no more than a total of 50 vehicles.

Note 5: The applicant will need to show proof of CPC by the nominated person and also submit a copy of their contract of employment at the time of application. This is all done, including the statement of the hours to be worked, by using form TM1.

- All applicants, or their nominated professionally competent person, must sign a legal undertaking declaring that they, and any staff employed by the company, will comply with:
  - laws relating to the driving and operation of the vehicles being used (these include any hired vehicles);
  - drivers' hours and records regulations;
  - regulations to prevent overloading;
  - speed limits;
  - vehicle-condition safety requirements;
  - defect reporting and rectification requirements;
  - the requirement to retain maintenance records for 15 months;
  - operating-centre vehicle authorization limits;
  - compliance with only using authorized operating centres;
  - I will notify the TC of any convictions against myself, or the company, business partner(s), the company directors, nominated transport manager/s named in this application, or employees or agents of the applicant for this licence;
  - I will ensure that the TC is notified within 28 days of any other notifiable changes;
  - For standard licence holders only the declaration also requires the applicant to declare that they have a UK address where all documentation can be found and that they access to at least one UK registered vehicle.

Now we can see the basis on which all applications are judged, and the absolute need that the criteria can be met and demonstrated, we can move on to the application and administrative processes.

Application process and traffic commissioners' roles

As we already mentioned, applications for operators' licences must be made to the DVSA at the Central Licensing Office (CLO) at least nine weeks before the licence is required. This application must also be accompanied by a non-refundable application fee.

Other facts include:

- The country is divided into eight different traffic areas.
- The TCs are appointed by the Secretary of State for Transport as DfT staff and are not directly accountable to the DVSA.

- Each TC is responsible for the licensing of operators in their own traffic area, and for taking action against drivers of both goods vehicles and passenger vehicles within said traffic area.
- Only one licence can be held in each traffic area but any number of operating centres can be held on that single licence.
- Northern Ireland has a separate system of operator licensing, overseen by the Department for Infrastructure (DfI).

Note: Operators holding licences in more than one traffic area will be given a 'Lead Traffic Commissioner'. Administration in these circumstances is undertaken by the Multi-licence Holder (MLH) team at the CLO.

The application process involves the TC seeking comments from both statutory objectors and local people in order to make a considered decision on whether or not to grant a licence. They do this in different ways. For example, in the case of statutory objectors, all applications appear in a fortnightly publication called *Applications and Decisions* (referred to as 'A and D' or 'As and Ds').This publication enables statutory objectors to object against the application.

Statutory objectors include the following:

- local authorities;
- local planning authorities;
- the police;
- the British Association of Removers;
- the Freight Transport Association;
- the Road Haulage Association;
- the Union of Shop, Distributive and Allied Workers;
- the Transport and General Workers' Union;
- the United Road Transport Union;
- the General and Municipal Workers' Union;
- the National Union of Rail, Maritime and Transport Workers.

Note: This list is currently under review by the Senior Traffic Commissioner.

All the above can only object to an application (or a major change to a licence, which is virtually the same procedure as for an initial application) on statutory grounds such as their belief, or knowledge, that the business does not have sufficient funding, that one or more directors do not have good repute or are not fit and proper, that the nominated person lacks professional competence, or other similar 'statutory' issues.

Local people use a different system, which is linked with the need for the applicant to take out an advertisement in a local newspaper, within a strict and important time period of 21 days before to 21 days after the date of application, to inform people in the area of their intention to open an operating centre. Local people are only able to make what are known as 'environmental representations'. These people need to be owners or occupiers of land or buildings in the vicinity of a proposed centre and must:

- make their representation within 21 days of the date of publication of the advertisement;
- ensure it is only on environmental grounds such as noise, emissions, possible obstruction, visual intrusion or vibration;
- ensure it is signed;
- ensure it is not vexatious or frivolous;
- send copies to both the TC and the applicant.

If either a statutory objection or an environmental representation is made, the TC will usually call a public inquiry and, depending upon the outcome of the inquiry, the licence may be rejected, granted in part, or granted in full.

A further difference between the two forms of objection/representation is that whilst statutory objectors and the applicant have 28 days following the publication of the decision in A and D to appeal against the decision, environmental representors have no direct right of appeal and are only able to combine with the statutory objectors as part of their appeal.

Once the decision is published in A and D, any appeal must be lodged within 28 days of the decision's publication. However, if the decision is not actually published in A and D within 21 days of the appellant being informed of the decision, the appellant has a further 49 days to lodge an appeal.

Initial appeals against decisions are made to the Administrative Chamber of the Upper Tribunal using form UT12. Should further actions be needed then the case would go on to be heard in the law courts in England and Wales or the Court of Session in Scotland.

The TC may agree to the continuation of an existing licence pending the outcome of an appeal, or they may not allow it to continue. Where it is not allowed to continue the appellant may request the Upper Tribunal to give a decision within 14 days.

Issue of the licence

The TC issues both the actual licence, which is referred to as form OL1, and authorized vehicle discs, referred to as form OL2. These discs are colour coded by type of licence, where an orange disc is used for a restricted licence, a blue disc is used for a standard national licence and a green disc is used for a standard international licence.

The discs need to be put in the windscreen of the vehicle to which they refer and are of a standard format that displays:

- the name of the operating person or company;
- the operator licence holder's reference number;
- the expiry date of the licence;
- the type of licence;
- the vehicle registration number.

The discs can only be used on the vehicle to which they apply and if they become illegible (perhaps by fading) they need to be replaced. In any case all discs must be placed in the vehicle within 28 days of being issued and returned within 28 days of the vehicle being removed from the fleet.

Other operational issues

- It may be the case that an existing operator needs a new 'O' licence within the prescribed nine-week application-processing period (perhaps when upgrading from a standard national to a standard international licence). In these cases they need to submit a form INT1 with their GV79 and apply for an interim licence.

  Interim licences have the word INTERIM in bold on the OL2 and, whilst they allow an operator to function whilst the application is being processed, they do not guarantee that the application itself will be successful.

- In addition to interim licences some companies may take over another company. In these cases, the main company, known as the holding company, may be able to include the vehicles of the subsidiary companies on its 'O' licence, providing that the holding company owns more than 50 per cent of the share capital.

- Schedule 4 is a system that enables an existing operator who takes over another operator's business in the same traffic area to take it over without the need to advertise in a local newspaper, providing that there are no material changes to the licence other than the change of ownership. Schedule 4 can also be used where the trading status of the licence holder changes but, again, there are no material changes as in cases where a sole trader forms a limited company.

- When hiring in vehicles, which must only be done providing there is a sufficient 'margin' on the licence to allow this, if the vehicle is hired without a driver it is the hirer who is responsible for it in relation to the 'O' licence. Where a vehicle is hired with a driver, like most subcontractors' vehicles, then it is the driver's employer who remains responsible.

- If a licence holder is asked by the police or a DVSA official to present the 'O' licence for inspection it can be presented within 14 days either at: 1) a police station of the operator's choice (if requested by the police); 2) the company office or operating centre (if requested by a DVSA official).

- 'O' licences are actually deemed to be 'continuous', insofar that if nothing changes then the licence can simply continue to run. However, the Traffic Commissioner reviews licences every five years to ensure things such as the details of the licence are still correct and to check there have been no compliance problems. If everything is in order, and providing the renewal fee is paid on time, the licence will remain valid. Should payment not be made on time the operator concerned will have to submit an application for a new licence, along with all the required procedures mentioned previously.

- The final issue we need to look at is the matter of the issue of community licences to standard international licence holders because, in addition to the OL1 and OL2, standard international licence holders are also issued with a community licence, which acts as a permit for them to operate throughout the EU and EFTA states. This is valid for five years and needs to be retained at the main operating centre. Certified copies of the community licence are issued for each vehicle and need to be carried on the vehicle when it is abroad.

We have now looked at criteria, applications, issue and operational factors but it is probably true to say that most operators will have to change, or modify the licence at some time or another. These changes need to be recorded by the TC and various forms and procedures, with and without time limits, are in place. However, minor changes such as a change of ownership of the business or the retirement of a director can be notified to the CLO by letter or through what is known as TAN, the Traffic Area Network computer system that provides a link from the DVSA website to Operator Licensing. Operators need to be registered to use TAN and use a password and PIN to access the service in order to make and record changes much more quickly.

As discussed above, there is a new electronic system offering a comprehensive range of new online services known as the Vehicle Operator Licensing (VOL) system, which operators will need to sign up to and use a user name and PIN number to access. The VOL will eventually replace TAN completely. Details about the VOL can be gained by contacting the CLO.

In any case, changes and variations to the 'O' licence are deemed to be major, medium or minor, and are grouped accordingly, as set out below.

Major changes and variations to the licence

Major changes usually require the full procedure in the same way as the initial application, including placing the advertisement, the A and D procedure and allowing at least nine weeks for the process. The only difference is that the forms used are not a GV79. The principal 'major' changes and the forms to be used are:

- Form GV79A which is the vehicle list which needs submitting when vehicles are changed.

- Form GV80 used in conjunction with Form GV79A to identify the actual new or old vehicles within the authorisation that are either coming on fleet or going off fleet.

- Form GV80A used to request a change to the type of 'O' Licence and to notify of an unexpected change to the competent person.

- Form GV81 used to apply for a new operating centre, or centres.

- Form GV81 also used for requesting to add additional vehicles in excess of the margin.*

- Form SUR1 is the form used when the licence is to be surrendered.

---

* In cases where additional vehicles are being applied for on form GV81 and this is granted, form GV79A (the fleet/vehicle list) will then need to be submitted for amending.

Medium changes to the licence

Medium changes are changes that do not have to go through the A and D procedure but they do require either using the VOL system, a written letter or the use of a form and they are mainly subject to some sort of time limit.

A list of medium changes, including the method of notification and any time limit are below:

- change of name or address of the business;
- prohibitions issued against an authorized fleet vehicle;
- loss of 'good repute' of the operator;
- bankruptcy of a director, partner or operator;
- ordinary change of transport manager (when notifying the TC of a change of transport manager by letter, a form TM1 and the original CPC of the new transport manager must accompany the letter).

Note: Notification without using VOL, of all, or any of the above needs to be sent by letter to the TC within 28 days of the event.

- Notification of the death of the operator or competent person must be sent to the TC as soon as possible. Where the death involves the competent person, form GV80A must be used. The TC can then allow six months, or up to nine months, for the licence to continue until it is either surrendered or able to meet the required criteria.
- Notification of the unexpected departure (usually dismissal) of, or change to, the competent person must be made as soon as possible using form GV80A. The TC can then allow six months, or up to nine months, for a replacement to be found.
- Notice of liquidation or receivership needs to be sent by letter to the TC before the actual order or declaration is made.
- Notification of a change of a partner or director must be made by letter to the TC as soon as possible.

Note: The term 'as soon as possible' means that it should be done as a matter of priority and, in any case, within a time limit of 28 days.

- Notification of any changes to the list of specified vehicles needs to be made within one month of the changes. Form GV79A (fleet list) and form GV80 (listing the new registration numbers and the old registration numbers) will also need to be submitted to the TC.
- Notification of additional vehicles within the margin needs to be made within one month of the vehicle(s) arriving. Form GV79A (fleet list), form GV80 (listing the new registration numbers) and the actual 'O' licence (OL1) will all need to be submitted to the TC.
- Notification of the transfer of vehicles to a different traffic area needs to be made to the new traffic area TC within three months of the vehicles being transferred. Form GV79A (fleet list), form GV80

(listing the transferred vehicle's registration number) and the actual 'O' licence (OL1) will all need to be submitted to the TC. Note that the transfer of vehicles within the same traffic area does not require any notification to be made to the TC.

Minor changes and requests for advice or clarification can be notified and requested by e-mail, the VOL system, letter or telephone. There is no laid-out procedure for these.

It is important to note that the whole area of operator licensing is being reviewed and major changes to the administration and current criteria used are expected to be revised in 2018. People studying for this examination and all operators should make serious efforts to keep up to date as various changes are announced and come into force.

Whilst we have now covered many aspects relating to the procedures, enforcement is the next issue we need to examine because enforcement is done under an operator monitoring and scoring system known as the Operator Compliance Risk Score (OCRS).

The Operator Compliance Risk Score (OCRS)

The Operator Compliance Risk Score (OCRS) is used by the DVSA to iden-tify operators who are, and who may be likely to be, non-compliant. The DVSA monitors and records non-compliance, both at the roadside and when vehicles are presented for test. Each non-compliance means that the operator gets a number of points added to their score, and operators with high scores are the ones who find themselves stopped more frequently and subject to more enforcement activity than those with low scores. In short, the system works on the principle that there is a greater 'risk' of high-scoring operators committing offences than those with low scores.

As mentioned, the scores result from both roadside (traffic) enforce-ment, covering such things as drivers' hours, overloading and similar issues, and roadworthiness, covering items such as annual tests and depot inspec-tions. A combined score is worked out by adding the total roadworthiness and traffic points together and dividing them by the total number of events the points came from. For example, if you have 160 roadworthiness points from 4 events and 150 traffic points from 4 events, this means you have a total of 310 points from 8 events. Your combined score is 310 divided by 8 = 38.75.

The scores reflect both these enforcement areas, effectively meaning that each operator actually has two scores that fit into bands referred to as:

- Red Band with traffic scores over 30 points and roadworthiness scores over 25 points.
- Amber Band with traffic scores of 6–30 points and roadworthiness scores of 11–25 points.
- Green Band with traffic scores of 5 or fewer points and roadworthiness scores of 10 or fewer points.
- Grey Band, which is the band used for new operators who have not received any sort of score, to date.

OCRS is based on data from enforcement over a three-year rolling period with data being updated on a weekly basis.

Importantly, scores can be amassed even if the operator is using a hired vehicle or if an outside contractor is used to present a vehicle for test and it does not pass.

There are also things known as 'sifted encounters'. A sifted encounter is where a DVSA examiner decides not to carry out a full inspection of the vehicle because it may be new or only just have been tested. In these cases no scores are awarded.

The scores for individual offences are graduated to ensure that more points are awarded for more serious issues. For example, in relation to roadworthiness, an immediate prohibition for bald tyres will attract 200 points, whereas an annual test failure will normally attract 25 points. For traffic offences, the most serious offences can carry 300 points.

There are a number of identified Most Serious Offences (MSOs) for which the DVSA will also issue 300 points. These are listed by the DVSA as:

- exceeding the six-day or fortnightly driving limits by more than 25 per cent;
- exceeding, during a daily working period, the maximum daily driving limit by a margin of more than 50 per cent without taking a break or without an uninterrupted rest period of at least 4.5 hours;
- using a fraudulent device able to modify the records of the recording equipment;
- not having a speed limiter as required by community law;
- using a fraudulent device able to modify the speed limiter;
- falsifying the record sheets of the tachograph;
- falsifying data downloaded from the tachograph and/or the driver card;
- driving with a driver card that has been falsified;
- driving with a driver card belonging to another driver;

- transporting regulated dangerous goods, without identifying them on the vehicle as dangerous goods, thus endangering lives or the environment to such an extent that it leads to a decision to immobilize the vehicle;

- serious overloading of a vehicle with a gross weight not exceeding 12 tonnes by a factor of 25 per cent or more;

- serious overloading of a vehicle with the gross weight exceeding 12 tonnes by a factor of 20 per cent or more.

Note: Whilst there are 12 points listed here, these most serious offences are often referred to as 'The Seven Deadly Sins'.

In fairness to operators the scores they have relate to offences committed in the past and, as time passes, the scores for offences are 'weighted' depending on how long it has been since the problem occurred. In line with the three-year rolling time period the scores are lessened by:

- first year the full score (100 per cent) is applied;

- second year 75 per cent of the score is applied;

- third year 50 per cent of the score is applied.

Whilst we have looked at ongoing monitoring we now need to look at other actions that can be taken against operators and drivers that relate to operator licensing.

Traffic Commissioners' powers and related offences

Where there is non-compliance with any of the terms of the 'Legal Undertaking' the TCs have a range of powers they may use against non-compliant operators and vocational drivers. These include:

- Revoking the licence. Revocation means that the licence is taken away and that the operator can no longer hold a licence. The terms of revocation may be for a given period or even for the life of the operator concerned.

- Curtailing the licence. Curtailment is when the TC either reduces the number of operating centres on a licence or reduces the number of vehicles on a licence because the operator concerned has shown they are unable to comply with a fleet or operation of a certain size.

- Suspending the licence. Suspending a licence means that the operation must cease for the given period of suspension, normally whilst improvements are made.

- Attaching conditions to the licence. Conditions of operation are put on licences where a relatively minor issue is encountered. Typically, conditions may restrict the times of operation of an operating centre or the routes to be used by LGVs to and from an operating centre.

- Taking action against vocational drivers. Whilst the Traffic Commissioners cannot remove the entitlement to drive a car (Category B) they do have the power to withdraw or suspend the vocational driving entitlements such as Category C or CE from drivers who commit offences.

Note: All operators who are disciplined in one way or another are allowed to request a public inquiry to be held and, if not happy with the result of that inquiry, they are entitled to appeal to the Upper Tribunal.

Whilst the Traffic Commissioners have certain powers, and do work with the courts, they are not actually entitled to fine operators. Fines and custodial sentences must be ordered through the legal system. For the purposes of the syllabus the 'O' licence-related offences and penalties are:

- Illegally operating goods vehicles without a valid operator's licence. Operating without a licence at all will result in a fine.

- Operating under a restricted licence for hire and reward operations will also result in a fine. However, if the operator is caught twice in five years, the licence is automatically revoked.

- Operating under a standard national licence when carrying out international hire and reward operations will also result in a fine.

It may appear that these 'fines' are quite minor in relation to the offences but they are the current levels of punishment in place and the ones you need to be aware of for your examinations.

Key points you need to know

- The 'O' licence criteria (including TM1).

- The 'O' licence application procedures.

- The issue details and operational issues.

- Forms to be used for changes and notification periods.

- The OCRS scoring system, in full (including MSOs).

- The powers of the Traffic Commissioners.

Notes

We have now covered operator licensing but it is absolutely essential for you to obtain a GV74 to gain a thorough understanding of this important topic and that you try to keep up to date with the many changes that are taking place and that will take place in the foreseeable future.

The syllabus now requires us to consider various aspects of international freight operations. We begin by looking at the documentation required when operating internationally.

Note: Some abbreviations may be used in the lists below but explanations will follow as we go through the rest of the syllabus.

Documentation for operating internationally

Documents required that relate to the vehicle include:

- The original vehicle registration certificate (V5C) or:
  - if the vehicle is new then form V379 is used;
  - if the vehicle is hired, form VE103 or the hirer's 'on-hire' documentation can be used.
- A certified copy of the community licence (already discussed).
- 'O' licence disc (OL2).
- Certificate of insurance and/or Green Card.

- Annual test certificate. This is not obligatory but is advisable.
- Vehicle checklist and vehicle security certificate to prove that anti-illegal immigrant procedures are being carried out.
- Vehicle approval certificate if operating under ADR, ATP or TIR (GV60).
- Vignettes, if applicable.
- Permits, if applicable.
- GB plate, unless there is a country identifier marking as a part of the registration number plate.
- Certificate of ownership for trailers for Italy and Germany.
- 'Euro Safe' certification when operating under ITF permits.
- Carnet de Passages en Douane (in order to temporarily import and re-export the vehicle into and out of some Middle Eastern countries).

Documents required that relate to the driver include:

- Passport (with at least six months' validity, if possible) and a visa, if required.
- Current full driving licence and/or an international driving permit (IDP).
- Qualification card for the driver CPC (DQC).
- Tachograph card and/or records.
- VTC card to show that the driver is qualified to carry any dangerous goods in the load.
- Letter of authority: a letter from the employer authorizing the driver to have possession of the vehicle.
- A blank European accident statement form (EAS), as discussed.
- An EHIC, as discussed.
- Driver nationality attestation*: drivers who are not EU nationals must carry a letter of attestation stating that they are lawfully employed by an EU operator. If this is the case, this should be accompanied by a valid work permit or visa.
- Letter of attestation (activities)*. When tachograph records are not available for all of the necessary previous days, a letter of attestation concerning rest periods should be carried.
- An authenticated prescription relating to any prescription medicines that are being taken.

- Proof that the driver is being paid at a rate that meets the requirements of the minimum wage for deliveries and collections in France and Germany and for cabotage operations (see below) in Austria.

- Any maps or detailed instructions.

---

* These attestations should not be confused with the informal attestation required by Austria, France and Germany relating to visiting drivers proving that their earnings are at appropriate levels.

Documents required that relate to the load include:

- CMR consignment note.

- General load documentation.

- Forms relating to the status and origin of the goods (eg EUR1, TAD, ATR).

- ADR document (referred to as a Dangerous Goods Note, DGN) and instructions in writing when carrying dangerous goods.

- Carnets if operating under TIR or ATA.

- Load logs and certificates, if carrying animals.

- Document de suivi for France, which gives details of the consignor, vehicle operator, driver and load.

Other documentation

A final document that may be required is a bill of lading. A bill of lading is used for some movements by sea, and acts as a receipt for the carrier, provides evidence of a contract of carriage and signifies 'title' to the goods, meaning that the person who holds the bill of lading may transfer ownership of the goods, if they so wish. It is sent to a bank in the country of delivery where the ultimate customer 'buys' it from the bank and then becomes the owner of the goods.

Bills of lading are described in different ways. They can be:

- clean bills, which means the goods have been received on the vessel and are in good condition;

- a dirty bill of lading, which means the goods were not in a good condition when received on board;

- a stale bill of lading, which means that the bill of lading arrived more than 21 days after the goods had left the UK.

We need now to expand on some of the points made in the lists above in order to try to identify different types of international freight movements.

International freight movements

For our purposes, we have to look at four different types of international goods movements:

- Cabotage: this is defined as 'domestic haulage undertaken by a foreign haulier'. For example, if a French-based haulier carried a load to London, unloaded and then reloaded in London for Manchester, the London to Manchester journey would be domestic haulage but the haulier would be 'foreign'. This would be termed 'cabotage'. Cabotage is only allowed within the EU and hauliers are only permitted to carry out three cabotage operations in any seven days whilst they are not in their 'home' member state. Cabotage is illegal outside the EU.

    We also briefly noted earlier that any cabotage operations may need the haulier to register for VAT in the country concerned.

- Third-country traffic: this is the term used to describe an operation where a vehicle from one country loads goods in a second country and delivers them to a third country. For example, a Spanish haulier loading in Madrid, delivering to Berlin, reloading in Munich, and delivering the goods loaded in Munich to Paris would be termed 'third-country traffic'.

- Through traffic: this is simply the term used to describe a movement where an operator licensed in one country loads goods in that country and delivers them to another country on a single journey. For example, if an Austrian haulier loaded goods in Vienna and delivered them to Paris, this would be termed 'through traffic'.

- Own-account operations: these are operations where a company moves its own goods and where proof of the fact that they are own goods may be required. This usually means that an own-account document needs to be carried to prove the status of the goods. Most own-account documents show details such as the name and address and type of company, a description of the goods, where they were loaded and where they are going, as well as details of the vehicle and route.

Having looked at the four principal types of movements, it is time to look at customs procedures, which support, monitor and control movements.

Customs procedures

Customs authorities are not only in place to control the flow of goods and people into and out of countries, they also act to prevent illegal immigration; control the import of illegal, restricted or non-compliant goods from foreign countries; collect duty on imported goods; and compile trade figures for the country concerned.

In order to collect duty and control goods, the customs authorities use a 'customs tariff', which is a list that categorizes all goods by giving them a customs code number.

For EU purposes, goods are also classified into two distinct groups:

- T1 goods, which are not deemed to be in 'free circulation', usually because there is still duty to be paid on them.*

- T2 goods, which are deemed to be in free circulation because duty has been paid on them. This means that T2 goods within the EU will normally not require any customs procedures when moved between member states.*

---

* A system known as community transit (CT) does apply when goods are moved across the EU via an EFTA country (eg goods from Greece to Denmark via Switzerland), some EU goods moved to the Channel Islands via the UK and non-EU goods where duty needs to be paid.

Community transit

Because community transit (CT) applies to both the EFTA and the EU, different terminology is used to identify the type of transit:

- Community transit applies to goods moved only within the EU.

- Common transit is the term used where goods travel through EU member states and either transit or are delivered to any of the EFTA countries (Norway, Liechtenstein, Switzerland and Iceland).

CT movements require the haulier, referred to as the CT principal, to take out a customs-approved guarantee, which is a 12-month guarantee that any duty, taxes or tariffs will be paid (available from Prudential Assurance Company, the RHA and the FTA). Guarantees can be set at 100 per cent, 50 per cent, or 30 per cent of the value of the goods and there are waivers, in limited circumstances, for some large operators.

The current and most common procedure for CT is a system known as the New Computerized Transit System (NCTS), which is an electronic system that HMRC use to:

- Create a movement reference number (MRN) for each separate movement of goods. This number will need to be quoted at the customs office of departure.
- Use the MRN to provide a Transit Accompanying Document (TAD) that will be generated by the office of departure and that will accompany the goods.

The older system, now largely replaced by NCTS, is a paper-based CT system that uses a Single Administrative Document (SAD) that accompanies the goods:

- The SAD is a combined import, export and transit declaration document.
- It is referred to as customs form C88.
- It is an eight-part form where:
  - Copies 1–3 remain in the country of export.
  - Copies 4–8 travel with the goods.

Note: If a CT consignment has to leave the EU in order to arrive at the final destination, as in the case of a common transit movement, Transit Advice Notes (TANs) are required. The first TAN needs to be presented at the point of departure* from the EU and the second TAN needs to be presented at the place of re-entry back into the EU.

---

* The point of departure from the EU is known as the Office of Transit. Offices of Transit are situated at locations such as the Swiss border where CT consignments need to transit Switzerland. The Office of Transit will have been notified of the expected arrival of the consignment through a 'Record of Anticipated Transit' having been sent to it from the office of departure.

Upon arrival at the Office of Transit the TAD is presented and upon departure from the Office of Transit sends confirmation to the original Customs Office of Departure that the goods have left the EU.

Whilst CT is most commonly used by most international hauliers there are other international movements to countries outside of the EU and the EFTA where permits may be required.

The EU trades not only between its member states and the EFTA countries, but it also has 'special trading relationships' with some other non-EU countries. Where such export arrangements are in place:

- A form EUR1 is used to prove that the goods originated from within the EU.
- Forms EUR1 are obtainable from the Chambers of Commerce.

In addition, goods in free circulation within the EU exported to Turkey require an ATR certificate. The ATR certificate provides proof of the origin of the goods to enable the customs authorities to establish whether or not any duty needs to be paid and, where duty is paid, the ATR certificate ensures preferential import rates.

Permits

Although permits are not normally required by UK operators operating in Europe, they are required for operations in other countries such as Russia, the Ukraine, some CIS states, Turkey and many Middle Eastern states. There are two types of permits:

- Bilateral permits that allow a vehicle to enter a specific country such as Russia or the Ukraine and to transit Turkey. Bilateral permits can be quota or non-quota in nature:
  - Quota permits are restricted in number by the International Transport Federation (ITF) to restrict certain flows of goods into, and out of, certain countries.
  - Non-quota permits are the more commonly used bilateral permits and are readily available.
- Multilateral permits, which are strictly controlled by the European Conference of Ministers of Transport (ECMT), a UNECE organization. These permits also come in two different forms:
  - Permits for general haulage, which allow 'tramping' between several different countries without the need for specific bilateral permits for each country (they are not allowed to be used for own-account movements or unaccompanied trailers).
  - Permits for household removals.

All ECMT permits are valid for 12 months (January to December), and their use has to be recorded in a monthly record book and monthly returns submitted. Operators who apply for ECMT permits but do not use them will normally have their allowance cut for the following year.

All permits are issued and controlled by the International Road Freight Office (IRFO), a DVSA department adjacent to the Eastern Traffic Area Office in Cambridge. Permit applications must be made at least five working days before intended use. And first time applicants also need to submit a copy of their 'O' licence with the initial application.

When a multilateral permit becomes time expired or a bilateral permit has been used, the operator must return the permit to the IRFO within 15 days.

Some goods that move to and from non-EU countries also need to be included on a customs document known as a 'carnet'.

Carnets

A customs carnet is really a form (usually like a ticket) that acts in the same way as a CT guarantee and that also simplifies many customs procedures for goods travelling outside the EU and EFTA.

The most commonly encountered carnet is a Transports Internationale Routiers (TIR) carnet. TIR is a convention that: 1) recognizes approved vehicles approved in any TIR signatory country; 2) reduces delays by reducing the amount of scrutiny of the goods carried.

TIR carnets are valid for a single outward or a single return journey only and are supplied in 4 volet, 6 volet, 14 volet and 20 volet options. The volet number applies to the number of carnets in the book containing them.

The carnet is presented at all frontier customs offices along the route as well as the office of departure and the office of destination. Whilst the TIR scheme is controlled by the International Road Transport Union (IRU), the carnets are available through the RHA and FTA. It is a requirement that completed carnet counterfoils are returned to the RHA or FTA by the operator within 10 days of the carnet being 'discharged' in the country of destination.

The carnets themselves are like tickets, which can be torn out of the book. The haulier produces one at the border point of entry and one at the border point of exit of each TIR signatory country, where each of the customs offices will retain a carnet. These carnets are then returned to the customs authority in the country of issue and act to prove that the goods came in and departed securely.

Customs authorities that only return a single carnet will normally be from the country of destination and will then be liable for any duty or tax that relates to the goods concerned. In addition, in the event of accidents, or where a TIR seal may be broken or removed, the carnet must be amended by the customs authorities of the country concerned.

The other key points that you need to know about TIR are that:

- Vehicles used under the TIR scheme need to be approved by the DVSA at a LGV test station.
- All TIR vehicles must be designed so that they can be sealed and there are no secret compartments.
- They must be constructed in a way that any unauthorized entry is easily noticeable.

- TIR-approved vehicles must carry blue-and-white TIR plates to the front and rear.

- The TIR plates must be prominently displayed when operating under TIR.

- The TIR plates must be able to be covered or removed when not operating under TIR.

- Box bodies and tilt trailers are commonly used for TIR work as they are capable of being sealed and, in the case of a tilt trailer, secured by a tricing line, over wooden slats and a cover.

- The approval certificate is form GV60.

- The original GV60 must be carried on the vehicle.

- Two colour photographs of the locking device must also be carried.

- A GV60 is valid for two years.

- If the GV60 is lost, the vehicle will need recertification.

- If the vehicle is sold it will need recertification as a GV60 is not transferable.

There are two more carnet systems we need to cover:

- Admission Temporaire (ATA) carnets are used for goods that require temporary import and/or re-export:

  - Typically, this applies to goods such as advertising material, musical instruments, broadcasting equipment and exhibition materials.

  - ATA carnets are valid for 12 months and can be used any number of times within that period providing that the goods mentioned are the same each time.

  - ATA carnets are issued by Chambers of Commerce who act as guarantor.

- Carnets de Passages en Douane, which are carnets that:

  - apply to the vehicle and not to the goods;

  - allow the import, and re-export, of the vehicle into countries in the Middle East and are no longer required in Europe;

  - require the applications to be made to the German organization known as ADAC Touring GmbH (ADAC) based in Munich;

  - are issued, following application to ADAC, either by the Federation Internationale de l'Automobile (FIA) or the Alliance Internationale de Tourisme (AIT).

Having discussed customs procedures relating to goods (and to vehicles), it is time to look at customs procedures for drivers and crew members.

The Schengen Agreement

The Schengen Agreement effectively acted to:

- remove all the EU's internal border controls;
- establish border controls at the EU's external borders;
- introduce a common visa policy for the whole of the EU;
- define the role of carriers in order to reduce illegal immigration;
- develop closer cooperation between national police forces;
- develop better coordinated surveillance procedures at borders;
- where possible, separate people travelling within the Schengen area from those arriving from countries outside the Schengen area at border points;
- create the Schengen Information System (SIS) (see below).

Note: Recently, following the flood of refugees and immigrants towards the EU, some internal controls have been reintroduced but these are not expected to be long-term measures.

Whilst the four EFTA countries (Iceland, Liechtenstein, Norway and Switzerland) also signed the Schengen Agreement, the UK and Republic of Ireland stayed outside of the agreement, whilst some of the newer EU member states still do not belong to Schengen but have applied to become signatories. These countries include Bulgaria, Croatia, Cyprus and Romania. In practice this means that drivers or crew members wishing to enter or leave any non-signatory country or candidate country need to carry passports.

Where UK passports are needed, the rules in regard of them include the facts that:

- Passports are issued by the UK Passport Authority (UKPA).
- Passports are valid for 10 years.
- Replacements normally need to be requested at least three months before they are required.
- Passports can be obtained at a higher cost using the 'express passport' system, but under this system the applicant must present themselves at the passport office.

As a final note about obtaining official documents, if a driver or crew member requires a visa as well as a passport, these are usually available from the embassy of the country concerned, although some countries do allow visas to be purchased at border points but this obviously causes delays. It should also be noted that some countries require a Letter of Invitation (LoI) from the organization based in the country concerned to validate the need for the visa. These LoIs must accompany the visa application, as might proof of in-date inoculations in a few specific countries.

As mentioned above, the creation of a Schengen Information System (SIS) was a part of Schengen. The SIS allows national border authorities and police forces to gain access to information and details of:

- persons wanted for arrest (for extradition);
- persons to whom entry has been refused;
- persons reported as missing;
- persons in need of police protection, or persons needing temporary police protection;
- persons required as witnesses in court proceedings;
- persons summoned to appear in court;
- persons under surveillance in relation to criminality or security;
- goods that have been lost or stolen.

From the above you can see that SIS is an information-gathering and sharing system that sees international cooperation as a key aspect of work largely aimed at the control of people and stolen goods.

In support of this, additional measures have been introduced in most EU member states requiring drivers and crew members to carry out ongoing checks in an attempt to reduce illegal immigration. For example, UK drivers must now:

- check the vehicle after every delivery or collection;
- check the vehicle after every rest or break period;
- check the vehicle at regular intervals throughout the journey;
- ensure the checks are for goods (drugs in particular) as well as for stowaways;
- keep a proper record that these checks have been carried out.

Guidance on checks, including items to check such as seals, locks, tool boxes, spare tyre racks and any spaces behind air deflection equipment, as well as under and on top of the vehicle and trailer, where possible, is available from the trade associations (FTA and RHA) and from HMRC. These bodies also advise drivers to use the facilities at ports of entry and departure such as CO_2 detectors, X-ray machines and thermal imaging cameras. Such is the importance of this matter that vehicle checks for illegal goods and stowaways is now an element of Module IV of the vocational driving licence system, and the UK Border Force have introduced a Civil Penalty Accreditation Scheme for hauliers to sign up to in order to show they are trying to stop 'illegals' entering the UK.

In spite of checks, illegal goods and immigrants do still make their way into the UK and drivers and operators are subject to fines (currently £2,000 for each illegal person) when this occurs, unless they can prove:

- that the driver could not have been in any way aware that the vehicle had been breached;
- that the driver had no reason to suspect that the vehicle had been breached;
- that the company had an 'effective' system of vehicle checks in operation;
- that the system, including record keeping, was working correctly.

Key points you need to know

- The documents required for the vehicle, driver and load.
- Definitions and examples of the types of traffic, including cabotage.
- T1 and T2 definitions and the CT and NCTS systems and documents.
- Types of permits and permit procedures.
- Types of carnets and carnet procedures.
- TIR vehicle requirements and documentation requirements.
- Key points on Schengen and the SIS.
- Key points on required vehicle checks.

In the next chapter we move on to cover another important area of the syllabus: the technical aspects and standards. In respect of the questions below, you may wish to complete them now or you may wish to do them later – the choice is yours.

Notes

Self-test example questions

OCR-type questions (multi-choice)

1 Form GV79E is used to provide the TC with:

  a Additional information relating to European operating centres and additional information about Level 4 fines.

  b Additional information relating to environmental matters.

  c Additional exempted vehicles powered by electricity.

  d Additional operating centres in the same traffic area and the surrender of an operator's licence.

2 The main difference between the two forms of objection/representation is that:

  a Whilst statutory objectors have 14 days following the publication of the decision in A and D to appeal against the decision, environmental representors have 21 days to make their appeal.

  b Whilst statutory objectors have 21 days following the publication of the decision in A and D to appeal against the decision, environmental representors have 28 days to make their appeal.

c Whilst statutory objectors have no direct right of appeal in spite of the fact that the decision is published in A and D, environmental representors have seven days to lodge an appeal and may allow statutory objectors to combine with them to strengthen their case.

d Whilst statutory objectors have 28 days following the publication of the decision in A and D to appeal against the decision, environmental representors have no direct right of appeal and are only able to combine with the statutory objectors as part of their appeal.

3 The information that can be found on an operator's licence disc (form OL1) includes i) the operator licence holder's reference number and ii) the expiry date of the licence.

These statements are:

a (i) true (ii) false;

b (i) false (ii) false;

c (i) false (ii) true;

d (i) true (ii) true.

4 Schedule 4 is a system that enables:

a An existing operator who takes over another operator's business in the same traffic area to take it over without the need to advertise in a local newspaper, providing that there are no material changes to the licence other than the change of ownership.

b A new operator who wants to upgrade their operator's licence to take over an existing licence providing that they advertise in a local newspaper and providing that there are no material changes to the licence other than the change of ownership.

c An existing operator to take over the operator's licence of a company that has gone into liquidation, providing there is no conflict of interest with another operator's business in the same traffic area as the company concerned, without the need to wait the full nine weeks, providing that there are no material changes to the licence other than the change of ownership.

d A restricted operator's licence holder to carry out hire and reward operations using vehicles hired in from a standard licence holder in a different traffic area, providing that there are no material changes to the licence other than the change of use.

5 What forms would be used to notify the Traffic Commissioner (TC) of an amendment when additional vehicles are permitted to be added to the licence, an application for a new operating centre and a request to change to the type of 'O' licence?

a Forms GV79, GV80A and GV81A respectively.

b Forms GV81, GV80 and GV74A respectively.

c Forms GV79A, GV81 and GV80A respectively.

d Forms GV80A, GV79A and GV81 respectively.

6 In relation to OCRS, the scores represent:

a Traffic and roadworthiness and a score of 6–30 points for traffic offences and 11–25 points for roadworthiness will normally mean an operator goes into the Red Band.

b Traffic and roadworthiness and a score of 50 points for traffic offences and 30 points for roadworthiness will normally mean an operator goes into the Red Band.

c Traffic and roadworthiness and a score of more than 25 points for traffic offences and 20 points for roadworthiness will normally mean an operator goes into the Red Band.

d Traffic and roadworthiness and a score of more than 30 points for traffic offences and 25 points for roadworthiness will normally mean an operator goes into the Red Band.

7 Curtailment of the operator's licence is an action that can be taken by the Traffic Commissioner (TC) to:

a Either reduce the number of operating centres on a licence or reduce the number of vehicles on a licence because the operator concerned has shown they are unable to comply with a fleet or operation of a certain size. They can also reduce licences, delete licences, attach conditions to licences and take actions against guilty drivers.

b Either reduce the number of operating centres on a licence or reduce the number of vehicles on a licence because the operator concerned has had maintenance problems and financial difficulties in relation to the size of the operation. They can also revoke licences, cancel licences, attach conditions to licences and take actions against any drivers.

c Either reduce the number of operating centres on a licence or reduce the number of vehicles on a licence because the operator concerned has shown they are unable to comply with a fleet or operation of a certain size. They can also revoke licences, suspend licences, attach conditions to licences and take actions against vocational drivers.

d Either reduce the number of licences held in the same traffic area, or reduce the number of vehicles in a nominated operating centre because the operator concerned has shown they are unable to comply with correct standards of operation. They can also revoke licences, fine operators, attach conditions to licences and fine drivers.

8 Why would a vocational driver need to carry a 'letter of attestation (activities)' and a 'driver nationality attestation'?

a A 'driver nationality attestation' is used by drivers who are EU nationals to state that they are lawfully employed by a non-EU operator and a 'letter of attestation (activities)' is used to explain why the driver is making manual records using a digital tachograph.

b A 'driver nationality attestation' is used by drivers who are not EU nationals to state that they are lawfully employed by an EU operator and a 'letter of attestation (activities)' is used to explain why all the normally required tachograph records are not available for examination by the authorities.

c A 'driver nationality attestation' is used by all foreign drivers who are visiting the UK to state that they are driving under an operator's licence issued in a different EU member state and a 'letter of attestation (activities)' is used to explain why the tachograph records may appear to show infringements committed earlier on the journey.

d A 'driver nationality attestation' is used by drivers who are not EU nationals to state that they have the correct visas and work permits to work in EU and EFTA countries and a 'letter of attestation (activities)' is used to explain to the enforcement authorities that the driver is not subject to any reduced rests or extended driving periods in the week concerned.

9 The customs use NCTS to:

    a Create a movement reference number (MRN) for each separate movement of goods. This number will need to be quoted at the customs office of departure for customs to provide a Transit Accompanying Document (TAD) that will be generated by the office of departure and that will accompany the goods.

    b Create an office of transit on the border of a neighbouring country for each separate movement of goods. The customs office of transit will inform the customs office of departure that the goods have arrived safely.

    c Create a Single Administration Document (SAD), which is an electronic document used to generate a movement customs tariff number (MCTN) for each separate movement of goods. This MCTN will need to be quoted at the customs offices of transit to enable customs to provide a Transit Advice Document (TAD) that will be returned to the customs office of departure.

    d Create movement reference numbers (MRNs) for bulk movements of multiple individual consignments. These numbers will need to be individualized to identify the consignor in each case and held at the customs office of departure for customs to trace the consignors in cases where duty and/or tariffs have not been paid.

10 In relation to the application and return of permits:

    a All permit applications need to be made to the International Road Freight Office (IRFO) in Leeds at least 14 working days before intended use. When a multilateral permit becomes time expired or a bilateral permit has been used, the operator must return the permit to the IRFO within 21 days.

    b All permit applications need to be made to the local International Road Freight Office (IRFO) in the operator's own traffic area at least seven working days before intended use. When a multilateral permit becomes time expired or a bilateral permit has been used, the operator must return the permit to the issuing traffic area office within 14 days.

    c All permit applications need to be made to a Chamber of Commerce prepared to act as a guarantor, at least 10 working days before intended use. When a multilateral permit becomes time expired or a bilateral permit has been used, the operator must return the Chamber of Commerce within 28 days.

d All permit applications need to be made to the International Road Freight Office (IRFO) in Cambridge at least five working days before intended use. When a multilateral permit becomes time expired or a bilateral permit has been used, the operator must return the permit to the IRFO within 15 days.

OCR case study-type question

See past papers referred to in Chapter 1.

CILT-type questions (short answer)

1 Briefly explain the purpose of form GV79E.

2 Outline the difference between statutory objectors' right to appeal against the granting of an operator's licence and the rights of appeal for environmental representors.

3 Briefly discuss:

a the role of a form OL1;

b what information will be found on form OL2.

4 Briefly explain the operator's licence system known as 'Schedule 4'.

5 Describe what forms GV79A, GV80A and GV81 would be used for in relation to operator licensing.

6 In relation to scores:

a What do the two scores used in the OCRS represent?

b What scores effectively put an operator into the Red Band?

7 The Traffic Commissioners (TCs) have the power to 'curtail' an operator's licence. What does 'curtail' actually mean in relation to operator licensing and what other powers do the TCs have?

8 Briefly explain the purpose of the two different types of 'driver attestations' that may need to be used by vocational drivers.

9 For what purpose would the customs authorities use the New Computerized Transit System (NCTS)?

10 Briefly explain the application procedure and surrender criteria when applying for and returning permits.

CILT-type question (long answer)

Discuss the application procedure and the criteria that need to be met when applying for an operator's licence.

Note: Because operator licensing and international operations are areas that are key to legal compliance and standards of operation, there will always be at least one long question relating to either of these subjects in both the OCR and CILT examinations.

Technical standards and technical aspects of operation

07

This is another large chapter covering many aspects of operation and the required syllabus. Importantly, it includes vehicle maintenance for which you need to download the DVSA Guide to Maintaining Road-worthiness, as many examination questions are based on its content in relation to maintenance standards, maintenance requirements and vehicle safety.

Specifically, the syllabus requires that you should:

- be familiar with the rules concerning the weights and dimensions of vehicles in the member states and the procedures to be followed in the case of abnormal loads that constitute an exception to these rules;

- be able to choose vehicles and their components (eg chassis, engine, transmission system, braking system) in accordance with the needs of the undertaking;

- be familiar with the formalities relating to the type approval, registration and technical inspection of these vehicles;

- understand what measures must be taken to reduce noise and to combat air pollution by motor vehicle exhaust emissions;

- be able to draw up periodic maintenance plans for the vehicles and their equipment;

- be familiar with the different types of cargo handling and loading devices (eg tailboards, containers, pallets) and be able to introduce procedures and issue instructions for loading and unloading goods (eg load distribution, stacking, stowing, blocking, and chocking);

- be familiar with the various techniques of 'piggy-back' and roll-on/roll-off combined transport;

- be able to implement procedures to comply with the rules on the carriage of dangerous goods and waste, notably those arising from Directive 2008/68/EC3 and Regulation (EC) No 1013/2006;

- be able to implement procedures to comply with the rules on the carriage of perishable foodstuffs, notably those arising from the Agreement on the International Carriage of Perishable Foodstuffs and on the Special Equipment to be used for such Carriage (ATP);

- be able to implement procedures to comply with the rules on the transport of livestock.

We begin with weights and dimensions and other subsections aimed at many facts and figures that relate to the Construction and Use Regulations (C&U) within the UK and other European requirements. These are mainly facts and figures and, as such, they rarely form parts of essay-style or long-scenario questions. However, you are required to have a factual understanding of these, and this knowledge is tested in the short-answer and multi-choice questions. The points you need to know are shown as bullet points wherever possible, with explanations if required.

UK maximum weights and dimensions

Note: The term 'air suspension' is used below as a common usage term but the actual term in the regulations is 'road friendly' suspension. In addition, 'ordinary suspension' would normally imply leaf spring suspension.

There are requirements relating to axle spread and types of operation – Table 7.1 contains the maximum dimensions, and it is these that you will need. In addition, note that the 12-metre length limit for a draw-bar trailer is the same as for a rigid vehicle because, in general terms, the C&U Regulations define a draw-bar trailer as a 'rigid vehicle'.

Note: In early 2017 an EU directive allowed trucks to run over their maximum permitted weights (for example, a 44-tonne vehicle operating at 45 tonnes) in order for it to be fitted with aerodynamic kits and/or be able to operate using alternative fuels. The implementation date of this directive within the UK is still awaited (see below).

TABLE 7.1   UK vehicle weights and dimensions

Vehicle	Max weight	Max length
2-axle rigid vehicle	18,000 kg	12.00 m
3-axle rigid with ordinary suspension	25,000 kg	12.00 m
3-axle rigid with air suspension	26,000 kg	12.00 m
4-axle rigid with ordinary suspension	30,000 kg	12.00 m
3-axle rigid with air suspension	32,000 kg	12.00 m
3-axle artic with ordinary suspension	25,000 kg	16.50 m
3-axle artic with air suspension	26,000 kg	16.50 m
4-axle artic with ordinary suspension	36,000 kg	16.50 m
4-axle artic with air suspension	38,000 kg	16.50 m
5-axle artic with any type of suspension	40,000 kg	16.50 m
6-axle artic with air suspension	44,000 kg	16.50 m
Low-loader combinations (as per axle configuration)		18.00 m
Conventional semi-trailers		13.60 m
4-axle draw bar with less than 3.0 m between the rear axle of the prime mover and the front axle of the trailer	30,000 kg	18.75 m
4-axle draw bar with more than 3.0 m between the rear axle of the prime mover and the front axle of the trailer	36,000 kg	18.75 m
5-axle draw bar with more than 3.0 m between the rear axle of the prime mover and the front axle of the trailer	40,000 kg	18.75 m
6-axle draw bar with more than 3.0 m between the rear axle of the prime mover and the front axle of the trailer	44,000 kg	18.75 m
Any draw-bar trailer		12.00 m

TABLE 7.2 UK axle weights

Axle type	Max weight
The sole driving axle of a vehicle	11,500 kg
A non-driving single axle	10,000 kg
A tandem bogie with a driving axle	19,000 kg
A tandem bogie with no driven axles	20,000 kg
A tri-axle bogie with no driven axles	24,000 kg

The figures found in Table 7.2 are, once again, maximum figures and will rely upon axle spread and other factors.

Because it is easy for drivers and operators to exceed axle weights there is a formula that can be used to calculate the axle loading for front axles. Whilst this formula does have limitations, in cases where the centre of gravity of the load cannot be accurately determined it is a formula you need to know. The formula is:

$$\frac{P \times D}{W}$$

Where P is the weight of the load, D is the distance of the centre of gravity of the load from the rear axle, W is the wheelbase of the vehicle.

What this means is that if you have an 8-tonne load on a rigid vehicle with a wheelbase of 10 metres and the centre of gravity of the load is 4.5 metres from the rear axle the weight on the front axle will be:

$$\frac{8 \times 4.5}{10} = \frac{36}{10} = \text{an axle load of 3.6 tonnes (3,600 kg) on the front axle}$$

Calculations for articulated vehicles are a little more complicated but the wheelbase, in these cases, is taken as the distance from the kingpin to the centre of the rear axle of the trailer.

Diminishing loads

Increasingly, drivers are required to deliver to more than one or two delivery points and in these circumstances there is a risk of individual axles becoming overloaded even though the overall weight of the load is being reduced as 'drops' are made. Such axle overloads are most often caused because the drops are made from the rear door of the vehicle and trailer, which acts to move the centre of gravity of the load forwards towards the front axle of the vehicle, or drive axle of the articulated unit.

To prevent these types of axle overloads, drivers may need to be given time on their schedule to move the remaining goods towards the rear of the vehicle or trailer and erect a false 'bulkhead' (usually of empty cages or pallets) at the front of the cargo space and then restack the remaining consignment.

Drivers need to be made aware of the problem of what is known as 'diminishing load syndrome' as axle overloads can be viewed as most serious offences by the DVSA.

UK vehicle weight enforcement

Where problems with loads and overloads occur, it is either the police or DVSA enforcement officers who take action against drivers and operators. Where a vehicle is suspected of being overweight it can be stopped by either the police or the DVSA enforcement teams and either weighed at the roadside or directed to a place of weighing. When it is directed to a place of weighing a form PG3 will be issued.

The PG3 instructs the driver to drive to a place of weighing, which must be within five miles of the place of issue. If the vehicle is subsequently weighed and found to be okay then the operator may claim all costs incurred with the diversion and delay to the vehicle. However, if the vehicle is found to be overloaded, having been diverted to a place of weighing, or at the roadside where either an axle is overloaded or the vehicle is found to be exceeding the authorized gross vehicle weight, then a form TE160P will be issued.

The form TE160P acts as a vehicle prohibition preventing the vehicle from proceeding until the overload is corrected. In addition, the operator must notify the Traffic Commissioner (TC) of the issue of this prohibition, which will also be logged against their OCRS and, if legal proceedings follow, they may be subject to a fine of up to £5,000.

Should an operator be charged with an overloading offence, there are two defences that they may submit. These are that:

- The vehicle was either proceeding to, or returning from, a place of weighing to ascertain whether or not it was in an overloaded condition.
- When the vehicle started the journey it was not overloaded and the overload was caused by an increase in the weight of the load of not

more than 5 per cent whilst the vehicle was in transit (as in the case of hay or straw due to heavy rain).

Before we move on to look at weights in Europe we should first briefly look at some of the definitions we find in the C&U Regulations as they clarify many of the abbreviations and acronyms used in the syllabus:

- GVW, MAM, PMW and GPW all mean the same thing. They refer to the maximum authorized weight of the vehicle and relate to gross vehicle weight, maximum authorized mass, permitted maximum weight and gross plated weight, respectively.

- GTW means gross train weight and refers to the maximum authorized weight of a draw-bar combination because these are termed 'road trains' in the C&U Regulations.

- MAW means maximum axle weight.

- GCW refers to the gross construction weight, which is a design weight provided by the manufacturer. As it is a design weight, within the UK, it always exceeds an 'authorized weight' such as the GVW.

- Kerbside weight means the weight of the vehicle, without the crew, but otherwise ready for work.

- Unladen weight means the weight of the vehicle as it left the production line. That means it is the weight of the vehicle without water, fuel, oil, batteries, spare wheel or equipment. It is NOT the kerbside weight.

European and international weights and dimensions

Whilst the C&U Regulations cover weights in the UK, an EU Directive (93/53), covers weights within the rest of the EU, although every member state is allowed to vary, within moderation, from the directive should it choose to do so. An outline of the European picture, including some non-EU countries, is found in Table 7.3.

It should be noted that these maximum weight examples are merely samples and not an exhaustive list but they do highlight the problems when transiting different countries, even within the EU. In addition, they also rely upon things such as types of operation, types of vehicle and axle spread.

TABLE 7.3   European maximum weights (all countries)

2-axle rigid vehicle	18,000 kg except: Belgium, France, Greece, Luxembourg, Norway and Portugal, where it is 19,000 kg; the Netherlands, where it is 21,500 kg
Any 3-axle rigid vehicle	26,000 kg except: Hungary, Malta and Romania, where it is 25,000 kg; Croatia and Moldova, where it is 24,000 kg
4-axle artics and road trains	36,000 kg except: Hungary, where it is 30,000 kg; Portugal 37,000 kg; Belarus, Denmark, France, Greece and Sweden 38,000 kg; Belgium and Norway 39,000 kg; Italy, Latvia and the Netherlands 40,000 kg; Luxembourg 44,000 kg
5-axle artics and road trains	40,000 kg except: Belgium, Czech Republic, Georgia, Ireland, Italy and Luxembourg, where it is 44,000 kg, Russia 38,000 kg; Netherlands 50,000 kg; Denmark 54,000 kg; Norway 56,000 kg; Finland and Sweden 60,000 kg
6-axle artics and road trains	44,000 kg except: Austria, Bulgaria, Croatia, Estonia, Germany, Latvia, Poland, Romania, Slovakia and Switzerland, where it is 40,000 kg; Czech Republic 48,000 kg; the Netherlands 50,000 kg; Sweden 60,000 kg

Vehicle dimensions (all countries)

Within the EU the dimensions of large goods vehicles are generally standardized to:

- Width   2.55 m
- Width (refrigerated vehicle)   2.60 m
- Length (rigid vehicle)   12.00 m
- Length (artic)   16.50 m
- Length (road train)   18.75 m

There are no EU variations although countries such as Finland, Norway and Sweden, where articulated combinations are authorized to pull two trailers, do have length limits to accommodate this concession.

In the UK there is currently a 10-year trial of longer vehicles to ascertain whether or not they should be allowed in order to increase payload space and reduce emissions. As mentioned above, there are also planned concessions where the maximum length of the vehicle can be exceeded in order to fit aerodynamic kits also aimed at reducing emissions. A further EU directive also allows vehicles to exceed their maximum length when this is caused by the fitting of equipment to act as a 'crumple zone'. This directive is also yet to be implemented in the UK.

In relation to the height of vehicles the EU has a general height limit of 4.00 metres. However, there are a few differences including:

- UK, France and Norway who have no set limit;
- Finland, where it is 4.20 m;
- Gibraltar, where it is 4.22 m;
- Sweden, where there is no set limit but where the bridges over the main network routes are set at 4.50 m.

Note: Specifically in the UK the following points are important:

- Any vehicle with an operating height exceeding 3.00 m must have a sign indicating the height of the vehicle fixed in the vehicle cab, or carry a route card or pre-set electronic route instructions for the driver to follow that avoids low bridges.
- Vehicles such as cranes and skip lorries must have a bell or buzzer to indicate that the jib or arms are raised and not stowed.
- All unmarked bridges have a minimum clearance of 5.03 m.

Having looked at the weights and dimensions of vehicles it is to be noted that some weights and dimensions in the UK and Europe may change in the future following trials on heavier vehicles, extended length trailers and the fitting of 'crumple' zones.

Whilst we have now covered most weights, we need to record the facts related to moving abnormal indivisible loads (AILs) where the normal weights and dimensions rules need to be exceeded.

Abnormal indivisible loads (AILs)

In the UK, AILs are moved under Special Types General Order (STGO) rules that categorize the vehicle and load into one of three categories. These are:

- Category 1: where the total weight of the vehicle and load does not exceed 50,000 kg (this is reduced to 46,000 kg where the combination only has five axles).
- Category 2: where the total weight of the vehicle and load does not exceed 80,000 kg (at least 6 axles required).
- Category 3: where the total weight of the vehicle and load does not exceed 150,000 kg (at least 6 axles required).

These rules also require that:

- The vehicle is marked with a placard that shows white letters on a black background showing either STGOI, STGOII or STGOIII to reflect the category of movement.
- The police, the highway authorities and any bridge or tunnel authorities are notified at least two days before any movement of up to 80,000 kg.
- The police, the highway authorities and any bridge or tunnel authorities are notified at least five days before any movement of loads exceeding 80,000 kg. Vehicles operating in excess of 150,000 kgs also need a special order issued by the Secretary of State.
- Speed limits are adhered to for:
  - Category 1: 60 mph on motorways, 50 mph on dual carriageways and 40 mph on single carriageways.
  - Category 2: 40 mph on motorways, 35 mph on dual carriageways and 30 mph on single carriageways.
  - Category 3: 40 mph on motorways, 35 mph on dual carriageways and 30 mph on single carriageways.

Notification can be done manually but it is normally done online using the Electronic Service Delivery for Abnormal Loads (ESDAL).

Most AILs will require some sort of statutory escort and escort vehicle to accompany the load. Where non-police escorts are used the escort must be:

- at least 18 years old;
- properly trained;
- using an escort vehicle which is constructed and fitted out to the required specification and properly marked.

Other AILs

Where the load may be extremely large, whether or not it is also very heavy, other rules apply to 'projecting and overhanging loads'. These include:

- Statutory attendants to be carried in or on the vehicle when the overall width exceeds 3.5 m.
- Statutory attendants to be carried in or on the vehicle when the overall length of the vehicle exceeds 25.9 m.

- Statutory attendants to be carried in or on the vehicle if a forward projection exceeds 2 m.
- Statutory attendants to be carried in or on the vehicle if a rear projection exceeds 3.05 m.

Note: The term 'overhanging' relates to the load exceeding the limits of the vehicle. There is another term 'overhang', which relates to the distance on a vehicle from the centre of the rear axle to the rearmost part of the vehicle. In this case the 'overhang' is a design feature where: 1) the overhang of a goods vehicle does not exceed 60 per cent of the vehicle's wheelbase; 2) the overhang of a motor tractor should not exceed 1.83 m.

Basically, the rules for projecting and overhanging AILs are that:

- Rearwards:
  - Loads projecting to the rear up to 2 m must be made 'clearly visible'.
  - Loads projecting to the rear 2 m to 3.05 m must be made 'clearly visible' using an end marker board.
  - Loads projecting to the rear 3.05 m to 5 m must be made 'clearly visible' using an end marker board and side marker boards; an attendant must be carried and it is subject to two days' notice to the authorities.
  - Loads projecting to the rear more than 5 m must be made 'clearly visible' using an end marker board, side marker boards and additional side marker boards; an attendant must be carried and it is subject to two days' notice to the authorities.
- Front:
  - Loads projecting to the front up to 2 m must be made 'clearly visible'.
  - Loads projecting to the front 2 m to 3.05 m must be made 'clearly visible' using an end marker board and side marker boards; an attendant must be carried.
  - Loads projecting to the front 3.05 m to 4.50 m must be made 'clearly visible' using an end marker board and side marker boards; an attendant must be carried and it is subject to two days' notice to the authorities.
  - Loads projecting to the front more than 4.50 m must be made 'clearly visible' using an end marker board, side marker boards and additional side marker boards; an attendant must be carried and it is subject to two days' notice to the authorities.

- Width:
  - Loads overhanging up to 305 mm and where the vehicle and load does not exceed 2.9 m do not need to be marked.
  - Loads overhanging over 305 mm and where the vehicle and load does not exceed 2.9 m: marker boards are required.
  - Loads overhanging where the vehicle and load exceeds 2.9 m up to 3.5 m: marker boards and two days' notification are required.
  - Loads overhanging where the vehicle and load exceeds 3.5 m up to 4.3 m: marker boards, an attendant and two days' notification are required.
  - Loads overhanging where the vehicle and load exceeds 4.3 m up to 5 m: marker boards, an attendant and five days' notification are required and they are subject to speed limits (see below).
  - Loads overhanging where the vehicle and load exceeds 5 m up to 6.1 m: marker boards, an attendant, five days' notification and DfT notification and approval are required, and they are subject to speed limits. These are:
    - 30 mph for a motorway;
    - 25 mph for a dual carriageway;
    - 20 mph for a single carriageway.

When moving loads of between 5 metres and 6.1 metres wide an additional form VR1 must be submitted to Highways England or ESDAL to inform them of the intention to move. Where the load exceeds 6.1 metres the form used is form BE16.

When marker boards are used, they must be of an approved type. These are red-and-white striped boards with an end marker being a small, equilateral (even-sided) triangle no smaller than 610 millimetres on any side and side markers being right-angled triangles where the height is no less than 610 millimetres and the length no less than 1,520 millimetres.

Where any part of the projecting load or any marker boards obscure any obligatory lights on the vehicle, alternative lights must be used and the end marker board, where used, must be capable of being lit at night and in poor weather conditions.

Also note that two days' notification to the police and an attendant is required for very long loads (not necessarily heavy loads) where the overall length of a rigid vehicle or semi-trailer (not including the tractor unit) and load exceeds 18.65 metres and where an articulated combination and load exceeds 25.9 metres.

The syllabus also requires you to be able to make the correct selection of vehicles most appropriate to your operational requirements and this will be our next area of study.

Vehicle and equipment criteria

Selecting the best vehicle and equipment is essential for any operation but it is not always that straightforward. In this small subsection we itemize the issues to be considered, over and above the make, distance from dealership, cost, leasing or purchasing and other general business issues, including:

- chassis/vehicle type;
- engine type;
- transmission;
- braking systems;
- additional considerations.

Chassis/vehicle type considerations

- number of axles;
- configuration (artic, draw-bar, rigid);
- gross weight;
- body type – for example:
  - Flat bed: versatile, easy to load, difficult to secure/sheet, vulnerable to the elements with poor security but available in many different forms (step frame, low loader, coil carrier, etc).
  - Tank: only suitable for liquids, powders and gases and needs regular tank testing.
  - Tipper: only suitable for bulk loads and relatively few other types of goods, not often suited to international work.
  - Curtain-sided: can be loaded and unloaded from the sides, quick to access the goods, medium security, good for many applications but not suitable for TIR operations.
  - Tilt: good for TIR operations, secure, usually only rear access but heavier than a curtain-sider.

- Box: good security, TIR compatible commonly used but only usually rear access.
- Demountable: good for urban deliveries, rapid turnaround time.
- Skeletal: good for ISO container and tank operation but little else.

Engine type

The type of engine is increasingly important, not least because of VED and other concessions for low-emission vehicles such as those fitted with Euro VI engines, but also because there are many hybrid engines coming on to the market and engines that use different fuels such as LPG, NGV and dual-fuel engines, and even some new vehicles that can use electric power for limited distances in the urban cycle.

In addition, the power output may also be a major factor when selecting the type of engine, depending on the planned operation of the vehicle, as may the availability of any alternative fuels when away from base.

Transmission

Drive trains are now more commonly automatic than manual with many semi-automatic options available. The main issue is the suitability of the transmission in relation to the type of operation, improved engine management and with 'simpler' transmissions often being seen as the preferred option for urban deliveries.

Braking systems

As all vehicles supplied by the major manufacturers are type approved, the choice of braking is usually down to what type of engine – or exhaust – braking is fitted, whether it is automatic or applied by the driver and how effective the different options are.

Additional considerations

These can relate to things such as:

- left- or right-hand drive;
- tyre and wheel specification;
- type of suspension;

- tail lifts and/or loading equipment;
- day cab versus night cab;
- pod versus sleeper cab;
- tracking and communication package;
- driver facilities such as fridge and cooker;
- livery options;
- leasing or buying;
- recyclability.

The list of additional considerations are only there as examples and are not meant to be exhaustive. Please also note the additional equipment and specification requirements for entering some restricted areas such as the London LEZ/CAZ.

Key points you need to know

- Weights and dimensions for all goods vehicles in the UK.
- Outline of main EU weights and dimensions.
- AIL categories, procedures and speed limits.
- Definition of overhang.
- Rules on projecting loads, including speed limits.
- Vehicle selection criteria.

Notes

....

....

....

....

....

....

....

....

....

....

We now need to look at the type approval processes, vehicle registration processes and technical inspections.

Vehicle type approval

C&U Regulations clearly require all vehicles to be of an approved type. Proof of 'type approval' comes in different forms, including:

- A Type Approval Certificate (TAC) for older vehicles manufactured inside the EU (these vehicles carry a type approval code with small 'e' such as e2).

- A Minister's Approval Certificate (MAC) for older vehicles manufactured outside the EU (these vehicles carry a type approval code with a capital 'E' such as E2).

- A Certificate of Conformity (CoC) for newer vehicles manufactured inside or outside the EU.

The old vehicle TAC and MAC system will eventually be phased out in favour of the TAC and CoC systems but, to date, both systems are in operation. The new system of type approval is somewhat more comprehensive and is outlined below.

Initial applications for a TAC need to be made by manufacturers to the Vehicle Certification Agency (VCA) in Bristol along with detailed drawings and specification data. Following the application the vehicle will be inspected by an authorized vehicle examiner to ensure it is of an approved type and, if the vehicle complies, a CoC will be issued. Once this is done the manufacturer may issue CoCs with each vehicle.

If the examiner refuses to issue a CoC, an appeal can be made by writing to the Goods Vehicle Centre (GVC) in Swansea, who will then forward it to the Secretary of State for Transport. The appeal must be made within 28 days of the refusal and must include on what grounds the appeal is being made.

Type approval, when granted, can be in one of three different formats:

- European Community Whole Vehicle Type Approval (ECWVTA) used by manufacturers selling vehicles throughout the EU.

- National Small Series Type Approval (NSSTA) used for small numbers of vehicles produced within the UK.

- Individual Vehicle Approval (IVA), where each individual vehicle needs to be examined and approved.

Note 1: The UK-based type approval systems (NSSTA and IVA) are part of the UK's Goods Vehicle National Type Approval (GVNTA) scheme. Under this the DfT can change the rules to include additional types of vehicles. This recently happened and now the following, previously exempted, vehicles all require type approval:

- vehicles used to carry AILs;
- recovery vehicles exceeding 12,000 kg GVW;
- engineering vehicles and highway testing vehicles using truck chassis;
- vehicles with moving mounted platforms on booms;
- crash-cushion vehicles, employed on highway maintenance.

Note 2: Under the IVA system, before a vehicle can be registered with the DVLA under the IVA scheme, it has to meet some criteria from the ECWVTA scheme in one of three ways:

- It must have full EU type approval through the Vehicle Certification Agency (VCA), which is an executive agency of the DfT.
- It must have National Small Series Type Approval (NSSTA) through the VCA.
- It must have approval through the IVA scheme controlled by the DVSA.

Having gained type approval, vehicles will then be required to be both 'plated' and tested – before, at the start of, and during their operational lives.

Plating and testing

Plating

The term 'plating' refers to the three types of 'plates' that can be found on, or relating to, a goods vehicle over 3,500 kg GVW:

1 The manufacturer's plate, which is often referred to as a VIN plate, is a metal plate fixed to the vehicle showing:
   - manufacturer's name;
   - vehicle and engine type;
   - chassis number;
   - axle weights;
   - GVW and GTW.

2 The DVSA plate, which is a paper plate issued when a vehicle is registered for the first time. It is known as a form VTG6A, and must be firmly fixed inside the cab of the vehicle within 14 days of it being issued.

3 Form VTG7A, which is a laminated copy of form VTG6A, which must be kept by the operator as a part of the vehicle's maintenance record.

Note: Since ECWVTA was introduced, new trailers are now issued with a unique ID number, which must be prominently displayed on the trailer, a VTG6A plate to be attached to the trailer and a VTG7A for retention by the operator. These are all issued by the DVSA.

Many operators, seeking to reduce VED, 'down plate' goods vehicles. Down plating is a system where the operator has the vehicle plated at a lower authorized maximum weight than the maximum weight permitted. For example, if an operator only carried light goods such as parcels but had a vehicle authorized to operate up to 40,000 kg GVW, they may choose to down plate the vehicle to an authorized GVW of 28,000 kg GVW and pay less VED. However, if they were caught operating over the 28,000-kg limit, then prosecution would follow and the OCRS would be affected.

If a plate is lost or damaged, replacements are available from the GVC in Swansea. Should an operator or driver be requested to produce a DVSA plate by a police officer, it must be produced at a police station of choice within seven days.

Testing

Once registered, the vehicle will become due for annual tests at either a Large Goods Vehicle Test Station or an Approved Test Facility (ATF). This test must be carried out by the end of the month of the anniversary of registration. For example, if the vehicle was registered on 8 January 2018, it would need to be tested before 31 January 2019.

Because trailers and semi-trailers are not registered in the same way as motor vehicles, when they are first purchased or leased, the rules are slightly different. In the case of trailers, they need to have their first test before the end of the month of the anniversary of the issue, by the DVSA, of the ID number and plates. For example, if the trailer ID and plates were issued by the DVSA on 16 February 2018, it would need to be tested by 28 February 2019.

A form VTG40 is used to book a test and it must be sent either to the intended test centre or the GVC in Swansea, requesting a test, at least one month before the test is actually required.

Single vehicle annual tests can also be booked electronically using the DVSA booking system known as eTB and payment made by credit or debit card. Multiple tests require operators to register with the DVSA and use a pre-paid account.

Testing of vehicles and trailers at test stations or ATFs applies to certain vehicles and trailers only, and you need to be aware that these are:

- rigid vehicles exceeding 3,500 kg GVW;
- all articulated vehicles and semi-trailers;*
- trailers (not being semi-trailers) over 1,020 kg unladen weight;
- converter dollies (which in effect act as a front axle, which are used to convert a semi-trailer to a trailer).

---

* All articulated vehicles and semi-trailers, even those that do not exceed 3,500 kg GVW, need to be tested at these stations and facilities because ordinary MOT test stations cannot test the fifth-wheel coupling arrangements.

There are rules relating to vehicles arriving for test and being tested; these include:

- All vehicles must arrive on time.
- All vehicles must be clean.
- All vehicles must have the appropriate paperwork.
- All vehicles must not be emitting excessive smoke.
- All vehicles used to carry dangerous goods must be unloaded.
- All vehicles used to carry dangerous goods must present a form VTG15 (Safe Examination Certificate) at the test.
- Failure to comply with any of the above will mean that the vehicle can be refused a test by the issue of a form VTG12.

Other issues

- If an appointment for a test needs to be cancelled by the operator, up to seven days before the test, they must inform the test station in writing, giving at least seven days' notice to the station concerned in order to get the test fee refunded.
- If a cancellation and refund is required within less than seven days of the test, the test station concerned must be notified immediately and documentary evidence presented within three working days of the appointed test.
- Where a vehicle arrives for a test with a minor defect, the DVSA examiner 'may' allow rectification during the test process.

- Where a vehicle fails a test, but is re-presented within 14 days of the original test, only the defective items causing the failure will be re-examined.

- After 14 days, a re-presented vehicle or trailer will need a complete new test.

- Applications for retests need to be made to a chosen test station at least seven days before the retest is required.

- Applications for retests that are made within 14 days of the original test can be made verbally to the station manager of the original test station, providing that three days' notice is given. In other cases, form VTG40 (see above) must be sent to the test station manager.

- When a test centre is temporarily unable to provide tests through staff sickness, or perhaps through fire, flood or inclement weather, a certificate of temporary exemption (VTG33) may be issued by the GVC in Swansea or the manager of a test centre:

  - These circumstances are deemed 'exceptional circumstances' and are defined as 'an accident, a fire, an epidemic, severe weather, a failure in the supply of essential services, or other unexpected happening'.

  - The certificate (VTG33) can act as a temporary test or plating certificate for up to a period of three months.

- Stolen or lost test certificates or plates are obtainable, for a fee, from the test station of issue.

Modifications

Where major modifications and alterations are made to goods vehicles, plating and testing certificates may need to be reissued. Where this is the case, the operator needs to inform the GVC by using form VTG10 and have the vehicle retested.

These circumstances relate to what are known as 'notifiable alterations' and specifically relate to alterations or changes to the:

- engine type;
- braking system;
- suspension;
- steering;
- tyre ply rating;
- chassis.

TABLE 7.4 Forms used for plating and testing

Form	Application
VTG5	Vehicle Test Certificate
VTG6A	DfT Plate
VTG7A	Laminated DfT Plate
VTG10	Notifiable Alteration
VTG12	Refusal to Test a Vehicle
VTG15	Safe Examination Certificate
VTG33	Temporary Test Exemption
VTG40	Application Form for an Annual Test

Before we move on to the Construction and Use (C&U) Regulations in detail, Table 7.4 summarizes the forms used for plating and testing – there are a number of them and their applications are often similar.

Vehicle testing is largely carried out to ascertain whether or not vehicles are able to meet the standards prescribed in the C&U Regulations, as examined below.

Construction and use (C&U) and lighting regulations

C&U Regulations

Again, given the nature of these subjects, we will try to use bullet points to cover each specific C&U item as you will only be expected to answer questions on these types of facts in brief, even though they do clearly form a requirement in the syllabus, which relates to vehicle testing and inspections.

In alphabetical order the C&U Regulations apply to:

- anti-spray devices;
- audible warning devices;
- brakes;
- bumpers;
- fuel tanks;

- ground clearance for trailers;
- mirrors;
- noise;
- safety glass;
- seat belts;
- side guards;
- silencers;
- smoke;
- speed limiters;
- speedometers;
- towing of vehicles;
- tyres;
- windscreen wipers and washers;
- wings.

All of the above – perhaps with the exception of ground clearance for trailers, power to weight ratios and towing trailers – are clearly items included in annual tests and in periodic safety inspections, as required under the operator licensing rules.

Also note the requirement that all new goods vehicles need to be fitted with Class V mirrors and the new requirement for the Direct Vision Standard aimed at reducing vehicle blindspots and being introduced over the next few years, where nearside clear panels are required, for operations in London. Operators should also make themselves aware of Construction Logistics and Community Standards (CLOCS) and the Fleet Operator Recognition Scheme (FORS) which both require certain levels of safety standards to be in place for operations in London and other cities.

Where examination questions may arise, the points you need are itemized below.

Brakes

The braking efficiencies:

- main (service) brake – 50 per cent;
- secondary brake – 25 per cent;
- parking brake – hold the vehicle on a gradient of at least 16 per cent.

Seat belts

- Seat belts and anchorage points must be maintained in a proper condition at all times.
- Anchorage points and load-bearing members within 30 cm of each anchorage point must at all times be free from serious corrosion, distortion or fracture.
- Where vehicles are equipped with seat belts, they must be worn.

The requirement to wear a seat belt does not apply when:

- reversing a vehicle;
- supervising a learner driver in a manoeuvre that includes reversing;
- the driver has a medical exemption;
- the driver is a taxi driver either seeking hire, answering a call for hire, or carrying a passenger for hire;
- the driver is driving a private hire vehicle being used to carry a passenger for hire;
- the driver is an examiner, carrying out a driving test, where wearing a seat belt would endanger themselves or any other person;
- travelling in a vehicle under trade plates to investigate or rectify a fault.

Tyres

- Different types of tyres must not be mixed on the same axle.
- On a two-axle vehicle, cross-ply tyres must not be fitted to the front (steering) axle if cross-ply tyres are fitted to the rear axle.
- Tyres are normally rated according to a load/speed index.
- Tyres manufactured after 1 July 2012 carry a label, or have a leaflet, stating:
  - external rolling noise;
  - fuel efficiency;
  - wet grip rating.
- There must be no cuts exceeding 25 mm or 10 per cent of the tyre width.
- There must be no ply or any cords visible.
- There must be no bulges or lumps.
- All tyres must be properly inflated to the correct pressure.

- Vehicles up to 3,500 kg GVW must have 1.6 mm depth of tread over the middle 75 per cent of the breadth of the tyre and around the entire outer circumference.

- For vehicles exceeding 3,500 kg MAM, there must be at least 1.0 mm depth of tread over 75 per cent of the breadth of the tyre, but tread pattern must be visible over the remaining 25 per cent. (The 1.0 mm must also be present right around the outer circumference).

Lighting regulations

Lighting regulations are our next area of study and one where we need to consider not only lights but other statutory 'visibility' issues. Again, we will bullet-point the salient issues.

First, let's look at the minimum number of obligatory lights that vehicles must have. These are:

- two front-position lights (sidelights);
- two dipped headlights (white or yellow);
- two main-beam headlights (white or yellow);
- one white rear registration plate light;
- two red rear-position lights;
- two red stop lamps;
- one red rear fog light;
- amber direction indicators:
  - one each side at the front;
  - up to two each side at the rear;
  - at least one side repeater set within 2,600 mm from the front of the vehicle.
- Amber hazard warning lights, only to be used to:
  - warn other drivers of a problem ahead; or
  - warn of the presence of the vehicle.
- Two red triangular rear reflectors, which are only obligatory for trailers – not motor vehicles.

Note 1: There has to be a tell-tale light in the cab to remind the driver when using main beam as opposed to dip-beam main beam.

Note 2: In place of sidelights, newer vehicles are often fitted with obligatory dim/dip lights to improve safety at night where sidelights may not give sufficient warning of the presence of the vehicle.

In addition to obligatory lights, there are lights such as:

- front fog lamps;
- reversing lights;
- working lamps;
- beacons, which include:
  - blue beacons used by the emergency services;
  - green beacons used by doctors;
  - red beacons used by bomb disposal teams;
  - amber beacons used for operations such as highway maintenance and vehicle recovery.

Other relevant points from the regulations include:

- Lights fitted to vehicles should not be set to dazzle other road users.
- Additional amber side-marker lights are required on new vehicles and trailers longer than 6 m in length.
- Amber side reflectors are required on vehicles over 5 m in length and on trailers over 6 m in length.
- End outline marker lights need to be fitted to all new vehicles and trailers exceeding 2.1 m in width.
- Front white reflectors are required to be fitted to all new trailers and semi-trailers.
- Red lights should not be shown to the front of a vehicle.
- White lights should not be shown to the rear (except reversing lights, rear number plate lights, interior lights and working lights).

The lighting regulations also apply to visibility markings, which we also need to consider.

Rear reflective plates must be fitted to:

- Vehicles exceeding 7,500 kg GVW.
- Trailers exceeding 3,500 kg GVW.
- Vehicles up to 13 m in length require a striped plate.
- Vehicles exceeding 13 m in length need a clear plate with an orange reflective border.
- Trailers up to 11 m in length require a striped plate.

- Trailers over 11 m in length but less than 13 m in length may use either a striped or a clear plate.
- Trailers over 13 m in length need a clear plate with an orange border.

Since 2011, goods vehicles exceeding 7,500 kg GVW and trailers exceeding 3,500 kg GVW must now be fitted with 'conspicuity markings'. These are reflective markers that give an outline of the vehicle or trailer and there are rules that apply to them. For example:

- The marking tape needs to be:
  - 60 mm in width;
  - rear marking tape needs to be red or yellow;
  - side marking tape needs to be yellow or white.
- Rear markings must be as close as possible to the edge of the vehicle.
- The horizontal and vertical markings to the rear should clearly outline the rear of the vehicle or trailer.
- Where the vehicle shape cannot be clearly defined, indicator line markings may be used.

As we have now looked at the regulations surrounding vehicle inspections it is worth quickly covering the issues relating to possible contravention and actual contravention of these rules and resulting penalties, where vehicles are found not to be fit and serviceable, as required by operator licensing rules and the regulations above.

Where DVSA examiners feel there may be a problem they have certain powers, such as:

- DVSA vehicle examiners are allowed, with the owner's consent, to enter premises at any reasonable time. However, if permission is not given at the time, they must give notice of their intentions to return, either: 1) verbally, giving 48 hours' notice; or 2) by recorded delivery, giving 72 hours' notice. (These time requirements do not have to be met if the vehicle has been involved in, or is believed to have been involved in, an accident.)
- Working with the police to prosecute drivers who obstruct authorized examiners.
- Issuing fixed penalties under the Graduated Fixed Penalty Scheme ('conditional offers' in Scotland) for minor offences such as a small hole in a light lens.
- Issuing fixed penalties with penalty points for serious offences, such as overloading or bald tyres.

- Immobilizing vehicles in serious cases until the issue causing the immobilization has been rectified. In these cases fines of up to £5,000 or even two years in prison may result.

- Taking into consideration any offences from the previous 28 days that can be detected from the driver's tachograph records or the vehicle VU. (This is a power which is only used when the offence detected at the time the vehicle was stopped would, in itself, result in a prosecution.)

When vehicles are examined there are a number of forms that the DVSA examiners can issue, depending upon their findings. The main forms are:

- PG9: this is a prohibition notice, prohibiting the use of a vehicle on the road:
  - A prohibition can be immediate or it can be deferred for up to 10 days.
  - Once a vehicle has been repaired, whilst the prohibition is still in force, the vehicle may be road tested within a three-mile radius of the place of repair.
  - The vehicle must be re-examined at a test station before the prohibition can be lifted.

Note: Where the PG9 is noted as a PG9S, this means that the offence is deemed to be severe and that prosecution will almost certainly follow. It also makes the offence likely to be marked as 'Most Serious' on the OCRS.

- PG9ABC: this is a combined Variation, Exemption and Refusal Notice used to vary the terms of a PG9 such as:
  - (PG9A): perhaps for varying the date that the prohibition is to take effect.
  - (PG9B): perhaps temporarily exempting the prohibition so that the vehicle can be safely moved to a nominated site.
  - PG9C: this is the part of the form used to notify of a refusal to lift the prohibition, when a vehicle is tested following a prohibition.
- PG9D: this is a continuation sheet, which is used when the number of defects and problems are too long to fit on either the PG9 or the PG9ABC.
- PG10: the form used to record the removal of the prohibition following a successful test, allowing the vehicle back into service.
- PG35ECDN or PGDN35: these are both forms used as Defect Notices and are issued at roadside checks where minor faults are detected. The defects need rectification but there is normally no

further action taken. The difference in the form coding is that the PGDN35 is a manually generated paper form while the PG35ECDN is computer generated, but they are both used for the same purpose.

- TE160DH: a prohibition notice resulting from drivers' hours and record-keeping offences.
- TE160P: a prohibition resulting from overloading.

Note 1: Operators must notify the Traffic Commissioner of all prohibitions they receive.

Note 2: Operators must retain all prohibitions and defect notices in the vehicle history file for a minimum period of 15 months.

Key points you need to know

- All type approval, plating and testing requirements and procedures.
- Outline of C&U Regulations.
- Detail of C&U requirements for brakes, seat belts and tyres.
- Outline of obligatory and optional lights.
- Rules on lights being shown to the front and rear.
- Rules on reflective rear plates and conspicuity marking.
- Powers of the DVSA examiners.
- Different forms used and their purpose/application.

Notes

....

....

....

....

....

....

....

....

....

That concludes a lot of information in relation to vehicle types, design, standards and related enforcement that may result from non-compliance. We now need to look at a different area of the syllabus: some of the measures that can be taken to reduce the noise of vehicles and air pollution caused by vehicles.

Emissions and noise

Whilst it can be argued that Euro VI emission standards and 'stop-start' engines are certainly aimed at reducing emissions, and things such as low-resistance tyres and electrically powered vehicles reduce noise, we need to consider several other technological issues. In relation to emissions these include:

- low-sulphur diesel;
- ultra-low-sulphur diesel;
- bio-diesel;
- hybrid vehicles – where gas or electricity is used in addition to the main engine, which is usually smaller than would otherwise be the case;
- alternative fuels – such as liquid petroleum gas (LPG) or compressed natural gas (CNG);
- exhaust gas recirculation (EGR) – where exhaust gases are simply recycled through the engine;
- selective catalytic reduction (SCR), which is used to reduce emissions of nitrogen oxides usually by using 'AdBlue', an ammonium-based fuel supplement;
- diesel particulate filters (DPF), which are used to reduce harmful particles from exhaust emissions.

In relation to noise from vehicles – ie made by horns, reversing 'bleepers', revving engines, loading and unloading and coupling and uncoupling of trailers – it is also important to consider noise from vehicle sites and facilities, including:

- workshops;
- radios;
- telephone speakers;
- fork trucks;
- compressors and other equipment.

Having covered that small requirement related to the environment, importantly, we can now move on to vehicle maintenance, which is examined in great detail and which you will need to study carefully, not least because of the safety and road safety implications and the requirements for compliance in relation to operator licensing.

Vehicle maintenance

This section is where you will need to download, or contact the DVSA for a copy of, the DVSA Guide to Maintaining Roadworthiness. It is free to download from the government website (www.gov.uk). You need this guide because it contains all the detailed information that goes to form the standards and requirements that the DVSA expect from an operator of goods vehicles, and these standards and requirements will be examined in some detail.

Importantly, we need to understand the general objectives and benefits that a properly structured maintenance regime can deliver and that vehicle maintenance systems are made up of different types of inspections and checks – and that they can be carried out in different ways.

The objectives of a maintenance programme should, in short, be to provide the business with:

- minimum administrative burden;
- minimum cost;
- minimum operational disruption;
- maximum levels of legal compliance.

These should lead to:

- maximum customer satisfaction;
- maximum vehicle availability;
- maximum earnings per vehicle;
- improved levels of operational reputation.

Let's now move on to periodic safety inspections (PSIs), which are the cornerstone to any planned preventative maintenance system.

Periodic safety inspections

When applying for an operator's licence, each applicant needs to declare how often they will have the vehicles inspected and who will carry out the inspections. At the time of application and throughout the life of an operator's licence, the applicant or operator will need to show the DVSA inspectors that they have safety inspections planned for at least the next six months, and ideally for 12 months, by using either a planning board or an electronic database system.

The safety inspections themselves are similar to a 'mini-MOT', where all the components related to the safety of a vehicle are inspected by a competent vehicle inspector at a facility that has to be of a certain standard.

These inspections are usually carried out every six weeks although the Traffic Commissioner (TC) can reduce that time if problems occur, or if the vehicles are engaged in particularly heavy work, or the TC may extend the period if the opposite circumstances prevail. However, in the case of trailers that are more than 12 years old, then 6 weekly inspections, or less, will always be required, irrespective of how often the trailers are used or their annual mileage.

In all cases, it is the applicant, or operator, who suggests a time period between inspections but it is always the TC who makes the final decision. To help applicants and operators the DVSA Guide has a graph that can be used to align individual operations with a suggested time period for safety inspections.

In addition to the fact that these periodic safety inspections can only be undertaken by technically competent safety inspectors, the inspection sheets and reports used by the inspectors must also be of an approved type.

Following each safety inspection, each report must provide the following information:

- the inspector's name;
- the date of the inspection;
- the name of the operator;
- the vehicle details;
- the odometer reading;
- the items to be inspected;
- the condition of these items at inspection;
- details of any defects found;
- a statement that any defects found have been repaired satisfactorily and by whom.

Approved safety inspection sheets and all other safety check and defect report sheets are available through trade associations such as the FTA or RHA. All records of the periodic safety inspections, including any remedial work following such an inspection, must be retained by the operator for at least 15 months and must be made available to the enforcement authorities 'upon request'.

Inspection choice

Most small operators elect to use an external maintenance provider to carry out the safety inspections. Larger operators may also elect to do this where the fleet is leased from a vehicle manufacturer but they may also elect to carry out the maintenance 'in-house'. The advantages and disadvantages of both of these choices are commonly included in the examinations. In either case, as mentioned above, the facilities must be of an approved standard, including the requirement for:

- undercover accommodation, complete with adequate lighting, for the largest vehicle in the fleet;
- appropriate tools and equipment for the fleet concerned, including:
  - steam or pressure-washing facilities;
  - access to exhaust emission-testing equipment;
  - access to brake and headlight-testing equipment.

Let us now look at the typical advantages and disadvantages of each of the choices. These are only listed as possible or potential issues and these lists are by no means meant to be exhaustive.

Advantages of systems of contracting out maintenance:

- no facility costs;
- no equipment costs;
- no staff costs;
- possible 'dealer' expertise;
- possible warranty requirements;
- 24/7 facilities are often available;
- possible fleet support scheme available;
- easier maintenance cost planning.

Disadvantages of systems of contracting out maintenance:

- possible increased costs;
- loss of control;

- loss of flexibility;
- usually increased vehicle downtime;
- possible quality issues;
- usually requires driver repatriation;
- problems more difficult to resolve.

Advantages of systems of in-house maintenance:

- retain overall control;
- staff are familiar with the vehicles in the fleet;
- staff are on-site so less downtime;
- some spare parts may be ordered in advance;
- able to prioritize work.

Disadvantages of systems of in-house maintenance:

- cost of the facility and facility upkeep;
- staff costs, including overtime, and weekend payments and training costs;
- cost of facility equipment;
- costs of stocking spare parts;
- time and costs associated with health and safety compliance.

If the inspections are to be carried out by an external maintenance provider there will need to be proof of a valid contract and copies of the forms to be used before the TC will approve the use of the nominated provider. However, whether the safety inspections are carried out in-house or externally, it is always the operator who remains responsible for the mechanical condition of the vehicles and not the maintainer. This is an important factor to consider, particularly given the link between maintenance, safety and OCRS.

In addition to the periodic inspection and maintenance of vehicles, there needs to be a check done every time a vehicle is 'first used'. This is normally a daily check, which is normally carried out by the driver, and consists of a walk-round check of the vehicle in order to ensure that items such as:

- The lights, horn, windscreen wiper/washers and similar items are operating correctly.
- The lights and number plates are clean and not damaged or missing.
- The tyres are inflated properly, not damaged and have sufficient tread.

- The wheel nuts are in place and are not loose and/or the plastic wheel nut indicators are properly aligned.
- The fluid levels, including fuel, are all okay.
- Warning systems are operating correctly.
- The vehicle is in good condition.
- Any trailer connections are properly made and secure.
- The load is secured correctly.

Again, the items above are only a sample but further detail is included in the DVSA Guide, including a sample of what the DVSA considers to be an acceptable check sheet for drivers to use.

In addition to the 'daily check' itself, there must also be an acceptable method for drivers to report any defects found. This requires that drivers' daily check sheets must also be able to record:

- details of the vehicle concerned (registration number);
- the identity of who reported the defect;
- the date when the defect was reported;
- a brief description of the defect;
- the defect having been rectified;
- who carried out the defect rectification (the fitter);
- when the rectification was carried out.

It is further recommended by the DVSA that operators should consider carrying out random vehicle checks on vehicles setting out from their premises in order to ensure that drivers are actually carrying out these daily checks.

All daily check sheets with defects recorded on them form a part of the vehicle history file and must be retained by the operator for a minimum of 15 months. Where there is no defect, the DVSA advises that the daily check sheets need only be retained for the period between each of the periodic safety inspections (normally six weeks).

As a final note in relation to drivers' daily checks, the DVSA recommends that all drivers are given either a letter or a handbook explaining the need for the daily check and the importance of it in relation to operator licensing. They also recommend that drivers acknowledge receipt of the letter or handbook.

Please make sure that you are fully familiar with all vehicle maintenance requirements before you sit your examination because it will be included as an important element of both the short-answer and long-answer questions.

Key points you need to know

- Typical noise and emission reduction measures.
- The principles of periodic safety inspections.
- Contents of safety inspections forms.
- The options of in-house and external vehicle maintenance systems.
- Driver daily check procedures.
- Drivers' defect reporting and rectification procedures.
- Retention periods for vehicle history data.
- Retention period for 'nil defect' daily check sheets.

Notes

....
....
....
....
....
....
....
....
....
....

Once again, we now come to a part of the syllabus where we can try to cover some of the subject matter using key/bullet-point notes: cargo handling and loading/unloading safety issues and companies that support transport operations, which are known as transport ancillaries.

Load safety

The DfT and the DVSA publish guides on the safety of loads. They are both free to download from the government website (www.gov.uk) and both complement each other. They are titled:

- Safety of Loads on Vehicles (published by the DfT).
- The DVSA Load Security Guide (published by the DVSA).

The DfT guide uses the principles that:

- No load must present a danger or be likely to cause harm to anyone.
- All loads must be properly secured.
- All loads must be carried on a suitable vehicle.
- Any vehicle used for any load must not be loaded in such a way that exceeds either an axle weight limit or the GVW of the vehicle.
- The driver should check load documentation, where possible, to check load weights.
- All load restraints must be capable of withstanding a force equivalent to the full weight of the load in a forward direction and half the weight of the load rearwards or to the side.
- The load is to be properly distributed within, or on, the vehicle as close to the centreline and headboard of the vehicle as possible.
- Heavy loads should be spread across the vehicle, where possible.
- Spacing pieces must be used if the load cannot be close to the trailer headboard, in order to prevent movement of the load.
- Heavy items must not be stowed on top of lighter items.
- The load platform and securing points need to be in good condition.
- Appropriate load-securing devices must be used for the load to be carried.
- Drivers should be trained to use load-securing equipment.
- Any loading/unloading mechanical handling equipment must only be operated by authorized staff.

The DVSA guide uses the principles that:

- The vehicle must be fit for purpose.
- The vehicle must be loaded correctly.
- The most appropriate securing method must be used.
- There must be 'adequate' load restraint.

These principles apply to all stakeholders in the loading, carriage and unloading of loads, including the loaders, drivers and managers, and take the form that everyone should assess the operation for risk and danger and be able to make improvements or changes, if required.

The DVSA guide also notes that the enforcement authorities will assess any danger and award penalties, which are graduated depending upon the severity of the problem.

For example, the DVSA vehicle examiners will consider questions such as:

- Can the load slide or topple forwards or backwards?
- Can the load slide or topple off the side?
- Is the load unstable?
- Is the load-securing equipment in poor condition?
- Is there anything loose that might fall off?
- Does the vehicle present an immediate likelihood of causing danger of injury due to its load security or stability?

They will then use a three-table matrix to determine the severity, looking at:

- the risk represented by the type of load;
- the type of load securing used;
- the appropriate action to be taken based on where a load and its security fit within the previous two tables relating to risk and load type.

Depending on these three tables, the offence (or breach) can result in anything from a warning to notification to the Traffic Commissioner (OCRS), up to a fine or even a custodial sentence.

Transport ancillaries

Our next area of the syllabus means that we now need to look at some additional support services offered by 'third parties' acting as general 'transport ancillaries' moving road freight in conjunction with other modes of transport. These include:

- ferry movements;
- container movements;
- intermodal movements.

Ferry movements

For your examination, you need to understand the advantages and disadvantages of roll-on/roll-off (ro-ro) ferries over the Channel Tunnel and the advantages and disadvantages of sending consignments accompanied (with the driver) or unaccompanied (trailer only). We list these below:

- Advantages of ro-ro ferries over the Channel Tunnel link (Eurotunnel):
  - can carry heavy AILs;
  - can carry oversized AILs;
  - more time for the driver to rest;
  - more departure and arrival destinations available;
  - Eurotunnel does not offer a full customs clearance facility;
  - ro-ro can offer accompanied and unaccompanied transit.
- Disadvantages of ro-ro ferries over the Channel Tunnel link (Eurotunnel):
  - longer loading/unloading times;
  - longer transit times;
  - affected by adverse weather conditions.
- Advantages of accompanied movements:
  - the driver is available to sort out any administrative problems;
  - shorter overall transit times;
  - increased security.
- Disadvantages of accompanied movements:
  - increased costs due to length of vehicle combination;
  - additional insurance costs;
  - international 'O' licence required;
  - premium vehicle usually required;
  - increased drivers' wages.
- Advantages of unaccompanied movements:
  - lower cost as length of vehicle combination reduced;
  - may not require an international 'O' licence;
  - improved driver and vehicle utilization;
  - may not require premium vehicle.
- Disadvantages of unaccompanied movements:
  - no driver to sort out any problems;
  - overall transit times are increased;

- less control over load;
- less control of trailer whereabouts;
- possible security issues;
- operator normally remains responsible to the client for the goods concerned.

The points above are not exhaustive but they are sufficient for examination purposes.

Container movements

Containers are usually handled in ports such as Felixstowe and London Gateway where they arrive by sea for transhipment to road or rail. The containers themselves are International Standards Organization (ISO) containers either 20 feet, 30 feet, or 40 feet in length and usually 8 feet or 8 feet 6 inches in height.

However, whilst the loading and unloading, registering, storage and distribution of these containers arriving and departing by sea is handled by third-party ancillaries, there are also inland rail/road-based systems such as Daventry International Rail Freight Terminal (DIRFT). In all cases, it is the ancillaries who also provide a full range of container services including container hire, container repair, container testing, container approval, container filling (stuffing) and container unloading (stripping).

Note: All containers must have a certified gross weight before they will be allowed to be loaded onto a deep water container ship. This rule does not apply to ro-ro services or short sea ferry services.

As a final note relating to movements of goods in containers, we need to understand that freight containers need to be kept fit and serviceable. This involves:

- having the containers examined by the HSE, or an HSE-approved organization;
- fixing a plate to each container that gives details of safety aspects such as safe load weights;
- ensuring that all freight containers are 'properly' maintained at all times.

Intermodal movements

Intermodal services are another service offered by third-party ancillaries. They are being offered within the UK albeit in a limited way (as from DIRFT above), but on mainland Europe they are more widely offered and used. Within the EU, the majority of intermodal services are operated and/or controlled by Novatrans who carry vehicles and trailers by rail. Novatrans also carry unaccompanied ISO container traffic, offering transhipment between road and rail and operating services between most major European cities. This Novatrans network serves countries including Austria, Belgium, Denmark, France, Germany, Greece, Hungary, Italy, Netherlands, Norway, Spain, Sweden, and Switzerland.

On services where both vehicles and drivers are carried, the drivers are accommodated in a passenger carriage where all normal services are available.

Key points you need to know

- The principles of load safety.
- The advantages and disadvantages of ro-ro versus Eurotunnel.
- The advantages and disadvantages of accompanied and unaccompanied movements.
- Services offered by container service providers.
- The main types of intermodal services.

Notes

....

....

....

....

....

....

....

....

....

....

Having now covered many aspects relating to technical services we turn to look at four very important types of service: dangerous goods, perishable foodstuffs, waste transport and livestock movements. It is important that you have a good understanding of all these types of services, especially dangerous goods and perishable foodstuffs, as they are often examined in detail.

Dangerous goods

The United Nations Economic Commission for Europe (UNECE) is the body that is responsible overall for most of the movements of dangerous goods by road. However, the rules themselves are laid out in a European Agreement known as ADR. ADR relates to international movements but most European countries have incorporated it (or most of it) into the regulations covering domestic movements. The ADR agreement is primarily aimed at ensuring all dangerous goods carried by road are classified, packaged, labelled and transported in line with laid-down standards (there are separate agreements for moving dangerous goods by rail, air and sea).

Classification of goods

Under ADR, all dangerous goods belong to a certain class. These are:

- Class 1: explosive substances and articles.
- Class 2: gases.
- Class 3: flammable liquids.
- Class 4.1: flammable solids.
- Class 4.2: substances liable to spontaneous combustion.
- Class 4.3: substances that emit flammable gases on contact with water.
- Class 5.1: oxidizing substances.
- Class 5.2: organic peroxides.
- Class 6.1: toxic substances.
- Class 6.2: infectious substances.
- Class 7: radioactive substances.
- Class 8: corrosive substances.
- Class 9: miscellaneous dangerous substances and articles.

In addition to the dangerous goods needing to be classified, they are each given a unique four-digit UN identification number, such as 1090 for acetone and 1133 for adhesives.

Packaging and labelling

Dangerous goods are also put into UN packing groups. These are:

- Packing Group 1: high hazard-level goods.
- Packing Group 2: medium hazard-level goods.
- Packing Group 3: low hazard-level goods.

It is the sender's responsibility to ensure that the goods in question are properly packaged and labelled in accordance with the ADR agreement, unless the quantity being carried is below certain set amounts. In these cases the goods are additionally given 'transport categories', depending upon the level of hazard (from Category 4 [minimal hazard] to Category 0 [extremely hazardous]) and the weight carried.

For example, categories and amounts carried in order to be exempted are as follows:

- Transport Category 4 goods – unlimited weight.
- Transport Category 3 goods – up to 1,000 kg.
- Transport Category 2 goods – up to 333 kg.
- Transport Category 1 goods – up to 20 kg.
- Transport Category 0 goods – 0 kg.

Vehicle marking

All vehicles carrying goods under ADR must show a rectangular orange plate to the front of the vehicle. In addition:

- Vehicles carrying packaged dangerous goods in any of the three packaging groups (above) must also show an additional rectangular orange plate at the rear of the vehicle.

- Tankers carrying a single substance on an international journey must show an additional subdivided orange plate at the rear that shows both the UN hazard identification code number (HIN), the UN identity number and a hazard diamond for the UN class of the goods (see below). These are known as Hazchem panels (or placards). There must be two further Hazchem panels fixed to each side of the vehicle.

Note 1: Where the dangerous goods are being moved in a tank container (ISO) and not in a tank vehicle or trailer, the Hazchem panels must be fixed to all four sides of the container.

Note 2: The only exceptions to these markings are when a tanker is carrying a single substance on a UK domestic journey, when the Hazchem panels on both sides and at the rear must show the UN hazard identity number (HIN), an emergency action code and an emergency contact number. For example, you may see a domestic placard that states 3YE – 1270. Whilst 1270 is the four-digit UN hazard identification number, the code 3YE is used by the emergency services as a guide to the severity of the hazard in cases of accidents or spillages (the letter 'E' actually requests consideration of evacuation of the vicinity).

Note 3: Where the dangerous goods are also classified as a 'marine pollu-tant', the vehicle must also show an 'environmentally hazardous substances' warning sign, which is a black-and-white picture of a fish and a tree. These signs are also required under the International Maritime Dangerous Goods (IMDG) rules when vehicles use ferries.

There are also dangerous goods that may be carried in what are known as 'limited quantities', where the vehicle carrying the goods may be exempt from ADR rules and transport categories. The term 'limited quantities' actu-ally refers to the size of the packaging unit (for instance small tubes of glue in boxes) and not always the weight of the whole consignment.

In short, limited quantities rules mean that, when dangerous goods are carried in small packages in vehicles exceeding 12,000 kg MAM and the total weight of the goods exceeds 8,000 kg, then the vehicle can either: 1) display orange plates to the front or rear; or 2) display an ADR 'limited quantity' plate to the front and rear of the vehicle, if preferred.

Note: A limited quantity plate is a white diamond with the top and bottom triangles shaded in black.

As an overview and guide, and because there are some minor differences between international movements and domestic movements, we can ease matters by summarizing as follows:

- All vehicles carrying goods under ADR must have a plain orange plate fixed to the front of the vehicle.

- All vehicles carrying packaged dangerous goods must have plain orange plates fixed to the front and rear of the vehicle.

- A UK-registered vehicle on an international journey needs orange plates at the front of the vehicle and Hazchem panels to the sides and rear of the vehicle.

- Dangerous goods moved in containers (ISO) must have Hazchem panels fixed to all four sides of the container.
- Dangerous goods moved in limited quantities can either have orange plates fixed to the front and rear of the vehicle or black-and-white limited quantity diamonds fixed to the front and rear of the vehicle.
- Where the dangerous goods are also classed as an environmentally hazardous substance, an additional black-and-white pollutant diamond must be fixed to the rear of the vehicle.

Note 1: A UK-registered vehicle on a UK domestic journey needs orange plates at the front and rear of the vehicle and Hazchem panels, with a contact telephone number, to the sides and rear of the vehicle. The telephone number is not required for international movements.

Note 2: Look out for vehicles with dangerous goods placarding, and practise identifying the types of loads they are carrying.

Vehicles and equipment

- All vehicles intended to be used under ADR must be initially examined and certified by the DfT for use under ADR (form ADR III).
- All certified vehicles must be recertified annually (normally at the annual test) (from ADR IIIS).
- Tank vehicles with a capacity of more than 1,000 litres can only be approved and examined by DfT examiners.
- Tank containers with a capacity of more than 3,000 litres can only be approved and examined by DfT examiners.
- Tank vehicles used under ADR must have a major tank inspection every six years.
- Tank vehicles used under ADR must have 'intermediate inspections', and be tested for leaks, every three years.
- Vehicles and trailers used under ADR must have antilock and endurance braking systems.
- Some vehicles used under ADR, especially when carrying flammable liquids, may also need to have circuit breakers that can be operated from inside and outside of the vehicle, as well as heat shields fitted to the engine compartment and exhaust system.

Equipment that must be carried on the vehicle in cases of emergency includes:

- at least two warning cones, triangles or amber flashing lights to warn other road users;
- at least one suitably sized wheel chock for both the vehicle and any trailer drawn, to secure the vehicle in position, if required;
- a hand lamp/torch that is flameproof and anti-static;
- high-viz clothing for the driver and any crew members;
- a spill kit to prevent spillage spreading;
- any PPE required when handling the goods in question;
- an eye bath/rinsing facility.

All vehicles operating under ADR must also carry certain levels of firefighting equipment. The requirements are as follows:

- Vehicles up to 3,500 kg GVW must have a minimum total capacity of 4 kg of extinguishant. This includes a minimum 2 kg extinguisher to be fitted inside the cab.
- Vehicles exceeding 3,500 kg GVW, but not exceeding 7,500 kg GVW must have a minimum total capacity of 8 kg of extinguishant. This includes a minimum 2 kg extinguisher fitted inside the cab and one other extinguisher that must have a minimum capacity of 6 kg.
- Vehicles exceeding 7,500 kg GVW must have a minimum total capacity of 12 kg of extinguishant. This includes a minimum 2 kg extinguisher fitted inside the cab and one other extinguisher that must have a minimum capacity of 6 kg (this could be a 10 kg extinguisher or a 6 kg extinguisher plus a 4 kg extinguisher).

It should be noted that extinguishers carried on the vehicle, but not in the cab, are usually placed in readily identifiable lockers or boxes on the vehicle or trailer and that all drivers and crew members must be properly trained in the use of the extinguishers they carry.

Documentation

So far we have dealt with areas where short-answer questions will form most of what will be required for the examinations. However, documentation is an area where both short and long questions may be asked. In particular, we need to look at two elements of documentation required under ADR. First there is the ADR Note (this is also sometimes referred to as the Dangerous Goods Note or the Transport Document). This note:

- Must be carried on the vehicle transporting the dangerous goods.
- Must be written in the language of the country of origin. (When the language of the country of origin is not German, French or English a copy of the ADR note in one of those languages must also be carried.)
- Must give a full description of the goods being carried including the:
  - UN identification number;
  - UN proper shipping name;
  - hazard class, including any secondary hazards;
  - packing group, if applicable;
  - tunnel code, if applicable (see below);
  - gross weight (in kilogrammes);
  - number and a description of the packages, if applicable;
  - name and address of the consignor;
  - name and address of the consignee.

Note: All ADR notes must be retained by the haulier for a minimum of three months following completion of the journey.

The second document that must accompany dangerous goods is known as 'Instructions in Writing'. These are generic and general instructions to the driver and the emergency services on what actions to take in cases of accidents or emergencies involving dangerous goods. They must explain how to:

- stop the engine, apply the braking system and isolate the battery, if possible;
- contact the emergency services and give them the relevant information;
- put on the 'high-viz' clothing and lay out the warning signs for other road users;
- avoid smoking or switching on any electrical equipment (this includes using e-cigarettes);
- make the transport documents available for the emergency services when they arrive;
- avoid coming into contact with spilled substances, fumes, smoke or dust, etc;

- remove any clothing or PPE that does become contaminated and how to dispose of it safely;
- use the fire extinguishers to extinguish any small fires, typically in the tyres, engine, brakes – but only if it is safe to do so;
- avoid tackling fires in load compartments involving the dangerous goods themselves;
- prevent spillages into watercourses and sewers by using the spill kit to contain the spillage;
- stay at a safe distance from the incident and to advise other bystanders to do the same;
- comply with any instructions given by the emergency services.

In addition, Instructions in Writing must:

- be completed in the language of the country of origin;
- be completed in a language able to be understood by the driver;
- be completed in the language of all countries of transit and the country of destination;
- be kept in the vehicle in a place and format that is clearly visible to any emergency services.

The two documents above are important because you may well be asked to discuss the content and differences between them. You might also be asked to explain what are known as 'tunnel codes'. These are codes associated with the risk of the release of toxic gases or liquids, fires and explosions in tunnels that road vehicles may transit.

Tunnels and dangerous goods are given codes to let the driver know of the potential risk in case of any emergency (as above) whilst the vehicle carrying dangerous goods is actually inside a tunnel.

As well as being entered onto the ADR note, tunnel codes are placed on routes leading towards tunnels but sufficiently away from the tunnel to allow the driver to stop and seek advice or to seek an alternative route, if required.

The codes are:

- Category A: no restrictions.
- Category B: risk of a large explosion.
- Category C: risk of a large or very large explosion or a large toxic release.
- Category D: risk of a large or very large explosion, a large toxic release or a large fire.

- Category E: restriction on the carriage of all dangerous goods in consignments of more than 8 tonnes.

As there are no restrictions for Code A goods or tunnels this code is not used at the roadside, allowing any driver who does not see a code prior to entering a tunnel to transit the tunnel without any restrictions.

Finally, in addition to the documentation relating specifically to dangerous goods we need to remember that the driver also needs to carry:

- their dangerous goods Vocational Training Certificate (VTC) (see notes below);
- the ADR approval certificate for the vehicle;
- any required authorization relating to the movement;
- a copy of the main text of any special agreement, (where the goods are covered by such an agreement);
- the IMDG documents, if using a ferry for a sea crossing.

Note 1: Under ADR, drivers must have a VTC for the classes of dangerous goods they carry. This VTC is valid for five years and must be carried by the driver.

Note 2: Even when handling 'limited quantities', all staff involved, including loaders and warehouse staff, must be trained in handling and storing the dangerous goods in question.

Note 3: Dangerous goods legislation is overseen and enforced by the HSE, the DVSA and the police.

Note 4: New security provisions in ADR, introduced to combat terrorism, have led to the introduction of a UK body known as the Transport Security Directorate of the Department for Transport (TRANSEC). TRANSEC provides guidance on dangerous goods movements and, in particular, can provide drivers with 'Dangerous Load Cards', which advise the driver of 'best practice' if they are stopped at a roadside vehicle checkpoint and have any concerns.

Note 5: Organizations carrying and storing dangerous goods must appoint a dangerous goods safety advisor (DGSA) qualified in the relevant classes of dangerous goods. Each DGSA is qualified for a period of five years, after which time they must requalify.

A DGSA is responsible for:

- advising on safety issues;
- checking the suitability of vehicles and equipment;
- monitoring safety compliance, safety training,* emergency procedures and equipment (including vehicles) used in connection with dangerous goods;

- investigating any accidents involving dangerous goods;
- preparing subsequent accident reports;
- preparing an annual company/organization report;
- ensuring all reports generated by the DGSA are retained for a minimum of five years.

---

* The DGSA is only responsible for monitoring the safety training, not for the actual delivery of the training.

For clarity, examples of hazard diamonds for single substances and other dangerous goods signs are shown in Figure 7.1, with the background colours indicated.

Dangerous goods are an important part of the syllabus and you need to know about them in some detail.

Key points you need to know

- UN classes and packaging and labelling requirements.
- Vehicle marking and limited quantities.
- Vehicle specification and equipment required.
- ADR note content and tunnel codes.
- 'Instructions in Writing' content and use.
- VTC validity.
- DGSA roles, responsibilities and validity.

Notes

....
....
....
....
....
....
....
....
....
....

FIGURE 7.1 Hazard diamonds

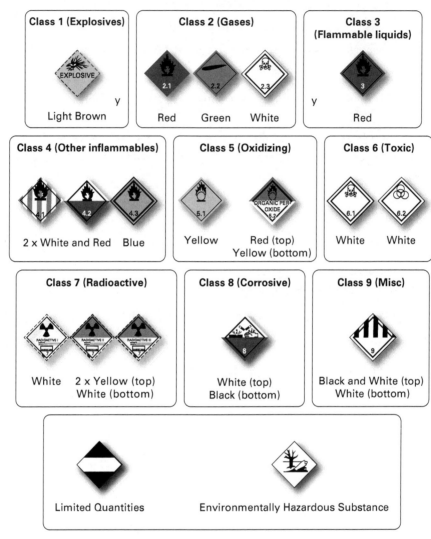

SOURCE: UNECE (ADR Regulations 2015)

Next we come to other types of goods where we will try to cover as much of the content as possible in bullet points. This does not mean that this content is less important than dangerous goods, but it is information more readily presented in single points. We begin with the carriage of perishable foodstuffs. First we deal with domestic (UK) legislation and then look at another UNECE agreement for international movements.

Perishable foodstuffs

Within the UK we have domestic hygiene regulations that apply to temperature-controlled movements and the movements of quick-frozen foods by road. These rules relate to:

- The need for vehicles to be constructed and maintained so that they can be properly cleaned.
- Food and non-food items being carried on the same vehicle.
- Foodstuffs and non-foodstuffs being prevented from becoming mixed or contaminated by each other.
- Bulk tankers having to be marked 'For Foodstuffs Only'.
- Driver personal hygiene and dress.
- Records of temperatures being produced, retained for at least 12 months and made available upon request by the authorities.
- Vehicles used for local distribution being fitted with a visible thermometer.
- Other vehicles being fitted with equipment that measures and records temperatures inside the load compartment.
- All recording equipment being accurate to within 1 °C.
- Records produced by the equipment being retained for at least 12 months and produced upon request by the authorities.
- Certain foods being carried within set temperature ranges. For example, the rules state that:
  - Under the UK's Quick-Frozen Foodstuffs Regulations, quick-frozen foodstuffs must be kept at a temperature no higher than –18 °C (+ or – 3 degrees).
  - Chilled foodstuffs must not exceed 8 °C.
  - Hot foodstuffs need to be kept at or above 63 °C.

International movements of perishable foodstuffs come under the UNECE agreement known as ATP. Whilst ATP only applies to transport, supporting regulations cover standards of hygiene and compliance right along the food supply chain and call for all risks to be risk assessed using an approach known as Hazard Analysis Critical Control Point (HACCP) principles, where risks are identified, eliminated as far as possible and records of risk assessment and actions taken and recorded.

ATP itself:

- provides a list of all the goods to which it is relevant;
- requires all vehicles and containers used to transport perishable foodstuffs to be tested and certified;*
- requires all signatory countries to recognize the agreed standards;
- sets common standards for temperature-control equipment and the testing of the equipment;
- applies to international journeys by road and rail;
- applies to sea journeys not exceeding 150 km;
- does not apply to the domestic legs of international journeys;
- applies to both hauliers and own-account operators.

---

* ATP equipment needs testing for efficient cooling by the Refrigerated Vehicle Test Centre, which is approved by the DfT. Following initial certification the vehicle or trailer will be authorized for ATP operations for six years. After the first six-year period the vehicle or trailer will become subject to examinations and certification every three years. Valid certificates need to be carried on the vehicle and made available upon request. However, because of the risk of loss or damage to the certificate, many operators choose to fit an ATP plate to the front or on the sides towards the front of the vehicle or trailer.

An ATP plate has blue letters on a white background and shows a reference code and the expiry date.

For example:

TPD
2021

All ATP movements need to be monitored using some form of thermograph to observe temperatures throughout the journey, and records of this monitoring need to be retained by the operator for 12 months.

Waste

To understand the rules on the carriage of waste, we first need to understand how 'waste' is defined. The EU defines waste in many different forms but it basically refers to it as substances and articles that are meant to be discarded or disposed of.

This means that damaged items, imperfect items, spoiled or contaminated items, residues, items no longer serviceable or required, and unusable offcuts and the like are all classed as 'waste'.

In the UK the Environmental Act requires all persons involved in the carriage of controlled waste – usually 'trade waste' but not waste taken on door-to-door collections from private households – to adopt a duty of care that ensures:

- all waste is taken to authorized waste transfer sites;
- all parties involved are named;
- all waste is properly described;
- all reasonable steps are taken to prevent the loss or escape of any waste (this may require the waste to be packaged);
- all records of waste transfers are retained for two years.

Note: Records of the movements must be retained by both the carrier and the waste transfer station for the two-year period mentioned above.

Once we have our waste items we are then only permitted to move them to a registered waste disposal or waste transfer site and, in order to do that, we, or the carrier we use, must be a registered waste carrier, properly registered with a Waste Regulatory Authority (WRA).

In the UK, the WRAs are:

- the Environment Agency in England and Wales;
- the Scottish Environmental Protection Agency in Scotland;
- the Environment and Heritage Service in Northern Ireland.

In order to be granted a licence by the WRAs the applicant must be deemed to be a 'fit and proper person' to hold a licence. In this case 'fit and proper' applies to previous convictions for environmental offences.

Waste carriers' licences come in two different formats: 'lower tier' licences, where the licence will automatically renew upon renewal; and 'upper tier' licences, in which the licence is normally valid for three years. Both versions of the licence appear on the public Registers of Waste Carriers.

Should a licence be refused, the applicant can appeal to the Secretary of State for the Environment, providing the appeal is made within 28 days of notification of refusal to grant the licence.

Licensed waste carriers must record every single waste movement they undertake and also record:

- a description of the waste;
- details of when the movement occurred;
- details of the volume involved;
- details of the collection and delivery points.

The records of the movements are often paper records but larger waste carriers may register to use the national Electronic Duty of Care (EDOC) programme, enabling them to complete and download waste transfer notes electronically.

International movements of waste are covered by an EU Directive. Under this Directive operators need:

- to be registered with a WRA in the UK;
- to ensure that the driver has the correct waste transfer note showing volume, collection and delivery points;
- details of the operator's UK waste carriers licence to be produced upon request.

Other issues include:

- Failure to comply with licensing provisions can lead to fines of up to £5,000.
- Imprisonment for up to five years and unlimited fines may be imposed for serious breaches of the regulations.
- Production of the waste carrier's licence is required even if the vehicle is operating abroad.
- The EU Directive 94/62 EC defines packaging waste and also sets recycling targets for packaging waste.
- The directive also requires producers of packaging waste to register and provide details of annual tonnages to be recycled or disposed of.
- The directive currently requires registered waste packaging producers to recover 92 per cent of their total annual packaging waste.
- Packaging recovery notes (PRNs), which are issued to the producer of the packaging waste by the reprocessing organization, are used as proof that the 92 per cent target has been met.

Livestock

When moving livestock the rules differ depending upon the type of livestock and the distance of the journey. For example, journeys of up to eight hours are treated differently to journeys exceeding eight hours. However, there are some general requirements irrespective of the journey or the livestock and these include:

- All vehicles used for the carriage of live animals being 'fit for purpose' and properly constructed and able to be cleaned properly.

- Sick animals, pregnant animals and some very young animals are not allowed to be transported.
- For journeys less than 65 km, the driver needs no formal training or experience.
- Where the pickup and delivery points on journeys under 65 km do not include a market, there is no need to clean the vehicle between each load (it must be cleaned in all other cases).
- All journeys over 65 km must be authorized.
- To become approved to operate authorized movements, the transporter must not have committed any serious infringements of animal welfare legislation in the past three years.
- Authorization to carry livestock lasts for five years and is granted by the Department for the Environment, Food and Rural Affairs (DEFRA).
- Records of all animal movements must be retained by the carrier for at least six months.

We now look at the under-eight-hour versus over-eight-hour journeys issues. Journeys up to eight hours (that exceed 65 kilometres) require that:

- A General Authorization from DEFRA is obtained before the movement.
- The carrier completes an Animal Transport Certificate (ATC), giving details of:
  - the carrier;
  - the animals moved;
  - the date of the movement;
  - the collection and delivery points.
- The ATC is carried on the vehicle during the journey and retained for six months.
- The animals must be rested for 24 hours following the journey.
- The driver must have been assessed and hold a certificate of competence in the care of animals. This is carried on the vehicle and must be retained for six months.

For longer journeys, exceeding eight hours, the rules are that:

- The carrier must be authorized by DEFRA and use a carrier's reference number on all documentation relating to the movement.
- A Special Authorization must be granted from DEFRA before the movement in question takes place.

- The carrier must complete a route plan and have it approved by the DEFRA Divisional Veterinary Manager (DVM) before the movement takes place.
- The driver must be properly trained and assessed in animal care.
- The animals must have sufficient bedding and food.
- The vehicle must be able to be compartmentalized into smaller subcompartments.
- The vehicle must have water fittings to provide the animals with drinking water.
- The vehicle must give access for the driver or crew to each level of the vehicle where animals are being carried.
- All new vehicles (since 2009) used for livestock and horse transport must be fitted with a satnav system.
- Pre-2009 vehicles used for livestock and horses nationally, for journeys up to 12 hours or, internationally, on journeys over eight hours' duration, must have a satnav system fitted.
- A journey log must be carried during the journey to record any accidents or incidents.
- The journey log must be signed and returned to the DVM within one month of the movement having been completed.
- A copy of the journey log must be retained by the carrier for at least three years.

Animals differ in their needs and their welfare requirements and the rules relating to feeding, watering and rest also differ. For example:

- Horses can only be transported for a maximum of 24 hours on a single journey, but must have food at least every eight hours and be given water at timed intervals.
- Pigs can also be transported for 24 hours but must have constant access to water throughout the transit time.
- Cattle and sheep (and goats) can only be transported for a maximum of 14 hours on a single journey before being given feed, water and being rested for at least one hour. After this one hour rest, they may be transported for another 14 hours.

Phytosanitary issues

Today, plant diseases cost governments many millions of pounds and, in an attempt to reduce these bills, regulations known as phytosanitary regulations have been introduced. Basically, they require drivers to produce phytosanitary certificates at non-EU national borders when the vehicle is carrying plants and plant products.

These certificates guarantee that the plants have been inspected before departure and found to be free from disease, infestation or any pests. These requirements are sometimes required for items such as wooden pallets, wood-based packaging and wood shavings, all of which are difficult to sterilize and may need to be fumigated or treated in some way before the journey, in order for a certificate (issued by the Forestry Commission) to be issued.

Key points you need to know

- UK perishable food carriage rules.
- ATP vehicle marking and testing requirements.
- ATP distances (sea).
- Waste carriage, licensing and records.
- EU waste requirements.
- Livestock general requirements.
- Livestock movements under and over eight hours.
- Phytosanitary issues.

Notes

....
....
....
....
....

....

....

....

....

....

Self-test example questions

OCR-type questions (multi-choice)

1 Which of the following formulae can be used to calculate the load on the front axle of a loaded rigid goods vehicle and what would the weight on the front axle be if the vehicle load weighed 6 tonnes, the vehicle had a wheelbase of 7 m and the centre of gravity of the load is 2.5 m from the rear axle?

a $\dfrac{P \times D}{W}$ and 2.14 tonnes respectively (working to 2 decimal points).

b $\dfrac{L \times W}{W}$ and 2.12 tonnes respectively (working to 2 decimal points).

c $\dfrac{W \times P}{D}$ and 2.10 tonnes respectively (working to 2 decimal points).

d $\dfrac{L \times D}{W}$ and 2.08 tonnes respectively (working to 2 decimal points).

2 Which of the following lists are the three formats used for UK type approval of vehicles and to what groups, or types, of vehicles do they apply?

a

- UK Vehicle Type Approval (UKVTA) used by manufacturers selling vehicles throughout the EU.

- National Series Type Approval (NSTA) used for small numbers of vehicles produced within the UK.

- Unique Vehicle Approval (UVA), where each individual vehicle needs to be examined and approved.

b

- European Community Vehicle Type Approval (ECVTA) used by manufacturers selling vehicles throughout the EU.
- International Small Series Type Approval (ISSTA) used for small numbers of vehicles produced within the UK.
- Single Vehicle Approval (SVA), where each individual vehicle needs to be examined and approved.

c

- European Community Whole Vehicle Type Approval (ECWVTA) used by manufacturers selling vehicles throughout the EU.
- National Small Series Type Approval (NSSTA) used for small numbers of vehicles produced within the UK.
- Individual Vehicle Approval (IVA), where each individual vehicle needs to be examined and approved.

d

- European Community Single Vehicle Type Approval (ECSVTA) used by manufacturers selling vehicles throughout the EU.
- National Major Series Type Approval (NMSTA) used for small numbers of vehicles produced within the UK.
- International and UK Single Vehicle Approval (IUKSVA), where each individual vehicle needs to be examined and approved.

3 When a DVSA vehicle examiner wishes to enter an operator's premises there are certain rules relating to the notice that must be given and the circumstances leading to the purpose of the visit. These include:

a DVSA vehicle examiners are allowed, with the owner's consent, to enter premises at any time, day or night. However, if permission is not given at the time, they must give notice of their intentions to return within 24 hours. This stated time requirement does not have to be met if the vehicle has been involved in, or is believed to have been involved in, an accident.

b DVSA vehicle examiners are allowed, with the owner's consent, to enter premises at any reasonable time. However, if permission is not given at the time, they must give notice of their intentions to return, either verbally, giving 48 hours' notice, or by recorded delivery, giving 72 hours' notice. These stated time requirements do not have to be met if the vehicle has been involved in, or is believed to have been involved in, an accident.

c DVSA vehicle examiners are allowed, with or without the owner's consent, to enter premises at any reasonable time to inspect any vehicles on the premises. However, if access is not made available or not possible, they may seek an injunction entitling them to immediate access and serve the injunction accordingly. These stated time requirements do not have to be met if the vehicle has been involved in, or is believed to have been involved in, an accident.

d DVSA vehicle examiners are not allowed to enter operational premises at any time unless accompanied by a police officer in uniform. However, if no search warrant has been issued they are entitled to have a warrant drawn up and return within 48 hours of the initial visit, or seek a court injunction, which must be served within 24 hours to enable them to enter the premises. These stated time requirements do not have to be met if the vehicle has been involved in, or is believed to have been involved in, an accident.

4 Which of the lists below contain two advantages of systems of contracting out maintenance and two disadvantages of systems of in-house maintenance?

a Advantages of contracted-out maintenance include:

- Time and costs associated with health and safety compliance.

- Easier maintenance cost planning.

Disadvantages of systems of in-house maintenance include:

- Cost of the facility and facility upkeep.

- No facility costs.

b Advantages of contracted-out maintenance include:

- Possible 'dealer' expertise.

- Costs of stocking spare parts of stocked spares.

Disadvantages of systems of in-house maintenance include:

- Cost of the facility and facility upkeep.

- Possible warranty requirements.

c Advantages of contracted-out maintenance include:

- 24/7 facilities are often available.

- Costs of stocking spare parts of stocked spares.

Disadvantages of systems of in-house maintenance include:

- Staff costs, including overtime, and weekend payments and training costs.

- Easier maintenance cost planning.

d Advantages of contracted-out maintenance include:

- No facility costs.

- Easier maintenance cost planning.

Disadvantages of systems of in-house maintenance include:

- Cost of facility equipment.

- Time and costs associated with health and safety compliance.

5 Which of the following most accurately describes the DVSA principles in relation to load security?

a The DVSA guide uses the principles that: the vehicle must never be overloaded; the vehicle must be loaded safely; the strongest securing method must be used; and there must be 'total' load restraint.

b The DVSA guide uses the principles that: the vehicle must be roadworthy; the driver must be properly trained; the securing method used must be 'adequate'; and there must be 'sufficient' load restraint.

c The DVSA guide uses the principles that: the vehicle must be fit for purpose; the vehicle must be loaded correctly; the most appropriate securing method must be used; and there must be 'adequate' load restraint.

d The DVSA guide uses the principles that: the vehicle must be 'appropriate'; the vehicle must be of the correct type and design; the securing method used must be type approved; and there must be 'certified anchor points' for load restraint devices.

6 The rules state that vehicles and trailers used for the carriage of perishable foodstuffs under the ATP must undergo which of the following requirements?

a They must undergo initial certification, which will be authorized for ATP operations for six years. After the first six-year period the vehicle or trailer will become subject to examinations and certification every three years.

b They must undergo initial certification, which will be authorized for ATP operations for five years. After the first five-year period the vehicle or trailer will become subject to examinations and certification every three years.

c They must undergo initial certification, which will be authorized for ATP operations for three years. After the first three-year period the vehicle or trailer will become subject to examinations and certification every 12 months.

d They must undergo initial certification, which will be authorized for ATP operations for two years. After the first two-year period the vehicle or trailer will become subject to examinations and certification every 12 months.

CILT-type questions (short answer)

1 Calculate the following:

a Give the formula used to calculate the axle weight on the front axle of a goods vehicle.

b Calculate the load on the front axle of a vehicle if you have a 6-tonne load on a rigid vehicle with a wheelbase of 7 m and the centre of gravity of the load is 2.5 m from the rear axle.

2 Briefly explain the three different formats of type approval available for UK vehicles and the circumstances where each format would be applied.

3 Briefly discuss the rules relating to DVSA vehicle inspectors seeking to gain access to a vehicle operator's operating centre.

4 Identify two advantages of systems of contracting out vehicle maintenance and two disadvantages of in-house vehicle maintenance.

5 The DVSA Load Security Guide uses four principles. What are they?

6 Briefly explain the rules in relation to the initial certification and subsequent certification of vehicles and trailers used for ATP operations.

CILT-type question (long answer)

Discuss the certification, examination and inspection criteria that apply to goods vehicles, trailers and equipment used to move dangerous goods under the ADR. Include in your answer details of the equipment, including firefighting equipment, required to be carried in/on the vehicle or trailer and the associated load documentation and its purpose and content.

Road safety

08

This chapter looks at many road safety issues including driver licensing, driver training, vehicle checking, road signage, road procedures, road accidents, security and the EU road network.

Specifically the syllabus requires that you should:

- know what qualifications are required for drivers (such as driving licence, medical certificates and certificates of fitness);

- be able to take the necessary steps to ensure that drivers comply with the traffic rules, prohibitions and restrictions in force in different member states (speed limits, priorities, waiting and parking restrictions, use of lights, road signs);

- be able to draw up instructions for drivers to check their compliance with the safety requirements concerning the condition of the vehicles, their equipment and cargo, and concerning preventive measures to be taken;

- be able to lay down procedures to be followed in the event of an accident and to implement appropriate procedures to prevent the recurrence of accidents or serious traffic offences;

- be able to implement procedures to properly secure goods and be familiar with the corresponding techniques;

- have elementary knowledge of the layout of the road network, including tunnels and ferry crossings in the member states.

In order to follow the sequence of the syllabus, we begin with driver licensing.

Driver licensing

There are some general rules that apply to driver licensing and actions to be taken by employers. These include:

- checking driving licences when first employing drivers;
- carrying out regular* checks of licences.

---

* The Senior Traffic Commissioner recommends that licences are checked, ideally, every three months or, in any case, every six months in order to ensure that the driver is still entitled to drive the vehicles they are required to drive. Where checks are done every three months they can be a random 50 per cent sample providing that all licences are checked every six months.

These checks were relatively easy in the days of the paper counterpart driving licences, as endorsements and offences were written there for all to see. However, since the abolition of the paper counterpart, the records of all endorsements and offences are held by the DVLA. This means that checking needs to be done in one of several ways, including:

- By a driver using the free View Driving Licence service at www.gov. uk/view-driving-licence and following the links. The links also allow the driver to share the information by obtaining a 'code' which may be used by an employer to also access the information.
- Using the DVLA's online 'Share Driving Licence Service' where the DVLA issues a code number that is valid for 21 days and which enables employers and drivers to check licence details, or share them.
- Using a DVLA telephone line, which requires the driver to call first to give permission for the employer to be given the details required.
- Finally, there is the DVLA Access to Driver Data (ADD) service, which is a B2B facility allowing employers to access live licence data relating to their employees providing that the employee agrees.

Drivers wishing to check their own driving licence details may also contact the DVLA by post. Employers may also use the post but must use a form D888/1 filled out by the driver to give permission for the check.

For non-UK driver checks there are different arrangements, for instance:

- The employer can call the DVLA Contact Centre by telephone with the driver being present and the details can be supplied at the time.
- The driver can contact the DVLA Contact Centre by telephone and give permission for the licence details to be released within seven days of the call being made.

Note 1: EU nationals are able to drive whatever categories of vehicles they have on their EU driving licences as all EU member states recognize the categories of other member states. (Drivers from Switzerland are also allowed to drive in the UK but must exchange their Swiss licence for an equivalent UK licence within 12 months.)

Note 2: Non-EU nationals are not entitled to drive any vehicles other than Category B (up to 3,500 kg GVW) and this entitlement is only valid for 12 months. After this time they must have gained a UK licence if they wish to continue to drive.

Note 3: The TCs have the power to take action against vocational drivers, up to and including suspension or revocation of the vocational categories. They cannot, as yet, suspend or revoke Category B (car) entitlement.

We now look at the requirements in relation to gaining vocational driving licences, which are classed as Categories C1, C1E, C and CE for goods vehicle drivers. A full explanation of the various driving licence categories is given below.

Driving licence categories and criteria

- Car, car-derived van and small goods vehicles:
  - Category B: vehicles not exceeding 3,500 kg GVW and vehicles with up to eight passenger seats.
  - Minimum age of driver: 17 years.
- Medium-sized goods vehicles:
  - Category C1: vehicles not exceeding 7,500 kg GVW towing trailers not exceeding 750 kg GVW.
  - Minimum age of driver: 18 years.
- Medium-sized goods vehicles:*
  - Category C1E: medium-sized goods vehicle not exceeding 7,500 kg GVW and trailer exceeding 750 kg GVW up to a maximum gross train weight (GTW) of 12,000 kg.
  - Minimum age of driver: 21 years.**
- Large rigid goods vehicles:
  - Category C: large rigid goods vehicle exceeding 7,500 kg GVW towing trailers not exceeding 750 kg GVW.
  - Minimum age of driver: 21 years.**
- Large goods vehicles towing trailers exceeding 750 kg GVW:

- Category CE: combinations of large goods vehicles towing trailers exceeding 750 kg GVW.
- Minimum age of driver: 21 years.**

---

* Young drivers may drive Category C1E vehicles with a Restricted C1E licence at the age of 18 providing that the combined weight of the vehicle and trailer combination does not exceed 7,500 kg.

** Young drivers may drive heavy goods vehicles (Category C, CE) from the age of 18 if they are:
- learning, or being trained to drive Category C or CE vehicles;
- learning or being trained to pass the Initial Driver CPC qualification (see below).

Note 1: There are some restrictions and also some concessions that apply to vocational driving licences such as:

- Restriction 107: restricting Category C1 drivers to driving vehicle combinations not exceeding 8,250 kg GTW.
- Restriction 103: restricted subject to the issue of a DCPC.
- Restriction 102: restricting Category CE drivers to driving draw bars only and not articulated combinations.
- Restriction 101: restricted to NOT driving for hire and reward.
- Restriction 106:[†] restricting all vocational drivers to driving vehicles with automatic gearboxes.

[†] Restriction 106 is a restriction that only applies to drivers who took their vocational driving test before 10 April 2014. It can now be removed providing that the driver concerned can prove that they passed their Category B (car) test in a manual vehicle.

Note 2: Drivers with Category C licences can currently drive solo tractor units, although this is expected to change some time in the near future.

Note 3: When checking the licences of foreign drivers from other EU countries a Restriction 69 may be found. This means that the driver has been convicted of a drink-drive offence and must have a breathalyser test before they can drive the vehicle on the public road.

First application for a vocational driving licence

The applicant must send the following to the DVLA in Swansea:

- current car licence (Category B);
- photocard application form D750;
- application form D2;
- medical form D4 (signed by a GP);
- driver CPC examination pass certificate (see below).

Note 1: Subsequent upgrades, perhaps from C to CE, will require the provisional vocational licence and the driving test pass certificate to be sent.

Note 2: Once acquired, if a driving licence cannot be produced at the time of request, it must be produced in person within seven days at a nominated police station.

Medical requirements

Again, car drivers and vocational drivers are treated differently. Car drivers are referred to as Group One drivers who simply need to declare any existing medical conditions when applying for a licence. Relevant conditions cover such things as epilepsy, Parkinson's disease, multiple sclerosis, brain tumours, strokes and other serious conditions.

Vocational drivers are referred to as Group Two drivers and these drivers need to have a medical examination, signed off by a doctor using a form D4, which is only valid for a period of four months from the date of the medical examination. In addition, the conditions that need to be declared by Group One drivers also need to be declared by Group Two drivers, and additional conditions or time limits apply. These include:

- visual problems;
- heart defects or heart operation;
- insulin-dependent diabetes;
- any hypoglycaemic event in the previous 12 months;
- epileptic attacks within the last 10 years;
- obstructive sleep apnoea syndrome (OSAS);
- any symptoms of stroke that last longer than one month.

Note 1: In June 2016, the DVLA announced that LGV drivers with non-insulin treated diabetes still need to inform the DVLA if they have suffered any of the below:

- 2 episodes of severe hypoglycaemia (help needed from another person) within the last 12 months;
- developed impaired awareness of hypoglycaemia;
- experienced any visual problems.

In addition, if a driver is taking insulin to treat their diabetes, they need to have:

- 3 months of continuous blood glucose readings available on a memory meter every time they apply for a licence;

- test their blood glucose no more than 2 hours before the start of their first journey and every 2 hours through the day;
- test their blood glucose and record their readings at least twice a day even when not driving.

DVLA has also announced that because most insulin-treated vocational (Group Two) drivers need to renew their licences every 12 months there is now a three year cycle for these renewals. As outlined below:

- First application or Year One – Self declaration, GP examination and independent diabetologist examination;
- Year Two – Self declaration and independent diabetologist examination;
- Year Three – Self declaration, GP examination and independent diabetologist examination.

Should a vocational licence be revoked due to medical issues, drivers can reapply to the DVLA but extensive checks will need to be made involving both the driver and the driver's GP.

Note 2: In addition to the medical declarations that drivers need to make, they must also disclose any convictions for vehicle overloading, vehicle condition or drivers' hours or records offences, which will need to be considered by the TCs as part of the overall application process. Should the application fail, the TCs' decision can be challenged by an appeal to a Magistrates' Court in England and Wales, or Sheriff Court in Scotland.

Driving tests and Driver Certificate of Professional Competence (DCPC)

The whole process of gaining a vocational driving licence also includes the need for drivers, who are not exempted and applying for a vocational licence for the first time, to pass an initial Driver Certificate of Professional Competence (DCPC) examination before they sit their vocational driving test.

The entire training programme consists of four separate modules:

- Module 1 parts a) and b): Theory and Hazard Perception Test, consisting of 100 multiple-choice theory questions (85 pass mark) and 19 hazard video clips (100 marks with 67 pass mark). Once this has been passed the physical driving test must be taken within a period of two years.

- Module 2: Initial Driver CPC Case Studies.
- Module 3: Practical Driving Test.*
- Module 4: Driver CPC Practical Test.

---

* Instruction for the practical test can only be provided by a person who has held that category of licence for at least three years. In addition, whilst under instruction to gain a vocational driving licence, learners may drive on motorways.

Once all modules have been completed, the driver will be issued with the vocational driving licence and a Driver Qualification Card (DQC) that is valid for five years. The DQC must be produced upon request and needs to be carried by the driver at all times when driving professionally if they are to avoid the risk of a fixed penalty fine.

Once the initial DQC has been issued, the driver becomes subject to periodic DCPC training that requires every vocational driver (unless exempt) to undergo 35 hours of training every five years.

This training is overseen by a body known as the Joint Approvals Unit for Periodic Training (JAUPT), based in Milton Keynes. JAUPT approves training providers, training courses and training deliverers. They also carry out on-site ad hoc audits at training delivery venues and set pre-arranged office audits at training providers' premises.

Note 1: There is no pass or fail element to the training, merely recorded attendance.

Note 2: The training sessions must normally be of at least seven hours' duration. (However, a course of seven hours may be split into two 3.5-hour parts, provided that the second part starts within 24 hours of completion of the first part.)

Test vehicles

All vehicles (post-2003) used for vocational driving tests must be fitted with an operational tachograph, ABS braking systems and a seat and seatbelt for use by the examiner.

Specifically, vehicles used for vocational driving tests must be of a certain specification. Some must also carry a minimum load as follows:

- Category C1:
  - a box body vehicle of at least 4,000 kg GVW;
  - a length of at least 5 m;
  - capable of a speed of at least 80 km per hour (kph);
  - no load requirements.

- Category C1E
  - a box body vehicle of at least 4,000 kg GVW;
  - capable of a speed of at least 80 kph;
  - a box body trailer of at least 2,000 kg GVW;
  - a combined length of at least 8 m;
  - loaded with 600 kg of bagged aggregate or one IBC** of that weight.

- Category C
  - a rigid goods box body vehicle of at least 12,000 kg GVW;
  - at least 8 m long but no longer than 12 m;
  - at least 2.4 m wide;
  - capable of a speed of at least 80 kph;
  - with either an automatic or manual gearbox;*
  - loaded with a minimum of 10,000 kg in 5 × 1,000-litre IBCs.**

- Category CE either:
  - any articulated vehicle of at least 20,000 kg GVW;
  - a box body semi-trailer;
  - at least 14 m long but no longer than 16.5 m;
  - at least 2.4 m wide;
  - capable of a speed of at least 80 kph;
  - with either an automatic or manual gearbox;*
  - loaded with a minimum of 15,000 kg in 8 × 1,000-litre IBCs.**

- or
  - a drawbar combination of at least 20,000 kg GVW;
  - both vehicle and trailer of box body design;
  - at least 14 m long but no longer than 18.75 m;
  - at least 2.4 m wide;
  - capable of a speed of at least 80 kph;
  - with either an automatic or manual gearbox;*

– with the prime mover loaded with a minimum of 10,000 kg in
5 × 1,000-litre IBCs** and the trailer loaded with a minimum of
5,000 kg in 3 × 1,000-litre IBCs.**

---

* The need for eight forward gears is no longer required. This allows the test to be taken in
either a manual or automatic vehicle and, providing the driver already has a manual entitlement for a car or lorry, they will be granted a full 'manual' entitlement, with or without
trailers (category B, BE, C, CE, C1, and C1E).

** IBCs are palletized intermediate bulk containers used to carry liquids. For test purposes the
IBCs must be filled with water to reach the required weights.

Renewals

Whilst Category B licences expire when the driver reaches the age of 70, vocational entitlements usually require renewal every five years. However, the
rules do vary depending upon the year the licence was originally granted.
The rules are as follows:

- Drivers acquiring their vocational licence before 19 January
  2013 have a licence valid until the age of 45. At 45 they will
  need a medical (using form D4) every five years to renew the
  licence and at age 65 the medical will need to be done
  annually.

- If an existing driver (pre-19 January 2013) renews their licence by
  supplying a new photograph, they will be issued with a new five-year
  licence.

- Vocational drivers over the age of 45 will need to supply a new
  photograph every 10 years (every other renewal).

- All vocational licences issued after 19 January 2013 are valid for five
  years.

- Drivers under the age of 45 passing their test after 13 January 2013
  will need to provide a self-declaration of fitness to drive at every
  five-year renewal up to the age of 45 and provide a new photograph
  every 10 years.

International driving permits

International driving permits (IDPs) are required by drivers who transit or
visit countries that do not recognize the standard UK/EU licence. These
countries include:

- most Middle Eastern states;
- Russia;
- Ukraine.

IDPs are valid for a period of 12 months and can be obtained from post offices, the AA, the RAC or Green Flag. The IDP is basically a small card with a photograph of the driver, endorsed by one of the issuing organizations.

Key points you need to know

- Licence check procedures and how to contact the DVLA.
- Licence categories, age limits and restrictions.
- Application procedure.
- Medical requirements.
- Driver CPC and training.
- Driving test vehicle specification and loads.
- Renewal periods and medical requirements.
- IDP applications, requirements and validity.

Notes

....
....
....
....
....
....
....
....
....

Whilst driver training and testing are statutory requirements we must also accept that once we have a licence, we need to keep within the law. Because of that fact, we will now look at road traffic rules and requirements in the UK and abroad.

UK traffic rules

In the UK, the 'rules of the road' are clearly published in the Highway Code. In addition, we already know that there are other rules relating to compliance covering such things as weight limits, drivers' hours, drivers' records and special rules for specific areas and so it is important that we have a good understanding of the main thrust of regulatory compliance. That said, we are again going to be looking at many factual figures and data and so in your examinations these areas will be largely examined by short-answer questions.

Let's begin with national speed limits on de-restricted roads where the national speed limits apply.

Speed limits (UK)

- Cars, car-derived vans and dual-purpose vehicles:*

single carriageway	dual carriageway	motorway
60 mph	70 mph	70 mph

* A dual-purpose vehicle is a vehicle with an unladen weight of less than 2,040 kg, able to carry both passengers and goods, which is fitted with a solid roof. Typically, these include estate cars, most 4×4s and some 'people carriers'.

- Small goods vehicles up to 3,500 kg GVW:*

single carriageway	dual carriageway	motorway
50 mph	60 mph	70 mph

- Medium-sized goods vehicles exceeding 3,500 kg GVW but not exceeding 7,500 kg GVW:*

single carriageway	dual carriageway	motorway
50 mph	60 mph	70 mph

* In effect this means that 3.5-tonne 'Transit'-type vans are subject to the same speed limits as 7.5-tonne vehicles.

- Cars and car-derived vans, small goods vehicles and medium-sized goods vehicles with trailers:

single carriageway	dual carriageway	motorway
50 mph	60 mph	60 mph

- Large goods vehicles, exceeding 7,500 kg GVW:

single carriageway	dual carriageway	motorway
50 mph*	60 mph*	60 mph*

---

* To date these limits only apply in England and Wales. The limits on single carriageways and dual carriageways in Scotland are 40 mph and 50 mph respectively.

Abnormal indivisible loads:

- Special Types General Order (STGO) Category 1 (50,000 kg GVW):

single carriageway	dual carriageway	motorway
40 mph	50 mph	60 mph

- Special Types General Order (STGO) Category 2 (80,000 kg GVW):

single carriageway	dual carriageway	motorway
30 mph	35 mph	40 mph

- Special Types General Order (STGO) Category 3 (150,000 kg GVW):

single carriageway	dual carriageway	motorway
30 mph	35 mph	40 mph

Note 1: Any type of vehicle towing a trailer cannot exceed 60 mph on a motorway. This also means that they cannot use the overtaking lane of a three-lane motorway.

Note 2: Speed limiters are set lower than 60 mph but there is no requirement to retro-fit speed limiters to older vehicles and so the 60 mph limit remains in force.

Note 3: The limits referred to apply to unrestricted (or de-restricted) roads. These are roads where street lamps (lampposts) are not present.

Clearly, most drivers are aware of the speed limits but, in recent years we have seen 'variable speed limits', 'average speed limits' and 20 mph speed limits introduced, as well as electronic detection, and so drivers need to take care that they comply at all times.

Non-compliance usually leads to a fixed penalty notice being issued and, where this is the case, the penalty must be paid within 28 days unless the driver elects to take the matter to court.

In addition, a fixed penalty is usually accompanied by the issue of three, or six, penalty points on the driver's licence and, as the Traffic Commissioners have the power to act against vocational licence holders, this can be a serious issue for a professional driver.

Height limits (UK)

There is no statutory height limit for vehicles in the UK. However:

- Bridges that are unmarked will have a height of at least 5.03 m.
- Electrical cables should be at least 5.79 m above the surface of the road.

Parking (UK)

For the purpose of the syllabus, we will look at motorways, clearways, yellow lines, pedestrian crossings, red routes, bus lanes and night-time parking.

Motorways and clearways

Vehicles are not allowed to park on motorways except on the hard shoulder, in cases of emergency or, in the case of goods vehicles, when directed to do so by the police, especially in relation to 'Operation Stack' on the M20 in Kent.

Because there are different types of clearways we need to consider each type in turn:

- Rural clearways, with or without a hard shoulder, have the same no-parking rules as motorways.
- Urban clearways also have no-parking rules at peak travel times but may allow temporary 'pick up and set down'.

Yellow lines

Yellow lines in line with the kerb mean that some sort of parking restrictions are in place. Two continuous yellow lines mean that there is no parking or waiting at any time of the day or night. One continuous yellow line means that there is no parking or waiting at set times; drivers need to check the accompanying notice plate to determine the actual restrictions.

Note: Lines at right angles to the kerb relate to loading and unloading restrictions, not parking.

Pedestrian crossings

In respect of pedestrian crossings, pedestrian zebra and pelican crossings and toucan crossings (where pedestrians and cyclists may all cross) are all bounded by zigzag markings. These zigzag markings indicate a no-parking area although vehicles may have to stop within these boundaries to allow people to cross.

Red routes

Red routes are major roads leading into and out of London and some primary routes in the West Midlands, where either a single red line or double red lines are painted in line with the kerb. In the same way as yellow lines, the double red lines apply to no parking at any time whilst a single red line will allow some relaxation at certain times.

Note 1: A similar system operates in Edinburgh where the road surface is green – these are known as 'greenways'.

Note 2: Red route clearways have clearly identifiable parking bays at set points that allow parking for short periods. White-coloured bays allow parking at any time whilst red-coloured bays only allow parking at set times.

Other issues

Other no-parking areas include bus lanes (and bus gates) although some relaxation may be made for essential deliveries where permission is given by a police officer or traffic warden.

In addition, the DfT recently announced that drivers of larger vehicles caught using mobile phones will now get a fine of £200 and 6 penalty points and that there is no opportunity to take any re-training instead of receiving these penalties.

The Highway Code also instructs that it is an offence to park in dangerous positions such as the brows of hills, on 'hump back' bridges and at road junctions; it should also be noted that if an accident is deemed to have been caused by the presence of a vehicle, the driver can be prosecuted whether or not he/she was actually in the vehicle at the time the accident happened.

Overnight parking

Parking at night is also an area where different rules apply, for example:

- Car-derived vans and small goods vehicles not exceeding 2,500 kg GVW may park on a road at night without lights if:
  - it is parked facing the direction of traffic;
  - it is parked parallel to the kerb;
  - it is more than 10 m away from any road junction;
  - the road is a restricted road (for example 30 mph).
- Goods vehicles exceeding 2,500 kg GVW parked on a road at night must have two white sidelights showing to the front and two red lights showing to the rear.

Note: This rule also applies to goods vehicles parked overnight in lay-bys unless the lay-by is physically separate from the main carriageway.

London Congestion Charging and Lorry Control Scheme

In relation to the London Congestion Charge:

- It operates from 7 am to 6 pm Monday to Friday.
- Failure to pay results in a Fixed Penalty Notice being issued to the registered keeper.
- The fine must be paid within 28 days.
- Vehicles with three or more outstanding penalty charges will be clamped or removed if detected.

The London Lorry Control Scheme is slightly different insofar that:

- It requires some operators to have a permit to enter most London boroughs during off-peak times.
- It requires operators to maximize use of the M25 and not to 'rat run' through the city.
- It requires set routes using major roads to be used to enter the city.
- It operates from:

– 9 pm to 7 am, Monday to Friday;

– 1 pm Saturday to 7 am Monday;

– all day Sunday.

Having covered what we need in relation to rules within the UK, we must now look at the situation in Europe.

European rules

We will again begin with speed limits for large goods vehicles. Throughout Europe all countries have a speed limit of 50 kph in built-up areas and this limit is generally rigidly enforced. However, speed limits on single carriageways, dual carriageways and motorways do vary:

- Single carriageways are generally subject to an 80 kph speed limit except for:
  - Luxembourg, where it is 75 kph;
  - Austria, Belarus, Bulgaria, Denmark, Greece, Hungary, Italy Lithuania, Poland and Slovenia, where it is 70 kph;
  - Belgium, France and Germany, where it is 60 kph.
- Dual carriageways are generally also subject to an 80 kph speed limit except for:
  - The UK, where it is 95 kph;
  - Belgium and Romania, where it is 90 kph;
  - Luxembourg, where it is 75 kph;
  - Austria, Belarus, Bulgaria, Denmark, Greece, Hungary, Italy and Slovenia, where it is 70 kph;
  - Germany, where it is 60 kph.
- Motorways are also generally subject to an 80 kph speed limit except for:
  - Romania, where it is 110 kph;
  - Bulgaria, where it is 100 kph;
  - The UK, where it is 95 kph;
  - Belarus, Belgium, Croatia, France, Lithuania, Luxembourg, Portugal and Spain, where it is 90 kph (Note: For draw bars in Spain the limit is 80 kph);
  - Greece and Slovenia, where it is 70 kph.

Specific European country regulations

The lists below include a sample of specific rules in some European countries and include rules relating to carrying and displaying warning triangles, in the case of a breakdown, in countries where rules relating to this apply:

Austria

- All foreign drivers must also be able to provide proof that their earnings are at least equivalent to the rate of the Austrian minimum wage when carrying out cabotage operations.
- Reflective jacket required by driver.
- Overtaking bans on some sections of road.
- Dangerous goods restrictions in some road tunnels.
- Winter tyres and/or snow chains compulsory on some roads during winter.
- Snow chains not permitted to be used in tunnels.
- Tyre tread depth varies with UK.
- A warning triangle is to be set 50 m to the rear of the vehicle, at least 1 m from the kerb and visible for 200 m.

Belgium

- All changes of direction to be indicated.
- No U-turns allowed.
- Rush-hour overtaking bans.
- Dangerous goods restrictions in some road tunnels.
- Exit from roundabouts must be indicated.
- Parking restrictions in built-up areas.
- Restricted use of cruise control.
- Studded tyres only allowed at certain times.
- Tyre tread depth varies with UK.
- A warning triangle is to be set 30 m to the rear of the vehicle on ordinary roads, 100 m to the rear of the vehicle on motorways.

Bulgaria

- Temporary vehicle prohibitions.
- Snow chains compulsory on some roads at certain times.
- A warning triangle is to be set 30 m to the rear of the vehicle.

Croatia

- Speed restrictions when raining and when roads are wet.
- Driving with headlights is obligatory during winter months.
- Snow chains or winter tyres compulsory at certain times.
- A warning triangle is required but vehicles with trailers need to carry two.

Czech Republic

- Dipped headlights compulsory at all times except during summer.
- A warning triangle is required.
- Snow chains compulsory at certain times.
- Studded tyres prohibited.
- Tyre tread depth varies with UK.

Denmark

- Dipped headlights compulsory at all times.
- Overtaking bans at certain times on some roads.
- Local vehicle prohibitions in some towns, cities and regions.
- Spare set of light bulbs must be carried.
- A warning triangle is required.

Finland

- Dipped headlights compulsory at all times.
- A maximum 200 l of diesel to be imported duty-free.
- Snow chains compulsory at certain times.
- Tyre tread depth varies with UK.
- A warning triangle is to be set 50 m to the rear of the vehicle and needs to be visible for 110 m.

France

- A minimum speed of 80 kph applies in the left-hand (overtaking) lane on motorways.
- Seasonal and weekend lorry bans.
- All changes of direction must be indicated.

- Spare set of light bulbs to be carried.
- Form VE103 required.
- Snow chains compulsory at certain times.
- Studded tyres generally banned.
- Possible fines for belly-tank fuel.
- Radar detection devices illegal.
- Safe distances must be set between moving vehicles.
- In poor weather conditions, the maximum speed limit on all roads is reduced to 50 kph (this may be increased to 80 kph if conditions improve).
- Drivers banned from using any earpiece capable of emitting sound.
- France is also pursuing a 'minimum wage' requirement in the same way as Germany (see below).
- A warning triangle is to be set 30 m to the rear of the vehicle and needs to be visible for 100 m.
- All foreign drivers must also be able to provide proof that their earnings are at least equivalent to the rate of the French minimum wage.

Note: Two disposable breathalysers also need to be carried on vehicles operating in France, although fines for not carrying them have not been enforced.

Germany

- All foreign drivers delivering or collecting from inside Germany currently require proof of payment at least to a level of the German minimum wage.
- Intention to leave roundabouts must be indicated.
- Drivers need to carry spare glasses or contact lenses.
- Snow chains compulsory at certain times.
- First-aid kit required.
- Spiked tyres prohibited.
- Amber flashing lights to be carried in case of breakdown.
- Tyre tread depth varies with UK.

- In poor weather conditions when visibility is reduced to less than 50 m, there is a maximum speed limit of 50 kph and overtaking is prohibited.
- A warning triangle needs to be set 100 m to the rear of the vehicle on ordinary roads, 250 m to the rear of the vehicle on motorways.

Greece

- Seasonal lorry bans on holiday routes.
- First-aid kit required.
- Fire extinguisher required.
- Use of the horn forbidden in towns except in an emergency.
- Tyre tread depth varies with UK.
- A warning triangle is to be set 55 m to the rear of the vehicle.

Hungary

- A special licence must be obtained from Budapest in order to transport dangerous goods.
- Dipped headlights required at all times.
- Goods vehicles must drive in inside lane unless overtaking.
- Intention to leave roundabouts must be indicated.
- Snow chains compulsory at certain times but must not be used on dry roads.
- A warning triangle is required.
- Tyre tread depth varies with UK.

Italy

- Additional fees and escorts required for some dangerous goods carried through some tunnels in Italy.
- Headlights to be used in tunnels and on motorways.
- Some overtaking bans in certain areas.
- Drivers and crew must wear reflective waistcoat when leaving the vehicle outside of built-up areas.
- Snow chains need to be carried during the winter and to be available, if required.
- Tyre tread depth varies with UK.

- In poor weather conditions with a visibility limit of less than 100 m, a maximum speed limit of 50 kph applies on all roads.
- It is mandatory for two facing vehicles turning left to turn in front of each other (rather than passing and turning behind).
- A warning triangle is to be set 50 m to the rear of the vehicle and needs to be visible for 100 m.

Note: On some alpine routes, vehicles must give way to post buses that have priority over all other traffic; where this applies the route is marked with signs showing a post horn.

Latvia

- Dipped headlights are required at all times between 1 October and 1 April.
- Vehicles must maintain certain distance requirements on some bridges.

Luxembourg

- Vehicle prohibitions and seasonal, weekend and night-time lorry bans.
- Vehicles under movement bans must not park on public roads.
- Designated transit routes to be followed.
- Restrictions on use of cruise control systems.
- Dipped headlights required at all times.
- Tyre tread depth varies with UK.
- A warning triangle is to be set 30 m to the rear of the vehicle.

Netherlands

- Tyre tread depth varies with UK.
- A warning triangle must be set 30 m to the rear of the vehicle, and needs to be visible for 250 m.
- The authorities will, if required, contact a driver's employer to prove that the driver is being paid at a rate at least equivalent to the Netherlands minimum wage rate.

Norway

- Dipped headlights required at all times.
- Tyre tread depth varies with UK at certain times of year and in certain areas.
- Snow chains compulsory at certain times.

- 600 l of diesel only to be imported.
- A warning triangle is required.

Poland

- Dipped headlights required at all times.
- Studded tyres are forbidden.
- Snow chains compulsory when indicated.
- A warning triangle is required.

Portugal

- Vehicles carrying dangerous goods must use dipped headlights at all times.
- Dipped headlights required in tunnels.
- First-aid kit required.
- Snow chains compulsory at certain times.
- Tyre tread depth varies with UK.
- Drivers and crew must wear 'hi-viz' jacket or tabard when leaving the vehicle outside of built-up areas.
- A warning triangle must be set 30 m to the rear of the vehicle and needs to be visible for 100 m.

Romania

- Dipped headlights required in tunnels, rain, fog and snow.
- Snow chains compulsory at certain times.
- Tyre tread depth varies with UK.
- Authorizations required for the carriage of waste.
- Radar detection devices illegal.
- A warning triangle is required.

Slovakia

- Dipped headlights required 15 October to 15 March.
- Limited seasonal, weekend and night-time lorry bans.
- Snow chains compulsory at certain times.
- A warning triangle is required.

Slovenia

- Dipped headlights required at all times.
- Seasonal, weekend and night-time lorry bans.
- Snow chains or winter tyres compulsory from 15 November to 15 March.
- Tyre tread depth varies with UK.
- It is an offence to pass a school bus that has stopped to pick up or drop off schoolchildren.
- A warning triangle is required but vehicles with trailers need to carry two.

Spain

- Dipped headlights required in tunnels.
- Two fire extinguishers required.
- Spare set of light bulbs to be carried.
- Spare spectacles or contact lenses to be carried.
- Tyre tread depth varies with UK.
- Drivers and crew must wear 'hi-viz' jacket or tabard when leaving a broken-down vehicle.
- Two warning triangles are required on some routes, where one is placed 50 m to the front of the vehicle and one is placed 50 m to the rear of the vehicle (other, minor routes only require one warning triangle to be set to the rear of the vehicle).

Sweden

- Dipped headlights required at all times.
- Spare set of bulbs required.
- Seasonal and weekend lorry bans.
- Tyre tread depth varies with UK.

Switzerland

- Spare set of bulbs required.
- Snow chains required, as indicated.
- Tyre tread depth varies with UK.
- A warning triangle is to be set 50 m to the rear of the vehicle on ordinary roads, 100 m to the rear of the vehicle on motorways.

As stated above, these lists are only included as samples of some of the complexity when operating goods vehicles in Europe.

European road signs

We have already mentioned road signs in Italy where a post horn is used as a sign that drivers must give way to post buses but, for syllabus purposes, you also need to know about other signs used in Europe, where an offence will be deemed to have been committed for any non-compliance, including:

- Signs in Luxembourg stating 'Transit France' or 'Transit Germany' that are posted on the authorized transit routes for drivers driving goods vehicles exceeding 3,500 kg GVW who are transiting the country and not delivering or collecting from within the country.
- Yellow diamond signs with a broad white border that are used to indicate who has priority.
- The same yellow-and-white sign with a black diagonal line through it to indicate the priority no longer applies.
- A sign of a red flame inside a red circle, used in France to indicate that vehicles carrying highly flammable goods are prohibited.
- Signs bearing the words 'Barrière de Dégel' used on minor routes in France, during periods of thawing snow, to prohibit large goods vehicles from using that route.

Whilst these four examples are relevant to the syllabus, drivers driving abroad will frequently encounter signs, rules and regulations that will be unfamiliar to them and they should try to clarify the situation as soon as possible.

Key points you need to know

- UK speed limits and categories of vehicles.
- AIL speed limits.
- Parking, red routes, congestion charging.
- European differences with UK.
- Specific European signs.

Note: As stated, because of the need to learn facts and figures in relation to these subjects, the related questions will be 'short questions'.

Notes

....

....

....

....

....

....

....

....

....

....

It is a fact that many prosecutions result from vehicles being in an unroadworthy or poor mechanical state, and so now we examine the daily vehicle checks that need to be carried out by drivers. We did look at these briefly earlier in the book but the syllabus requires that we now examine them in more detail so that you are able to 'instruct drivers' accordingly.

Drivers' daily ('first use') checks

This is another area where you will benefit from having your DVSA Guide to Maintaining Roadworthiness with you for the examination, as it clearly identifies all the items that drivers need to check.

Earlier in the book we examined what drivers need to check on a vehicle when they first take it over, including such things as:

- lights, mirrors and glass (including lens covers);
- tyre tread depth (1 mm for vehicles over 3,500 kg GVW; 1.6 mm for vehicles under 3,500 kg GVW;
- wheel fastenings;
- fluid levels;

- windscreen washer and wiper operation;
- any leaks;
- damage and body condition;
- seat-belt operation;
- audible warnings;
- load security;
- a whole host of additional items depending upon the type of vehicle concerned.

As the syllabus requires you to 'instruct drivers' in vehicle checks you need to use the Guide to Maintaining Roadworthiness to identify the checks needed and you need to ensure that your instruction sheet has a header that provides details of:

- the vehicle registration or fleet number;
- the make and model of the vehicle;
- the odometer reading;
- any trailer number, if applicable;
- the driver's name;
- the date.

In addition, there needs to be boxes to record:

- 'nil defects' against each item and also at the bottom of the sheet (where a driver would normally sign);
- a space for the driver to give a brief description of the defect;
- a brief explanation of where the driver needs to hand in the defect report;
- a space for the fitter to provide their name and the date of rectification.

Finally, please note that if the examination question asks you to send a draft sheet, in a report, to your transport manager (TM) or managing director (MD), you should write a top header to make the answer look like some sort of report by including:

- what the report is about (drivers' daily checks);
- who it is from (ie you);
- who it is to (ie TM or MD);
- the date.

Those four items as an initial part of your answer will be awarded marks, so please read the question carefully.

Having completed first-use checks and defect reporting we now look at road traffic accidents.

Road traffic accidents/collisions

Today, the term road traffic accident (RTA) is often replaced by road traffic collision or road traffic incident in an attempt not to apportion blame. However, there is no definition of either of these two phrases and so we will use road traffic accident, of which there is a statutory definition – a road traffic accident is said to occur when:

- any person other than the driver is injured;
- damage is caused to another vehicle;
- damage is caused to property on or next to the road;
- injury is caused to a domestic animal (mule, ass, dog, horse, cattle, goat, sheep and pig).

Because there is a statutory definition, there are also statutory actions that must be taken. These include:

- After a road traffic accident the drivers must stop.
- Drivers must provide details of the vehicle registration number, their name and address and the name and address of the vehicle owner/operator if requested to do so by any person with reasonable grounds for requiring that information.
- If the driver is not able to exchange details as required, the accident must be reported to the police as 'soon as is reasonably practicable' and in any case within 24 hours.
- If any person is injured the driver must produce a certificate of insurance for the vehicle concerned. If the insurance certificate is not immediately available, it must be produced at a police station within seven days.

Note 1: The main charges relating to RTAs are failing to stop and failing to report an accident.

Note 2: In cases where accidents involve large vehicles, where the driver may be unaware of the accident, the prosecuting council, in order for the prosecution to succeed, must be able to prove that the driver knew an accident had taken place and, with that knowledge, did not stop.

Actions to be taken in the event of an RTA

- Drivers should take care of anyone in danger or in need of medical assistance, providing they can do this without causing further injury.
- The technique known as DR-ABC (danger-response-airway-breathing-circulation or compressions) should be used on anyone seriously injured, if required.
- Drivers must not admit any degree of liability for the accident.
- Drivers need to exchange details with the other driver and/or any person with reasonable grounds' for requiring details.
- Drivers should try to get witness details as soon as possible, before witnesses leave the scene.
- Drivers should record details of the accident and try to take pictures, make notes or draw diagrams, to record such things as the positions of vehicles, skid marks and road layout, if possible.
- Drivers must comply with instructions or orders from the emergency services.

Within the next few days drivers will need to fill out some form of report relating to what happened. In this report they will usually be asked to draw a detailed sketch with approximate distances entered on it and record items such as:

- damage to the vehicles;
- injuries to any persons;
- vehicle speed at the time;
- speed of the other vehicle(s) at the time;
- signals given by any vehicles involved;
- weather conditions at the time;
- state of the road surface at the location;
- positions of any road signs or road markings at the location;
- traffic volume at the time;
- witness details obtained at the time.

Following accidents many organizations expect the driver concerned to undertake a 'driving assessment', which may include defensive driving techniques and safe driving practices. The organization concerned may also fit vehicles with forward-facing cameras.

Many insurance providers now supply two-part accident forms where summary details of accidents and vehicle, driver, operator and insurance details can be recorded and one copy given to the other driver. This is also the case in Europe where a European Accident Statement (EAS) is usually provided by insurance companies.

The EAS, which is a model, self-duplicating form, as mentioned above, provides a common method for drivers to record the information that their insurance company will require and to endorse the facts with a signature.

Note: If planning to travel abroad please check your insurance is valid and, if 'self-insured', please note that European cover will only be up to the basic level of 'third party' cover and additional cover may need to be taken out.

Please also note that many EU countries have laid down standard procedures for actions to be taken in the event of an RTA. These actions typically include:

- switching off the engine;
- preventing further injury;
- preventing fire;
- notifying the emergency services and obtaining and exchanging information with the other party.

Security of goods

We need to appreciate that 'security' can refer to the safety of the load in relation to it being secured in or on the vehicle; security of the load against pilferage or theft; and security of the load against the elements. We will try to cover all these areas as we go along.

The vehicle

Certainly, box-body vehicles and 'tilt' trailers, as well as being acceptable for TIR movements, offer better all-round security, but some have vulnerable fibreglass roofs (aimed at reducing weight), whilst others have different doors or shutters, or may lack sufficient internal load-securing points for part loads. All these issues need to be considered against the goods to be carried and the route to be taken.

The driver

Many cases of 'lost' or stolen goods involve the driver being complicit in some way. It is absolutely vital that we can trust the driver, irrespective of whether they are employees, agency drivers or subcontractors, and checks may need to be made.

The drivers also need to be briefed in security measures that should be taken in relation to things such as the operation of alarms and immobilizers, overnight parking, stopping for breaks, possible bogus officials, hitchhikers, breakdown procedures, contact procedures, route variations and not talking to others about loads being carried.

The load documentation

Drivers need to be able to check the load against the load documentation, whenever possible, to ensure that what is on the vehicle is what is being declared on the accompanying paperwork. This is often difficult if a vehicle is sealed, but there may be an opportunity for this type of check as the vehicle is being unloaded in order to prevent any bogus claims of 'shortages' or 'damages'.

The route

As mentioned above, the route taken needs to avoid danger areas and 'danger times' and regular runs should consider using varying routes so that the vehicle is not in the same place, at the same time, every day or week.

Routes in Europe may be somewhat more vulnerable to criminal activity than many routes solely located in the UK, although advice on 'high risk' areas can be obtained from the trade associations and perhaps even other operators who are familiar with the route to be taken.

As we can see, security involves many aspects of movements, including constant vigilance whilst the goods are in transit.

We are now approaching the end of the syllabus requirements. However, we still need to cover the planning of international journeys and the EU road network, which we look at below.

Planning international journeys

Planning journeys in advance of departure is absolutely vital when we need to move vehicles and goods abroad. We already know that different countries have lorry bans and lorry restrictions at different times of the week and year, and that there are restrictions on many types of goods being moved and routes that may be taken.

What we also need to plan for are things such as scheduling times, connecting with ferries and arrival times at delivery points if we are to avoid lost time and poor utilization of our vehicles and drivers.

Additional factors, such as drivers' hours regulations, speed limits, weight restrictions, tolls, fuelling points, breakdown services and available fleet support whilst abroad also need to be considered. Further to this we may need to make plans in relation to carrying consumable spares and driver supplies, foreign currency, as well as possibly needing to plan for items such as driver passport validity, DQC and tacho-card validity, letters of attestation, visa requirements, permits, or even getting the vehicle headlight beams reset, as well as any other items where there may be the potential for delays caused by problems with the authorities.

In spite of a whole range of planning requirements we must, most importantly, ensure that we plan (and normally book in advance) for the vehicle to use the most appropriate cross-channel, or other, ferry link. In addition, we must allow time for paperwork at the ports and appreciate that driving within UK port areas is now classed as 'driving' for EU drivers' hours purposes.

Before we look at the main ferry services available to UK-based operators, we need to understand that the Channel Tunnel link from Ashford (which has a limited customs facility) to Sangatte is a major cross-channel link that does not depend upon weather or sea conditions, and that some ferry services do not operate all the year round but are dependent upon the volumes of goods to be moved.

Below is a summary of some of the main ro-ro ferry options and ports available (although not necessarily available for 12 months every year) for UK operators moving goods between the UK, Ireland and Europe.

UK Port	Destination
Cairnryan	Belfast, Larne (Northern Ireland)
Dover	Calais (France)
Fishguard	Rosslare (Ireland)
Harwich	Esjberg (Denmark), Hook of Holland
Holyhead	Dún Laoghaire, Dublin (Ireland)

Hull	Rotterdam, Zeebrugge (Netherlands)
Immingham	Gothenburg (Sweden)
Liverpool	Belfast (Northern Ireland)
Newcastle	Bergen (Norway), Gothenburg (Sweden), Stavanger (Norway)
Newhaven	Dieppe (France)
Pembroke Dock	Rosslare (Ireland)
Plymouth	Roscoff (France), Santander (Spain)
Poole	Cherbourg (France), Santander (Spain)
Portsmouth	Caen, Cherbourg, Le Havre, St Malo (all France), Bilbao (Spain)

Note: These 'sample' services are not exhaustive but they are a picture of some of the services available to operators and, whilst it may seem expensive and time-consuming to use a ferry from Plymouth to Santander, it may allow the driver to take a reduced weekly rest in-transit, instead of the vehicle needing to be parked and not moving.

Our final subject is the European road network, known as the 'E' road network.

European road network

The 'Accord européen sur les grandes routes de trafic international', a UNECE agreement known as the AGR agreement, specifies main routes throughout Europe, which are deemed to be of 'strategic' importance to the effective movement of both goods and people.

The agreement sets the standards of construction for these roads and identifies them with common signage. Note that in the UK, although we have 'E' roads as part of the AGR agreement, we do not mark them separately in the same way as do mainland European countries.

The stated advantage of using common signage is that it makes it easier for drivers to follow these principal routes. Accordingly, signs are coloured green and white and use an 'E' prefix before the number of the road. For main roads, the numbering begins at E1, with a second digit that is an even number for east–west routes and an odd number for north–south routes. For example: E12 is an east–west route from Mo i Rana in Norway, across Sweden to Helsinki in Finland, whilst the E11 begins in Vierzon and ends in Montpellier.

In these examples, the E12 crosses borders but the E11 is wholly within France. It should also be noted that, in addition to crossing borders, these routes stretch out of Europe into Central Asia. This is simply because the AGR agreement is a UNECE agreement and countries such as Uzbekistan and Kyrgyzstan are UNECE signatory members. The sign pictured in Figure 8.1 relates to the E40, which is the longest E route, stretching some 8,000 kilometres from France to Kazakhstan. Main roads have two digits but minor routes, albeit still strategically important, have three digits, such as the E201 in southern Ireland.

When using these E routes we also need to consider the most suitable border crossing points on these routes, and the syllabus requires that you have some knowledge of the principal border crossing points where natural barriers (such as water or mountains) exist. In addition to the Channel Tunnel link from the UK, this means that you also need to be aware of points such as:

- the Mont Blanc Tunnel between France and Italy;
- the Fréjus Tunnel between France and Italy;
- the Somport Tunnel between France and Spain;
- the Øresund link (bridge and tunnel between Sweden and Denmark).

These final points conclude the requirements of the syllabus and, as you can see, much of the content where facts are listed will mean that these topics will be mostly subject to short questions and answers in the examinations.

FIGURE 8.1 E40 signage

Key points you need to know

- How to construct a driver's daily check sheet and the items that must be included on a driver's daily check sheet.
- The considerations to be made in relation to the security of goods.
- Journey-planning considerations.
- Ferry services.
- AGR markings and numbering system.
- Principal border barrier points.

Notes

....

....

....

....

....

....

....

Self-test example questions

OCR-type questions (multi-choice)

1 In addition to ADD, which of the following are three of the main methods that can be used to check the vocational driving licence entitlements of an EU vocational driver?

   a The three ways include: contacting the DVLA's Data Subject Enquiry Department at Swansea for a printout of the licence details; using the DVLA's online 'Share Driving Licence Service' where the DVLA issues a code number that is valid for 21 days; or using a DVLA telephone line, which requires the driver to call first to give permission for the employer to be given the details required.

b The three ways include: contacting the DVLA's Vocational Driver Enquiry Department at Swansea for a printout of the licence details; using the DVLA's online 'Vocational Driving Licence Service' where the DVLA issues a smart card; or using a DVLA telephone line, which requires the employer to call first to verify employment details.

c The three ways include: contacting the DVLA's Protected Data Enquiry Department at Swansea for a printout of the licence details; using the DVLA's online 'Employer Driving Licence Service' where the DVLA issues a password that is valid for 28 days; or using a DVLA telephone line, which requires the driver to call and obtain the details to give to their employer.

d The three ways include: contacting the DVLA's Personnel Enquiry Department at Swansea for a printout of the licence details; using the DVLA's online 'Driving Licence Information Service' where the DVLA registers the employer and issues a reference number that is valid for 12 months; or using an automatic DVLA telephone line, which takes the caller's details and then enables a telephone call handler to call back with the details.

2 Why would a driver need to apply for an international driving permit (IDP)? Where can they be obtained and how long are they valid?

a IDPs are required by drivers who transit or visit countries that do not recognize the standard UK/EU licence. These are Azerbaijan, Egypt, Morocco, Russia, Syria and the Ukraine. IDPs can be obtained from the International Road Freight Office (IRFO) and are valid for a single trip.

b IDPs are required by drivers who transit or visit countries that do not recognize the standard UK/EU licence. These are Belarus, Georgia, Iraq, Russia and the Ukraine. IDPs can be obtained from post offices, the AA, the RAC or Green Flag and are valid for three years.

c IDPs are required by drivers who transit or visit countries that do not recognize the standard UK/EU licence. These are most Middle Eastern states, Russia and the Ukraine. IDPs can be obtained from post offices, the AA, the RAC or Green Flag and are valid for 12 months.

d IDPs are required by drivers who transit or visit countries that do not recognize the standard UK/EU licence. These are Albania, Kosovo,

Russia, Turkey and the Ukraine. IDPs can be obtained from the DVLA and are valid for five years.

3 i) Car-derived vans and small goods vehicles not exceeding 2,500 kg GVW may park on a road at night without lights providing it is parked facing the direction of traffic, it is parked parallel to the kerb, it is more than 10 m away from any road junction and if the road is a restricted road (for example 30 mph). ii) Goods vehicles exceeding 2,500 kg GVW parked on a road at night must have two white sidelights showing to the front and two red lights showing to the rear. These statements are:

a (i) false (ii) false;

b (i) true (ii) true;

c (i) false (ii) true;

d (i) true (ii) false.

4 In what country would you encounter a road sign with a red flame inside a red circle and a road sign bearing the words 'Barrières de Dégel' and what do these signs indicate?

a The country is Switzerland and the sign of a red flame inside a red circle is used to indicate that vehicles carrying highly flammable goods are prohibited; signs bearing the words 'Barrières de Dégel' are used on high roads in the winter to indicate that the road has been closed due to high snow falls or icy conditions.

b The country is Austria and the sign of a red flame inside a red circle is used to indicate that vehicles carrying highly flammable goods are prohibited; signs bearing the words 'Barrières de Dégel' are used on toll routes to indicate that toll booths with barriers are in operation ahead.

c The country is Belgium and the sign of a red flame inside a red circle is used to indicate that vehicles carrying highly flammable goods are prohibited; signs bearing the words 'Barrières de Dégel' are used on major motorway routes to prohibit all goods vehicles from using that route.

d The country is France and the sign of a red flame inside a red circle is used to indicate that vehicles carrying highly flammable goods are prohibited; signs bearing the words 'Barrières de Dégel' are used on minor routes during periods of thawing snow, to prohibit large goods vehicles from using that route.

5 Which of the following lists are all statutory actions that drivers must take in the event of a road traffic accident in the UK where no one is actually injured?

a The drivers must stop. Drivers must provide details of the vehicle insurers, their driving licence, name and address and the name and address of the vehicle owner/operator if requested to do so by any person with reasonable grounds for requiring that information. If the driver is not able to exchange details as required, the accident must be reported to the police as 'soon as is reasonably practicable' and in any case within 12 hours.

b The drivers must stop. Drivers must provide details of the vehicle registration number, their name and address and the name and address of the vehicle owner/operator if requested to do so by any person with reasonable grounds for requiring that information. If the driver is not able to exchange details as required, the accident must be reported to the police as 'soon as is reasonably practicable' and in any case within 24 hours.

c The drivers must stop. Drivers must provide details of the vehicle damage, a contact telephone number, their name and address and the name and address of the vehicle owner/operator if requested to do so by any person with reasonable grounds for requiring that information. If the driver is not able to exchange details as required, the accident must be reported to the police as 'soon as is reasonably practicable' and in any case within 36 hours.

d The drivers must stop. Drivers must provide details of the vehicle registration number, their name and address and the name and address of the vehicle owner/operator if requested to do so by any person who claims to be a witness. If the driver is not able to exchange details as required, the accident must be reported to the police as 'soon as is reasonably practicable' and in any case within 48 hours.

6 Which of the following explanations most accurately describes the AGR system of road marking?

a The AGR system consists of signs that are coloured red and white and use an 'E' prefix before the number of the road. For main roads, the numbering begins at E10, with a third digit that is an even number for east–west routes and an odd number for north–south routes. Minor AGR routes have only two digits.

b The AGR system consists of signs that are coloured black and white and use an 'E' prefix before the number of the road. For main roads, the numbering begins at E3, with a second digit that is an odd number for east–west routes and an even number for north–south routes. Minor AGR routes have the same numbers of digits.

c The AGR system consists of signs that are coloured green and white and use an 'E' prefix before the number of the road. For main roads, the numbering begins at E1, with a second digit that is an even number for east–west routes and an odd number for north–south routes. Minor AGR routes have three digits.

d The AGR system consists of signs that are coloured blue and white and use an 'E' prefix before the number of the road. For main roads, the numbering begins at E2, with a second digit that is an odd number for east–west routes and an even number for north–south routes. Minor AGR routes have smaller digits.

CILT-type questions (short answer)

1 In addition to ADD, briefly discuss the other three methods that can be used to contact the DVLA in order to check the vocational driving entitlements of an EU vocational driver.

2 Briefly explain why a driver would need an international driving permit (IDP), where IDPs can be obtained and their validity.

3 Outline the different requirements for parking on a road at night for goods vehicles not exceeding 2,500 kg GVW and goods vehicles exceeding 2,500 kg GVW.

4 Explain what a sign of a red flame inside a red circle indicates and what the words 'Barrière de Dégel' are used for – and the country where these could be posted.

5 Outline the statutory actions that drivers must take in the case of a road traffic accident in the UK where no one is actually injured.

6 Briefly explain the AGR system of road numbering.

CILT-type question (long answer)

Explain the procedures for first applying for a vocational driving licence, the driving test, issue of the licence and DQC, the specification of a test vehicle for a Category C licence and the criteria to be met and rules to be observed when renewing a vocational driving licence.

It has to be accepted that this is an extensive syllabus that requires you to have knowledge of the subject areas but also to be able to apply that knowledge, as you would be expected to as a transport manager. Good luck with your studies and for any future progression and studies that we hope may be triggered by this insight into the road freight transport industry.

Note: As a final note, it is hoped that you can see the importance of obtaining all the guides referred to in the notes, because they are vital for both study and for use in the examinations themselves.

ANSWERS TO SELF-TEST QUESTIONS

The answers below are only guides to demonstrate the 'types' of answers that will be expected in the examinations. You will also note that the answers do not run in sequence with the notes. This is because the different multi-choice and short-answer questions appear on different examination papers. For example, Paper One of the CILT examinations covers Chapters 1, 2, 5 and 6 whilst Paper Two covers Chapters 3, 4, 7 and 8. This pattern is also reflected in the OCR multi-choice examinations.

You will also note that there are different numbers of multi-choice and short-answer questions relating to each chapter. This is because the numbers of questions relate to each unit you will expect to find on each examination paper. In addition, because of the nature of the OCR case studies, in that they vary for each examination, it is better for the reader to download past case studies from the OCR website, where they are free to download. If this is not an option then please note that the CILT long questions are certainly of the right structure to act as examples of typical OCR case-study questions.

Because of these facts we will put the questions below in line with the papers in which they will be found, and in the approximate numbers that will form each paper.

Paper One

Civil law answers (three questions)

OCR multi-choice answers

1 = A, B and C

2 = C

3 = D

CILT short answers

1 The groups who do not have the capacity to enter into legally binding business contracts include people under the age of 18, people of unsound mind and people under the influence of alcohol or drugs so that they simply do not know what they are doing.

2 The 'reservations box' on a CMR note is for the receiving driver to note any reservations he/she may have about the load, such as any damage, or if they were unable to check the load upon taking it over, or any other uncertainties relating to the consignment in question.

3 Clearing houses are organizations that act to provide operators with customers who need goods moving. In principle, clearing houses act as a point of contact between those requiring transport and those able to provide it. Groupage operators provide the means for customers with less than full loads, or even individual items, to move their goods as cost-effectively as possible by pulling together 'grouped' loads of smaller consignments into larger unit loads.

CILT long answer

1 First, there must be an initial offer made by an offeror to an offeree. The offer needs to be specific and have at least some outline terms.

2 Second, providing that the initial offer is not withdrawn at this stage, the next component of a contract is acceptance. All the offeree needs to do to accept is to give a positive (affirmative) response to the offer made from the offeror. It is vital that acceptance is relayed to the offeror or there is no acceptance. However, it must be noted that acceptance is deemed to have been made once any letter, signed form or other document enters the postal system, whether or not it has been delivered.

3 The third component is termed 'consideration'. Consideration is required if a contract is to be deemed legally binding and is based upon a common law principle that only transactions and bargaining can be supported in law, not simple promises. In short this means that both parties need to gain, or lose, something by forming a contract.

4 The fourth component is 'capacity'. Capacity relates to the ability of a person to enter into a legally binding contract. This means that contracts cannot be deemed legal if any person attempting to form a business contract is either under 18 years of age, of unsound mind or under the influence of alcohol or drugs so that they simply do not know what they are doing.

5 The next component is 'intention'. There must be an intention, by all the parties concerned, to form a legally binding relationship. It is not allowed to 'hoodwink', or fool someone into forming a contract if they never intended to do so.

6 The next required component is that every contract must in itself be legal. If a contract is related to any unlawful act or breaking the law then it would not be deemed to be legally binding.

7 Our last required component is 'formalities'. This means that, if the contract specifies specific terms, conditions or instructions, then any deviation from those requests that were itemized in the contract would break the terms of the contract because these 'formalities' had not been observed.

Commercial law answers (two questions)

OCR multi-choice answers

1 = D

2 = A

CILT short answers

1 The main disbenefits include: that the sole trader cannot limit their liability and if they go bankrupt they can lose everything; sole traders need to work to earn and so sickness and holidays can prove costly and long-term illness may force closure. In cases where the sole trader may need to hire someone to cover for them, or employ someone to help, some existing customers may resent the 'new face' or feel that they have been relegated to a poorer standard of service.

2 A company voluntary arrangement (CVA) is an arrangement, brokered by an insolvency practitioner, to pay creditors who are owed a minimum of 75 per cent of the total debts of a company over an agreed fixed period of time. Once the creditors have met and

agreed to the CVA the company is classed as 'solvent' and can carry on trading providing it makes the payments to the insolvency practitioner, as agreed.

CILT long answer

Company auditors are appointed at the AGM by a vote held by the shareholders. The company auditor has a duty to provide an independent report to inform the shareholders of the true financial position of the company. The auditor actually has a duty to the shareholders, and not to the directors or the company itself, to carry out this task. In cases where the company is a plc or a private limited company with a turnover exceeding £6.5 million, as well as having to produce an independent report the auditor must also be totally independent from the company concerned.

A company secretary is not needed in a private limited company but all plcs must have a company secretary whose duties include:

- ensuring that, at all times, the company is able to meet the requirements of all legislation, including the Companies Act;
- compiling and maintaining all company registers;
- organizing all company meetings and keeping records of the minutes;
- ensuring that the records of meetings and any resolutions passed are available for inspection at the company's registered office;
- ensuring that the records of meetings and any resolutions passed are retained for 10 years.

In the cases of plcs only, the company secretary must also:

- be suitably qualified in an appropriate profession (such as being an accountant, a barrister, a solicitor or chartered secretary); or
- be able to demonstrate sufficient prior experience as a company secretary.

Ordinary shares are the type of shares that are usually held by ordinary shareholders. They not only give the shareholder the right to vote at the AGM but they also offer the chance of a dividend. The dividend payable will normally be related to a percentage of the total profit of the company. Should a loss be reported the ordinary shareholder may get nothing at all. Preference shares are seen as a 'lower risk' option for shareholders. Preference shares pay out a fixed dividend irrespective of the level of profit of the company. However, like ordinary shares, there may be no dividend if the company fails to make any profit and a loss is reported. Because there is less risk, providing some sort of profit is reported, preference share-holders usually have no voting rights at the AGM.

Business and financial management of the undertaking answers (five questions)

OCR multi-choice answers

1 = B

2 = C

3 = D

4 = D

5 = A

CILT short answers

1 Working capital is calculated as current assets minus current liabilities and capital employed is calculated as the fixed assets plus the working capital. It can also be described as the fixed and current assets minus the current liabilities.

2 Whilst the P&L is an important management tool it does have the limitation that it is all historic information. This means that many organizations produce P&Ls for their own management purposes, several times a year in order to be made aware of any unplanned changes and to enable them to take any remedial action much quicker.

3 Direct costs are drivers' wages, fuel, vehicle maintenance and tyres; indirect costs are directors' salaries, advertising, rent, and heating and light.

4 The four Ps determine the marketing strategy of a product because:

- The 'product' needs to be suitable and appropriate for the intended market.
- The 'price' needs to reflect the product's quality and characteristics.
- The 'place' of sale needs to be suitable for the product.
- The way the product is 'promoted' needs to attract suitable buyers.

5 DAT helps buyers and sellers using containerized consignments. It is the seller who pays for the carriage to a nominated terminal at the place of destination, except for any costs related to import clearance. It is also the seller who assumes all risks for loss or damage right up to the point that the goods are unloaded at the named terminal at the port or place of destination.

CILT long answer

Costs:

Driver's costs = 2 × £75.00 plus 1 × £30.00 = £180.00.

Fuel costs = 1,860/3 = 620 L @ £1.05 per litre = £651.00.

Tyre costs = £0.04 × 1,860 = £ 74.40.

Maintenance costs = £0.05 × 1,860 = £ 93.00.

Ferry costs = £20.50 × 16.50 m = £338.25.

Tolls, etc = £265.00.

Total costs in GBP = £1,601.65.

Plus profit @ 12 per cent = £ 192.20.

Cost plus profit = £1,793.85.

Cost plus profit per pallet = £1,793.85/26 = £68.99.

Cost plus profit per pallet in euros = £68.99 × £1.35 = €93.14 per pallet.

Note: In the OCR case study and the CILT long questions there will always be a finance question. These usually relate to cash flow, budgeting, P&L accounts, balance sheets or costings.

Access to the market answers (10 questions)

OCR multi-choice answers

1 = B

2 = D

3 = D

4 = A

5 = C

6 = D

7 = C

8 = B

9 = A

10 = D

CILT short answers

1 Should there be issues about the environmental 'suitability' of the proposed operating centre, the Traffic Commissioners request the completion of form GV79E, which is used to provide additional environmental information.

2 The main difference between the two forms of objection/representation is that whilst statutory objectors have 28 days following the publication of the decision in A and D to appeal against the decision, environmental representors have no direct right of appeal and are only able to combine with the statutory objectors as part of their appeal.

3

a The actual operator's licence is referred to as form OL1.

b The vehicle discs are form OL2 and need to display:

– the name of the operating person or company;

– the operator licence holder's reference number;

– the expiry date of the licence;

– the type of licence;

– the vehicle registration number.

4 Schedule 4 is a system that enables an existing operator who takes over another operator's business in the same traffic area to take it over without the need to advertise in a local newspaper, providing that there are no material changes to the licence other than the change of ownership. Schedule 4 can also be used where the trading status of the licence holder changes but, again, there are no material changes, as in cases where a sole trader forms a limited company.

5 All the forms relate to making major changes of the 'O' licence. Form GV79A is the fleet/vehicle list, which will need to be submitted for amending when additional vehicles are permitted to be added to the licence. Form GV80A is used to request a change to the type of 'O' licence and form GV81 is used to apply for a new operating centre, or centres, and for requesting to add additional vehicles in excess of the margin.

6

  a The scores represent both roadside 'traffic' enforcement, covering such things as drivers' hours, overloading and similar issues; and 'roadworthiness', covering items such as annual tests and depot inspections.

  b An operator with a traffic score of over 30 points and a roadworthiness score over 25 points will normally go into the Red Band.

7 Curtailment is when the Traffic Commissioners either reduce the number of operating centres on a licence or reduce the number of vehicles on a licence because the operator concerned has shown they are unable to comply with a fleet or operation of a certain size. They can also revoke licences, suspend licences, attach conditions to licences and take actions against vocational drivers.

8 First, there is a 'driver nationality attestation', which is used by drivers who are not EU nationals to state that they are lawfully employed by an EU operator. Second, there is a 'Letter of Attestation (Activities)', used to explain why all the normally required tachograph records are not available for examination by the authorities.

9 The customs use NCTS to create a movement reference number (MRN) for each separate movement of goods. This number will need to be quoted at the customs office of departure for customs to provide a Transit Accompanying Document (TAD) that will be generated by the office of departure and that will accompany the goods.

10 All permit applications need to be made to the International Road Freight Office (IRFO) in Cambridge, at least five working days before intended use. First-time applicants also need to submit a copy of their 'O' licence with the initial application. When a multilateral permit becomes time expired (12 months, January to December), or a bilateral permit has been used, the operator must return the permit to the IRFO within 15 days.

CILT long answer

Should you require an operator's licence ('O' licence) all applications must be made to the DVSA Central Licensing Office (CLO) in Leeds, using a form GV79, which must be submitted at least nine weeks before you want the licence to commence. Applicants must advertise that they intend to open an operating centre and the advertisement must appear in a newspaper that is available in the area of the proposed operating centre. The full page of the newspaper containing the advertisement must be sent to the CLO with GV79.

As there are three types of 'O' licence, the type of licence you wish to apply for also determines the criteria that need to be met. General criteria include the fact that any person applying for any type of 'O' licence has to be a 'fit and proper person'. To meet this criteria every applicant must declare any previous convictions within the last five years that relate to vehicles and vehicle operation. Every applicant must have a suitable 'operating centre'. This is defined as a place where the vehicle, or vehicles, will usually be kept, and it must be large enough to hold all the vehicles concerned and have safe access and egress. The centre must also be suitable in relation to the environment. In deciding this, the Traffic Commissioners will consider the following:

- the nature and use of land in the vicinity of the operating centre and the effect that granting the application would be likely to have on the environment;

- the extent to which granting a licence, which will materially change the use of an existing (or previously used) operating centre, will harm the environment in the vicinity;

- in cases where land has not previously been used as an operating centre, any planning application or planning permission relating to the operating centre or the land in the vicinity;

- the number type and size of the authorized vehicles that will use the centre;

- the parking arrangements for the authorized vehicles that will use the operating centre;

- the nature and times of use of the operating centre;

- the nature and times of use of any equipment at the operating centre;

- the number and frequency of vehicles that would be entering and leaving the operating centre.

Applicants must demonstrate to the Traffic Commissioner that they will maintain their vehicles correctly. In order to do that they must:

- declare who is to maintain the vehicles and, if it is an external maintenance provider, submit a maintenance contract;

- submit samples of the forms to be used for both vehicle safety inspections and for drivers' daily checks and defect reporting;

- declare the proposed periods between planned safety inspections;
- demonstrate that they have a planning system for all vehicle safety inspections that can show planned inspection for a minimum period of six months in advance;
- declare they will retain all the vehicle maintenance records for a minimum period of 15 months.

There are, however, additional criteria to be met when applying for a standard operator's licence. For instance, the applicant for any standard licence must be able to prove to the Traffic Commissioners that they have sufficient 'financial standing' to operate any proposed fleet of vehicles. In order to do this they must demonstrate that they have, or can have, access to a figure of €9,000 for the first vehicle and €5,000 for each subsequent vehicle authorized. This is higher than for a restricted licence. Applicants must also declare any, and all, previous bankruptcy or financial failures.

Applicants for standard licences also need to demonstrate that they are not only 'fit and proper', as defined above, but that they also have 'good repute'. To ascertain whether or not this is so the Traffic Commissioners will look at any 'relevant' (criminal) unspent convictions that either resulted in a fine more than £2,500 or 60 hours of community service (or equivalent), or any more serious offences.

Applicants for standard licences must nominate a person who is deemed to be 'professionally competent' in road freight operations. In addition, this person must be able to prove that they have 'effective control' of the fleet.

Finally, all standard licence applicants, or their nominated professionally competent person, must sign a legal undertaking declaring that they, and any staff employed by the company, will comply with the following:

- laws relating to the driving and operation of the vehicles being used;
- drivers' hours and records regulations;
- regulations to prevent overloading;
- speed limits;
- vehicle condition safety requirements;
- defect reporting and rectification requirements;
- the requirement to retain maintenance records for 15 months;
- operating-centre vehicle authorization limits;
- notifying the TC of any convictions against themselves, or the company, business partner(s), the company directors or any nominated transport manager/s named in the application, or employees or agents of the applicant for a licence;

- ensure that the TC is notified within 28 days of any other notifiable changes;
- declaring that they have a UK address where all documentation can be found and that they have access to at least one UK registered vehicle.

Chapters 1, 2, 5 and 6 that comprise Paper One are now complete and we can go on to look at the remaining chapters and subjects that make up Paper Two.

Paper Two

Social law answers (four questions)

OCR multi-choice answers

1 = C

2 = B

3 = B

4 = D

CILT short answers

1

a A prohibition notice will be issued if an HSE inspector has reason to believe that whatever activities are being carried out may result in either a serious danger to health or a serious risk of injury.

b Improvement notices are issued by HSE inspectors to correct situations where they can clearly see that some sort of lesser breach of the regulations is occurring, and is likely to continue to occur.

2

Step 1: the employer must send a written statement outlining the reason for the intended action and invite the employee to attend a meeting, where the employee is able to be represented, so that matters can be discussed.

Step 2: following the meeting the employee must be told of any decision made by the employer, before any disciplinary action can actually begin.

Step 3: the employee must be permitted to have the right to appeal the decision made.

3 The three business circumstances include: where a business no longer carries out the type of work or business the employee was employed for; where the business no longer carries out business in the place or location where the employee is employed; and where a business no longer requires the employee to carry out a particular type of work.

4 Where a driver's card is lost the driver may drive without the card for a maximum of 15 calendar days, providing that he/she produces two printouts – one at the start of the journey/daily duty and another at the end. Both printouts must be marked with the driver's name or driver card or licence number and signature, and manual entries made need to show periods of other work, availability and rest or break. The driver must also report the problem to the DVLA and apply for a new card within seven calendar days of the loss.

CILT long answer (also to be used by OCR candidates)

Time	Activity	Notes
0	Start Work	
06.00 – 06.15	Check Vehicle	
06.15	Depart Manchester	
06.15 – 10.45	Drive to Dover	4.5 hrs
10.45 – 11.30	Break	
11.30 – 13.45	Drive to Dover	2.25 hrs = 6.75 hrs (540/80)
13.45 – 14.15	POA waiting for Ferry	(Known departure time)
14.15 – 14.30	Embarkation	15 mins driving
14.30 – 16.00	Ferry Crossing (POA)	
16.00 – 16.15	Disembarkation	15 mins driving
Switch to UTC+1		
17.15 – 19.00	Driving to Paris	1.75 hrs = 4.5 hrs
19.00 – 19.45	Break	
19.45 – 20.45	Driving to Paris	1 hr drive = 10 hrs driving

(Continued)

(*Continued*)

Time	Activity	Notes
20.45 – 05.45	Reduced Daily Rest	
05.45 – 06.00	Start Work – Daily Check	
06.00 – 06.45	Drive to Paris	45 min = 3.25 hrs Cal–Paris
06.45 – 09.45	Unloading	3 hrs
09.45 – 11.45	Driving to Marseille	2 hrs driving
11.45 – 12.00	15 min RTD/EU break	6 hrs duty (split EU break)
12.00 – 14.30	Driving to Marseille	2.5 hrs (4.5 hrs)
14.30 – 15.00	Break	2nd part of EU split break
15.00 – 19.30	Driving to Marseille	4.5 hrs
19.30 – 20.15	Break	
20.15 – 20.45	Driving to Marseille	15 hrs duty and 2nd EU extended driving period (9.5)
20.45 – 05.45	2nd Reduced Daily Rest	9 hrs
05.45 – 06.00	Start work– Daily Check	
06.00 – 08.30	Drive to Marseille	2.5 hrs = 12 hrs
08.30 – 11.30	Unloading in Marseille	3 hrs
11.30 – 11.45	Driving to Milan	15 mins driving
11.45 – 12.00	15min RTD/EU break	6 hrs duty (split EU break)
12.00 – 16.15	Driving to Milan	4.25 hr (4.5 total)
16.15 – 16.45	Break	2nd part of EU split break
16.45 – 18.15	Driving to Milan	1.5 hrs (6 hr total)
18.15	Arrive in Milan	

These types of questions are ALWAYS included as 'long questions' by both OCR and the CILT and often involve ferries and different time zones. You must read the set questions really carefully to ensure that you get all the facts and answer exactly what is required.

Fiscal law answers

OCR multi-choice answers

1 = D

2 = B

3 = A

4 = C

CILT short answers

1 This is done by HMRC issuing the company with a Certificate of Status, which is valid for a period of 12 months. The claim is then made online using the HMRC website and the foreign VAT reclaim portal. HMRC then forwards the claim to the relevant country for the payment to be made. All claims must be submitted within nine months of the tax year in which the relevant expense was incurred.

2 Germany has a Motorway User Charge (LKW-Maut) where a prepayment is made or post-payment is collected through a GPS-based system requiring an electronic device to be fitted to the vehicle. Germany also has additional tolls for vehicles exceeding 7.5 tonnes GVW; these are levied by extending the toll charges to include additional major roads on the federal road network.

3 They must either submit their income tax declaration forms to HMRC no later than 31 October each year using self-assessment forms, or alternatively they may choose to use 'online' self-assessment, in which case they have until 31 January to submit their forms. In either case, if the forms are submitted one day late HMRC will issue a fine of £100 to the individual concerned.

4 Recovery vehicles over 7,500 kg but not exceeding 44,000 kg, are subject to speed limits of 60 mph on a motorway, 50 mph on a dual carriageway and 40 mph on a single carriageway; recovery vehicles operating in excess of 44 tonnes are subject to speed limits of 40 mph on a motorway, 30 mph on a dual carriageway and 30 mph on a single carriageway.

CILT long answer

Where the operator applies for first registration the following documents must be produced by post to DVLA in Swansea:

- a completed application form (form V55/1 or V55/2);
- the initial registration fee;
- the appropriate vehicle excise duty fee;
- the vehicle suppliers' invoice with Certificate of Conformity (CoC);
- proof of identity (usually by producing a passport or photocard driving licence).

A similar process applies to VED renewals at the DVLA, although some vehicle VED renewals are able to be done completely online. This is made possible by the DVLA holding records relating to test certificates and vehicle insurance validity. However, it is also still possible to renew VED at selected post offices.

For renewals at post offices you must provide:

- the V11 renewal form sent by the DVLA;
- a valid certificate of insurance;
- a current test certificate;
- a Reduced Pollution Certificate, if applicable;
- the appropriate vehicle excise duty fee.

VED for all vehicles can be purchased monthly or six-monthly by a normal payment or by direct debit at a 5 per cent surcharge, or for 12 months by a single payment, and runs from the first day of each month (only full months can be purchased). This process is the same as that applied to private cars.

To qualify for a Reduced Pollution Discount, which applies to some vehicles exceeding 12,000 kg MAM, which are subject to discounts through the HGV Road User Levy charging system, a vehicle must be able to meet emission standards 'better than the levels required by law for that type of vehicle at the time of registration, based on the "Euro" emission levels of Euro I–Euro VI'. This definition means that all newly registered large goods vehicles in the UK must now conform to Euro VI emission standards.

In the case of older vehicles, emissions can be reduced by retro-fitting items such as particulate traps, systems that recirculate the exhaust gases or by fitting new, more efficient engines.

Upgrading the emissions standards of vehicles is particularly relevant at the present time because since April 2015, vehicles fitted with early

Euro II and III engines were issued with a final reduced pollution certificate. In turn, reduced pollution certificates ceased to be issued for these vehicles after 31 March 2016, and all reduced pollution certificates for these vehicles expired in February 2017. The whole scheme including certificates for Euro IV and V engines finished in December 2017 and the reductions for reduced emissions are now included in bands of the HGV Road User Levy.

In order to be exempted from VED the vehicle must be registered or operated as below:

- vehicles used by the armed forces or the Crown;

- police, fire, ambulance and mine-rescue vehicles;

- vehicles manufactured before 1 January 1976;

- a vehicle travelling to and from a test station, providing this is the only purpose of the journey, and the test appointment has been pre-booked;

- agricultural tractors;

- certain vehicles used for the carriage of people with disabilities, which are not ambulances, but need to be identified as ambulances.

Technical standards and technical aspects of operation answers

OCR multi-choice answers

1 = A

2 = C

3 = B

4 = D

5 = C

6 = A

CILT short answers

1

    a The formula is $\dfrac{P \times D}{W}$

Where:

- – P is the weight of the load;
- – D is the distance of the centre of gravity of the load from the rear axle;
- – W is the wheelbase of the vehicle.

b $\dfrac{6 \times 2.5}{7} = \dfrac{15}{7}$ = an axle load of 2.14 tonnes on the front axle.

(Working to two decimal points.)

2 The three different formats are:
- – European Community Whole Vehicle Type Approval (ECWVTA) used by manufacturers selling vehicles throughout the EU.
- – National Small Series Type Approval (NSSTA) used for small numbers of vehicles produced within the UK.
- – Individual Vehicle Approval (IVA), where each individual vehicle needs to be examined and approved.

3 DVSA vehicle examiners are allowed, with the owner's consent, to enter premises at any reasonable time. However, if permission is not given at the time, they must give notice of their intentions to return, either verbally, giving 48 hours' notice, or by recorded delivery, giving 72 hours' notice. These stated time requirements do not have to be met if the vehicle has been involved in, or is believed to have been involved in, an accident.

4 Any TWO advantages of systems of contracting out maintenance from:
- – no facility costs;
- – no equipment costs;
- – no staff costs;
- – possible 'dealer' expertise;
- – possible warranty requirements;
- – 24/7 facilities are often available;
- – possible fleet support scheme available;
- – easier maintenance cost planning.

Any TWO disadvantages of systems of in-house maintenance from:
- – cost of the facility and facility upkeep;

- staff costs, including overtime, and weekend payments and training costs;

- cost of facility equipment;

- costs of stocking spare parts of stocked spares;

- time and costs associated with health and safety compliance.

5 The DVSA guide uses the principles that: the vehicle must be fit for purpose; the vehicle must be loaded correctly; the most appropriate securing method must be used; there must be 'adequate' load restraint.

6 Following initial certification the vehicle or trailer will be authorized for ATP operations for six years. After the first six-year period the vehicle or trailer will become subject to examinations and certification every three years.

CILT long answer

Criteria in relation to vehicles and equipment include:

- All vehicles intended to be used under ADR must be initially examined and certified by the DfT for use under ADR.

- All certified vehicles must be re-certified annually (normally at the annual test).

- Tank vehicles with a capacity of more than 1,000 l can only be approved and examined by DfT examiners.

- Tank containers with a capacity of more than 3,000 l can only be approved and examined by DfT examiners.

- Tank vehicles used under ADR must have a major tank inspection every six years.

- Tank vehicles used under ADR must have 'intermediate inspections', and be tested for leaks every three years.

- Vehicles and trailers used under ADR must have antilock and endurance braking systems.

- Some vehicles used under ADR, especially when carrying flammable liquids, may also need to have circuit breakers that can be operated from inside and outside of the vehicle, as well as heat shields fitted to the engine compartment and exhaust system.

Equipment that must be carried on the vehicle in cases of emergency includes:

- at least two warning cones, triangles or amber flashing lights to warn other road users;
- at least one suitably sized wheel chock for both the vehicle and any trailer drawn, to secure the vehicle in position, if required;
- a handlamp/torch that is flameproof and anti-static;
- high-viz clothing for the driver and any crew members;
- a spill kit to prevent spillage spreading;
- any PPE required when handling the goods in question;
- an eye bath/rinsing facility.

All vehicles operating under ADR must also carry certain levels of fire-fighting equipment. The requirements are as follows:

- Vehicles up to 3,500 kg GVW must have a minimum total capacity of 4 kg of extinguishant. This includes a minimum 2 kg extinguisher to be fitted inside the cab.
- Vehicles exceeding 3,500 kg GVW, but not exceeding 7,500 kg GVW must have a minimum total capacity of 8 kg of extinguishant. This includes a minimum 2 kg extinguisher fitted inside the cab and one other extinguisher that must have a minimum capacity of 6 kg.
- Vehicles exceeding 7,500 kg GVW must have a minimum total capacity of 12 kg of extinguishant. This includes a minimum 2 kg extinguisher fitted inside the cab and one other extinguisher that must have a minimum capacity of 6 kg (this could be a 10 kg extinguisher or a 6 kg extinguisher plus a 4 kg extinguisher).

In relation to load documentation (not driver documentation) firstly there is the ADR Note, also sometimes referred to as the Dangerous Goods Note or the Transport Document). This note:

- Must be carried on the vehicle transporting the dangerous goods.
- Must be written in the language of the country of origin. (When the language of the country of origin is not German, French or English a copy of the ADR note in one of those languages must also be carried.)

- Must give a full description of the goods being carried including the:
  - UN identification number;
  - UN proper shipping name;
  - hazard class, including any secondary hazards;
  - packing group, if applicable;
  - tunnel code, if applicable (see below);
  - gross weight (in kg);
  - number and a description of the packages, if applicable;
  - name and address of the consignor;
  - name and address of the consignee.

The second document that must accompany dangerous goods is known as 'Instructions in Writing'. These are generic and general instructions to the driver and the emergency services on what actions to take in cases of accidents or emergencies involving dangerous goods. They must explain how to:

- Stop the engine, apply the braking system and isolate the battery, if possible.
- Contact the emergency services and give them the relevant information.
- Put on the 'high-viz' clothing and lay out the warning signs for other road users.
- Avoid smoking or switching on any electrical equipment (this includes using e-cigarettes).
- Make the transport documents available for the emergency services when they arrive.
- Avoid coming into contact with spilled substances, fumes, smoke or dust, etc.
- Remove any clothing or PPE that becomes contaminated and dispose of it safely.
- Use the fire extinguishers to extinguish any small fires, typically in the tyres, engine, brakes, but only if it is safe to do so.
- Avoid tackling fires in load compartments involving the dangerous goods themselves.
- Prevent spillages into watercourses and sewers by using the spill kit to contain the spillage.

- Stay at a safe distance from the incident and to advise other bystanders to do the same.
- Comply with any instructions given by the emergency services.

In addition, 'Instructions in Writing' must:

- be completed in the language of the country of origin;
- be completed in a language able to be understood by the driver;
- be completed in the language of all countries of transit and the country of destination;
- be kept in the vehicle in a place and format that is clearly visible to any emergency services.

Road safety answers

OCR multi-choice answers

1 = A

2 = C

3 = B

4 = D

5 = B

6 = C

CILT short answers

1 Three ways include: contacting the DVLA's Data Subject Enquiry Department at Swansea for a printout of the licence details (this requires consent from the driver concerned and payment of a fee); using the DVLA's online 'Share Driving Licence Service' where the DVLA issues a code number that is valid for 21 days; or using a DVLA telephone line, which requires the driver to call first to give permission for the employer to be given the details required. Other methods include using the DVLA's Access to Driver Data Service (ADD) or by writing and using the postal service.

2 IDPs are required by drivers who transit or visit countries that do not recognize the standard UK/EU licence. These countries include:

- Albania;
- Belarus;
- most Middle Eastern states;

- Russia;

- Ukraine.

IDPs can be obtained from post offices, the AA, the RAC or Green Flag and are valid for 12 months.

3 Parking at night is also an area where different rules apply. For example:

Car-derived vans and small goods vehicles not exceeding 2,500 kg GVW may park on a road at night without lights if:

- it is parked facing the direction of traffic;

- it is parked parallel to the kerb;

- it is more than 10 m away from any road junction;

- the road is a restricted road (for example 30 mph).

Goods vehicles exceeding 2,500 kg GVW parked on a road at night must have:

- two white sidelights showing to the front and two red lights showing to the rear.

4 A sign of a red flame inside a red circle is used in France to indicate that vehicles carrying highly flammable goods are prohibited; and signs bearing the words 'Barrière de Dégel' are used on minor routes, also in France, during periods of thawing snow, to prohibit large goods vehicles from using that route.

5 Statutory actions following a road traffic accident in the UK where no one is injured include:

- The drivers must stop.

- Drivers must provide details of the vehicle registration number, their name and address and the name and address of the vehicle owner/operator if requested to do so by any person with reasonable grounds for requiring that information.

- If the driver is not able to exchange details as required, the accident must be reported to the police as 'soon as is reasonably practicable' and in any case within 24 hours.

6 The AGR system consists of signs that are coloured green and white and use an 'E' prefix before the number of the road. For main roads, the numbering begins at E1, with a second digit that is an even number for east–west routes and an odd number for north–south routes. Minor AGR routes have three digits.

CILT long answer

When first applying for a vocational driving licence the applicant must send the following to the DVLA in Swansea:

- current car licence (Category B);
- photocard application form D750;
- application form D2;
- medical form D4 (signed by a GP);
- driver CPC examination pass certificate.

The driving test itself consists of different modules, including the need for drivers, who are not exempted and applying for a vocational licence for the first time, to pass an Initial Driver Certificate of Professional Competence (DCPC) examination before they sit their vocational driving test.

The entire training programme consists of four separate modules:

- Module 1 parts a) and b): Theory and Hazard Perception Test – consisting of 100 multiple-choice theory questions (85 pass mark) and 19 hazard video clips (100 marks with 67 pass mark). Once this has been passed, the physical driving test must be taken within a period of two years.
- Module 2: Initial Driver CPC Case Studies.
- Module 3: Practical Driving Test.
- Module 4: Driver CPC Practical Test.

Once all modules have been completed, the driver will be issued with the vocational driving licence and a Driver Qualification Card (DQC) that is valid for five years. The DQC must be produced upon request and needs to be carried by the driver at all times when driving professionally if they are to avoid the risk of a fixed penalty fine.

Once the initial DQC has been issued, the driver becomes subject to periodic DCPC training that requires every vocational driver (unless exempt) to undergo 35 hours' training every five years.

All vehicles (post-2003) used for vocational driving tests must be fitted with an operational tachograph, ABS braking systems and a seat and seatbelt for use by the examiner.

Specifically, vehicles used for vocational driving tests must be of a certain specification. A vehicle to be used for a Category C licence must also carry a minimum load, as detailed below:

- a rigid goods box body vehicle of at least 12,000 kg GVW;
- at least 8 metres long but no longer than 12 metres;
- at least 2.4 metres wide;
- capable of a speed of at least 80 kph;
- with either an automatic or manual gearbox;
- loaded with a minimum of 10,000 kg in 5 × 1,000 l IBCs filled with water.

Vocational entitlements usually require renewal every five years. However, the rules do vary depending upon the year the licence was originally granted. The rules are as follows:

- Drivers acquiring their vocational licence before 19 January 2013 have a licence valid until the age of 45. At 45 they will need a medical (using form D4) every five years to renew the licence and at age 65 the medical will need to be done annually.
- If an existing driver (pre-19 January 2013) renews their licence by supplying a new photograph, they will be issued with a new five-year licence.
- Vocational drivers over the age of 45 will need to supply a new photograph every 10 years (every other renewal).
- All vocational licences issued after 19 January 2013 are valid for five years.
- Drivers under the age of 45 passing their test after January 13 2013 will need to provide a self-declaration of fitness to drive at every five-year renewal up to the age of 45 and provide a new photograph every 10 years.

Notes

These self-test answers are the final element of this self-study book, which has been specifically designed to enable learners to sit CPC examinations, using the two most popular methods available, namely the OCR route and the CILT route. The book, as explained at the outset, is also designed to provide up-to-date information for transport professionals and it is hoped that the reader can clearly see that the book sets out, and hopefully accomplishes, its aim to provide often complex information in a way that meets the needs of modern transport professionals.

ONLINE RESOURCES

The below documents are available on the UK government website (www.gov.uk):

DVSA Code of Practice Guide to Maintaining Roadworthiness

DVSA Code of Practice Safety of Loads on Vehicles

DVSA Guidance: Load Securing: Vehicle Operator Guidance

DVSA Overview of Operator Compliance Risk Scores

Goods Vehicle Guide to Operator Licensing (GV74)

Rules on Drivers' Hours and Tachographs Goods Vehicles in GB and Europe (GV262)

Other websites:

DfT: www.dft.gov.uk

DVLA: www.dvla.gov.uk

DVLA: www.gov.uk/contact-the-dvla

DVSA: www.gov.uk/government/organisations/vehicle-and-operator-services-agency

HSE: www.hse.gov.uk

INDEX

Note: bold page numbers indicate figures; italic numbers indicate tables.

abbreviations and acronyms 251
abnormal indivisible loads (AILs) 253–57, 318
acceptance in contracts 11, 347
access to the market *see* market, access to
accidents/collisions 76–78, 333–35, 343, 345, 366, 367
accounts
　acid test ratio 169–70
　balance sheets 166–70
　capital employed 166
　requirement to produce 165
　trading and profit and loss (P&L) account 170–73, *171–72*
　working capital ratio 166, 168–69
acid test ratio 169–70
acronyms 251
Admission Temporaire (ATA) carnets 235
ADR agreement 285
ADR Notes 290
Advisory, Conciliation and Arbitration Service (ACAS) 59–60
agents, principals and 16
AGR agreement 338–39, 343–44, 345, 367
analogue tachographs 112–13, **113**
animals, movement of 298–300
annual general meetings (AGMs) 45–46
antenatal care, time off for 95–96
area representatives 56–57
Articles of Association 40
ATP 295–96, 306, 363
auditors 45, 53, 349
Austria, traffic rules in 323
authority 189
automatic number plate recognition (ANPR) 145, 148, 198, 202
auxiliaries *see* transport auxiliaries
axle weights 247, 249, *249*

balance sheets 166–70, *167–68*
banks 161
Belgium, traffic rules in 323
bilateral permits 233–34
bills of exchange 164
bills of lading 229
blindspots 266
braking systems 258, 266

budgets 174–78, *176*, *177*
Bulgaria, traffic rules in 323
bus lanes and gates 320
businesses
　annual general meetings (AGMs) 45–46
　Articles of Association 40
　auditors 45, 53, 349
　Certificates of Incorporation 40–41
　closure of 48–51
　communication in 189–90
　company secretaries 44–45, 53, 349
　compulsory insurance 198–99
　data protection 194–95
　directors' role and duties 43–44
　discipline procedures 190–91
　discretionary business insurance 199–201
　employers' liability insurance 198–99
　grievance procedures 190–91
　insurance 196–201
　limited companies 36–38
　management definitions 188–90
　market research 191–92
　marketing 192–94, 206–07, 208, 350
　Memorandum of Association 39–40
　motor vehicle taxation (VED) 140–44
　objectives 188
　partnerships 30, 32–35
　private limited companies 30, 37, 39
　public limited companies 30, 37–38, 39, 41
　public relations 195
　register, company 41–42
　registration procedures 39–42
　shareholders 46
　shares 46–47, 53, 349–50
　sole traders 29, 30–31
　stationery 41
　Statutory Off Road Notification (SORN) 144
　structure of organizations 187–88
　value-added tax (VAT) 137–40
　see also financial management

cabotage 230
capacity to enter into contracts 12, 26, 346, 348

capital employed 166, 208, 350
carnets 234–36
Carnets de Passage en Douane 235
cash flow budgets 174, 175–76, *176*
Central Arbitration Committee (CAC) 60
Certificates of Conformity 260
Certificates of Incorporation 40–41
Certificates of Insurance 197–98
certification officers 57
Chartered Institute of Logistics
        and Transport (CILT) examination
        route 4–5
chassis considerations 257–58
CIP – carriage and insurance paid 203
civil law *see* contracts
clean air zones (CAZs) 146–47
clearing houses 24, 27, 346, 347
closed-circuit television (CCTV) 201
closure of businesses 48–51
CMR *see* Convention Relative au Contrat
        de Transport International de
        Marchandises par Route (CMR)
CMR notes 18–20, **19**, 26, 27, 346, 347
collective bargaining 57
collisions 76–78, 333–35, 345, 366
commercial law
        'plying for trade', conditions and
                formalities for 29–30
        see also businesses; financial
                management
common carriers 14
common law 9–10
communication in organizations 189–90,
        201
community transit (CT) 231–33
companies *see* businesses
company directors 43–44
company secretaries 44–45, 53, 349
company voluntary arrangements (CVAs)
        50, 53, 348–49
compensation claims 20
compulsory business insurance 198–99
compulsory winding up of companies
        50–51
conditions of carriage
        areas covered 14–15
        international 17–24
configuration of costs 182–83
congestion charging 146
consideration in contracts 11, 347
consignment notes, CMR 18–20, **19**, 26,
        27, 346, 347
consolidation services 24–25, 27, 346,
        347
conspicuity markings 270

Construction and Use (C&U) regulations
        265–68
container movements 283
contracts
        acceptance of Offers 11, 347
        capacity 12, 26, 27, 346, 347, 348
        of carriage 13–16
        components of 11–12, 27, 347–48
        conditions of carriage 14–24
        consideration 11, 347
        defined 10
        exemption clauses 15–16
        formalities 12, 348
        intention 12, 348
        law governing 9–10
        legality 12, 348
        lien 15
        offers 11, 347
        principals and agents 16
        subcontractors 15
Control of Substances Hazardous to Health
        (COSHH) Regulations 76
Convention Relative au Contrat de
        Transport International de
        Marchandises par Route (CMR)
        17–24, 26, 346
coordination 189
corporate manslaughter 80
corporation tax 153
COSHH *see* Control of Substances
        Hazardous to Health (COSHH)
        Regulations
cost centres 178
cost units 178
costs 178–83, 206, 208, 209, 350, 351
CPT – carriage paid 203
credit cards, company 162–63
credit notes 162
Croatia, traffic rules in 324
curtailment 225, 241–42, 244, 353
customer monitoring systems 202
customs procedures 231–36, 243, 353
Czech Republic, traffic rules in 324

daily checks by drivers 277–78, 331–33
dangerous goods
        ADR agreement 285
        ADR Notes 290
        classification of goods 285
        documentation 289–93
        equipment to be carried 289
        firefighting equipment 289
        hazard diamonds **294**
        Hazchem panels 286–87
        identification number 286

Instructions in Writing 290–91
labelling 286
limited quantities 287
marking on vehicles 286–88
packaging 286
safety advisors 292–93
Transport Security Directorate of the
    Department for Transport
    (TRANSEC) 292
tunnel codes 291–92
United Nations Economic Commission
    for Europe (UNECE) 285
vehicles and equipment 286–89, 306,
    363–66
DAP – delivered at place 204
DAT – delivered at terminal 204, 207–08,
    351
data protection 194–95
DDP – delivered duty paid 204
debit notes 162
debt factoring 165
Deeds of Partnership 32–33
defects, reporting 278
delegation 189
Denmark, traffic rules in 324
dependents' leave 98
deposit systems 126
depreciation 183–86, *184*, *185*
derogations 104
diabetics, insulin-dependent 311–12
digital tachographs 116–21, **117**
dimensions *see* weights and dimensions
diminishing loads 249–50
direct costs 178
directives, EU 10
directors, role and duties of 43–44
disciplinary procedures 89, 131–32,
    190–91, 350, 356
discretionary business insurance 199–201
dismissal
    challenging 91–92
    fair 89–90
    redundancy 92–94, 133, 350
    unfair 90–92
display screen equipment 71
distribution services 25
downplating 262
Driver Qualification Card (DPC) 128
drivers
    daily checks by 277–78, 331–33
    Driver Certificate of Professional
        Competence (DCPC) 128–30,
        312–15, 368
    licensing 307–12, 340, 344, 345, 346,
        366, 368–69

monitoring systems 202
nationality attestation 228, 242, 244,
    353
security of goods 336 .
training and testing 128–30
see also rights of employees
drivers' hours
    British domestic rules 106–07
    calculating arrival 134–36, 357–58
    co-liability 128
    definitions 100–03
    deposit systems 126
    derogations 104
    EU Drivers' Hours Regulations
        100–04
    European Agreement on International
        Road Transport (AETR) 106
    exemptions from EU rules 103–04
    Group One/Two drivers 106–07
    GV262 form 100, 111
    Horizontal Amending Directive (HAD)
        108–09
    military reservists' rest periods 103
    offences against regulations 125–26
    penalties 126
    powers of DVSA vehicle examiners 127
    record keeping 123–25
    sanctions 127
    tachographs 112–23, 133–34, 357
    under mixed rules 110, 124
    working time rules 104–05
DVSA Guide to Maintaining
    Roadworthiness 274
DVSA vehicle examiners, powers of 127

emergency services 75
emissions 273
employees
    health and safety responsibilities 65, 73
    information on health and safety for 73
    involvement of in changes 87
    see also drivers; rights of employees
employers
    driver licensing, responsibilities
        regarding 307–12
    employers' liability insurance 81,
        198–99
    health and safety responsibilities 65–68,
        74
employment, terms of 83–84
Employment Appeal Tribunals (EAT) 60
employment tribunals 91–92
engine type 258
Environment Agency (EA) 63–64
equal pay 86

equipment
    and health and safety 70
    see also vehicle and equipment criteria;
        vehicles
estimates 161
European Accident Statement (EAS) 198,
    335
European Agreement on International Road
    Transport (AETR) 106
European health insurance cards (EHIC) 200
European Union (EU) 6–8
    Drivers' Hours Regulations 100–04
    Framework Directive 1992 69–71
    legislation 10
    road network 338–39
    signage 338–39, **339**
    tolls 148–51
    traffic rules 322–31
    VAT 139–40
    weights and dimensions 251–53, *252*
    Working Time Directive (WTD) 84–85
    working time rules 104–05
examinations 3–6
exemption clauses 15–16
EXW – ex works 203

fair dismissal 89–90
FCA – free carrier 203
ferry movements 281–83, 337–38
fidelity guarantees 200
financial management
    accounts 165–74, *167–68*
    acid test ratio 169–70
    bills of exchange 164
    budgets 174–78, *176*, *177*
    capital employed 166, 208, 350
    cash flow 174–78
    company credit cards 162–63
    costs 178–83, 206, 208, 209, 350, 351
    credit notes 162
    debit notes 162
    debt factoring 165
    depreciation 183–86, *184*, *185*
    estimates 161
    insurance 196–201
    invoices 162
    letters of credit 164
    long-term financing 165
    orders 162
    payment of accounts 162–64
    pro-forma invoices 162
    promissory notes 164
    quotations 161–62
    short-term financing 164–65
    statements 162

trading and profit and loss (P&L)
    account 170–73, *171–72*, 205–06,
    208, 350
transaction documents 161–62
working capital ratio 166, 168–69, 205,
    208, 350
Finland, traffic rules in 324
fire safety 79–80
firefighting equipment 289
first aid 79
fiscal law
    congestion charging 146
    HGV Road User Levy 144–45
    low emission zones (LEZs) 146–47
    motor vehicle taxation (VED) 140–44,
        159, 360–61
    tolls 147–51, 157–58, 159, 359
    value-added tax (VAT) 137–40, 157,
        159, 359
fixed costs 178, 179
fixed penalty notices 126
fleet administration systems 202
flexible working 95
foodstuffs, perishable 295–96, 305–06, 361
formalities in contracts 12, 348
four Ps 192–93, 206–07, 208
France, traffic rules in 324–25
Freedom of Information Act 195
freight forwarders 25

gender, equal pay and 86
Germany, traffic rules in 325–26
global positioning systems (GPS) 201
goods-in-transit insurance 199–200
Greece, traffic rules in 326
'Green Card' insurance 198
grievance procedures 89, 190–91
Group One/Two drivers 106–07
groupage operators 24–25, 27, 346, 347
guarantee payments 86
Guide to Operator Licensing 210
GV74 210
GV79E 213, 239, 244, 351
GV262 100, 111

hazard diamonds **294**
Hazchem panels 286–87
health and safety
    competent person as representative
        73–74
    Control of Substances Hazardous to
        Health (COSHH) Regulations 76
    corporate manslaughter 80
    display screen equipment 71
    emergency services 75

employees' responsibilities 65, 73
employers' responsibilities 65–68, 74
Environment Agency (EA) 63–64
equipment 70
EU Framework Directive 1992 69–71
fire safety 79–80
first aid 79
Health and Safety at Work Act 1974
  (HASAWA) 65, 69
Health and Safety Executive (HSE)
  62–63
improvement notices 63, 131, 134, 356
information on for employees 73
inspectors 62–63
Lifting Operations and Lifting
  Equipment Regulations (LOLER) 80
load safety 279–81
London, standards for operations in
  266
Management of Health and Safety
  Regulations 1999 71–75
manual handling 70–71
noise 80
personal protective equipment (PPE) 71
prohibition notices 63, 131, 134, 356
Reporting of Injuries, Diseases and
  Dangerous Occurrences (RIDDOR)
  76–78
risk assessment 72–73, 79–80
safety policy statements 67
safety representatives/committees 67–68
Smoke-free (Premises and Enforcement)
  Regulations 2006 78–79
surveillance 74
temporary staff 74
training 73
workplace 70
see also road safety
Health and Safety at Work Act 1974
  (HASAWA) 65, 69
Health and Safety Executive (HSE) 62–63
Health and Safety (First Aid) Regulations
  1981 79
height limits 319
HGV Road User Levy 144–45
Horizontal Amending Directive (HAD)
  84–85, 108–09
Hungary, traffic rules in 326
hygiene regulations 295

immigration, illegal 237–38
improvement notices 63, 131, 134, 356
incidents, reporting 76–78
income tax
  employed staff 152–53

self-employed 152, 158, 159, 359
Incoterms 202–04, 207–08, 351
indirect costs 178
individual voluntary arrangements
  (IVAs) 49
industrial action 56, 57–58
industrial tribunals
  Advisory, Conciliation and Arbitration
    Service (ACAS) 59–60
  Employment Appeal Tribunals
    (EAT) 60
information and communication technology
  (ICT) 201–02
insolvency 49–51
inspections, safety 275–78, 303–04, 306,
  361, 362
Instructions in Writing 290–91
insulin-dependent diabetics 311–12
insurance 196–201, 335
intention in contracts 12, 348
intermodel movements 283–84
international conditions of carriage 17–24
international operations
  bills of lading 229
  carnets 234–36
  community transit (CT) 231–33
  customs procedures 231–36, 243, 353
  documentation for 227–29
  driver nationality attestation 228, 244
  drivers nationality attestation 242, 353
  driving permits 315–16
  freight movements 230
  illegal immigration 237–38
  letters of attestation 228, 242, 244,
    353
  Letters of Invitation (LoI) 237
  movement reference numbers (MRNs)
    232
  New Computerized Transit System
    (NCTS) 231–32, 244, 353
  passports 236–37
  perishable foodstuffs 295–96
  permits 233–34, 243, 341–42, 344,
    353, 366–67
  planning journeys 337–40
  road safety 337–40
  Schengen Agreement 236–38
  Single Administrative Documents (SADs)
    232
  Transit Accompanying Documents
    (TADs) 232, 253
  Transit Advice Notes (TANs) 232
  visas 237
  waste carriage 298
  weights and dimensions 251–53, 252

invoices 139, 162
Italy, traffic rules in 326–27
itemized pay statements 86

Joint Approvals Unit for Periodic Training (JAUPT) 129

key performance indicators (KPIs) 189

Labour Relations (Consolidation) Act 1992 55–57
Latvia, traffic rules in 327
legality of contracts 12, 348
legislation
    Control of Substances Hazardous to Health (COSHH) Regulations 76
    data protection 194–95
    EU Framework Directive 1992 69–71
    Freedom of Information Act 195
    Health and Safety (First Aid) Regulations 1981 79
    Health and Safety at Work Act 1974 (HASAWA) 65, 69
    Labour Relations (Consolidation) Act 1992 55–57
    Lifting Operations and Lifting Equipment Regulations (LOLER) 80
    Management of Health and Safety Regulations 1999 71–75
    Reporting of Injuries, Diseases and Dangerous Occurrences (RIDDOR) 76–78
    Smoke-free (Premises and Enforcement) Regulations 2006 78–79
    Transfer of Undertakings (Protection of Employment) Regulations (TUPE) 84
    Working Time Directive (WTD) 84–85
less than container loads (LCL) 24
Letter of Invitation (LoI) 237
letters of attestation 228, 242, 244, 353
letters of credit 164
liabilities
    carrier's 21–23
    employers' liability insurance 81, 198–99
    limited 20
    limited companies 36–38
    partners' 33–34
    public liability insurance 199
    senders 20–21
licensed insolvency practitioners 51
licensing
    drivers 307–12, 340, 344, 345, 366, 368–69
    operator 211–23, 240–42, 245, 353–56
    waste carriage 297–98

lien 15
life-cycle, product 192
Lifting Operations and Lifting Equipment Regulations (LOLER) 80
Lighting Regulations 268–72
limited companies 36–38
limited liability 20, 34, 39
liquidators 51
livestock movements 298–300
living wage 86
load documentation 336
load safety 279–81, 305, 306, 361, 363
loans, short-term 164–65
London Congestion Charge 321
London Lorry Control Scheme 321–22
low emission zones (LEZs) 146–47
Luxembourg, traffic rules in 327

maintenance of vehicles
    contracting out or in-house 276–77, 304–05, 306, 361, 362–63
    daily checks 277–78, 331–33
    defects, reporting 278
    DVSA Guide to Maintaining Roadworthiness 274
    objective of programme of 274
    safety inspections 275–78, 303–04, 306, 361, 362
management definitions 188–90
Management of Health and Safety Regulations 1999 71–75
manual handling 70–71
maritime insurance 199
market, access to
    international operations, documentation for 227–29
    objection/representation 217–18, 239–40, 244, 351
    Operator Compliance Risk Score (OCRS) 223–25, 241, 244, 353
    operator licensing 211–23, 240–42, 244, 245, 351, 352, 353–56
    Traffic Commissioners 216–18, 225–26, 244
market research 191–92
marketing 192–94, 206–07, 208, 350
maternity rights 95–97
medical requirements 311–12
medical suspension 98
Memorandum of Association 39–40
military reservists' rest periods 103
minimum wage 86
mirrors 266
mobile phones 320
modifications to vehicles 264

Most Serious Offences (MSOs) 224–25
motor vehicle insurance 197–98
motor vehicle taxation (VED) 140–44, 159, 360–61
motorways 319, 322
movement reference numbers (MRNs) 232, 243, 353
multilateral permits 233–34

National Insurance (NI) 81, 153
Netherlands, traffic rules in 327
New Computerized Transit System (NCTS) 231–32, 244, 353
noise 80, 273
noncompliance by operators 223–25
Norway, traffic rules in 327–28
notice periods 88
notifiable alterations to vehicles 264

'O' licences 211–23
objection/representation 217–18, 239–40, 351
objectives 188
offers in contracts 11, 347
operational budgets 174, 176–78, 177
operational costing 178–83
Operator Compliance Risk Score (OCRS) 223–25, 241, 353
operator licensing 211–23, 240–42, 245, 353–56
orders 162
ordinary shares 47, 53, 349–50
organizations see businesses
overhanging 255–56
overnight parking 321
own-account operations 230
Oxford Cambridge Royal Society of Arts (OCR) examination route 4

parental leave 97–98
parking 319–22, 342, 344, 366, 367
partnerships 30, 32–35, 39, 152
passports 236–37
paternity leave 97
'pay as you earn' (PAYE) 152
pay statements 86
payment of accounts 162–64
pedestrian crossings 320
penalties 126
performance management 189
periods of notice 88
perishable foodstuffs 295–96, 305–06, 361
permits 233–34, 243–44, 315–16, 341–42, 344, 353, 366–67
personal protective equipment (PPE) 71

PG3 forms 250
PG9 forms 271
PG10 forms 271
PG35ECDN/PGDN35 forms 271–72
phytosanitary regulations 301
picketing 57–58
plants, movement of 301
plating 261–62, 265
'plying for trade', conditions and formalities for 29–30
Poland, traffic rules in 328
Portugal, traffic rules in 328
powers of DVSA vehicle examiners 127
preference shares 47, 53, 349–50
principals and agents 16
private carriers 14
private limited companies 30, 37, 39, 44–45, 45
pro-forma invoices 162
product life-cycle 192
professional negligence insurance 199
profit and loss (P&L) account 170–73, 171–72, 205–06, 350
prohibition notices 63, 131, 134, 356
promissory notes 164
property insurance 200
prospectuses 41
public duties 94–95
public highway damage insurance 200–01
public liability insurance 199
public limited companies (plcs) 30, 37–38, 39, 41, 45
public relations 195

quick assets ratio 169–70
quotations 161–62

ratios
    acid test 169–70
    quick assets 169–70
    working capital 166, 168–69
record keeping 123–25
recovery vehicles 153–55, 158, 159, 359
red routes 320
reducing-balance depreciation 185, 185–86
redundancy 92–94, 133, 357
reflective plates 269–70
register, company 41–42
registration procedures for companies 39–42
regulations, EU 10
renewal of driver licences 315
Reporting of Injuries, Diseases and Dangerous Occurrences (RIDDOR) 76–78

responsibilities and liabilities
  carrier's 21–23
  senders 20–21
responsibility 189
RIDDOR *see* Reporting of Injuries, Diseases
    and Dangerous Occurrences
    (RIDDOR)
rights of employees
  dependents' leave 98
  disciplinary procedures 89, 131–32,
    134, 350, 356
  equal pay 86
  fair dismissal 89–90
  flexible working 95
  grievance procedures 89
  guarantee payments 86
  involvement of employees 87
  itemized pay statements 86
  maternity rights 95–97
  medical suspension 98
  minimum wage 86
  paternity leave 97
  periods of notice 88
  public duties 94–95
  redundancy 92–94, 133, 357
  shared parental leave 97–98
  statutory sick pay (SSP) 87
  terms of employment 83–84
  Transfer of Undertakings (Protection of
    Employment) Regulations
    (TUPE) 84
  unfair dismissal 90–92
  working time 84–85
risk assessment 72–73, 79–80
road safety
  accidents/collisions 333–35, 343, 345,
    366, 367
  AGR agreement 338–39, 343–44, 345,
    367
  daily checks by drivers 331–33
  Driver Certificate of Professional
    Competence (DCPC) 312–15
  driver licensing 307–12, 340, 344, 345,
    366, 368–69
  height limits 319
  international driving permits 315–16
  international journeys 337–40
  London Congestion Charge 321
  London Lorry Control Scheme 321–22
  medical requirements 311–12
  parking 319–22, 342, 344, 366, 367
  road signs 330
  security of goods 335–36
  signage 330, 338–39, **339**, 342–43, 344,
    367
  speed limits 317–19, 322
  testing, driver 312–15
  traffic rules (EU) 322–31
  traffic rules (UK) 317–22
road signs 330, 338–39, **339**, 342–43, 344,
    367
road traffic accidents/collisions 333–35
Romania, traffic rules in 328
routes and security 336
routing software 201
running costs 180

safety
  inspections 275–78, 303–04, 306, 361,
    362
  load 279–81, 305, 361
  see also road safety
safety inspections 275–78
safety policy statements 67
safety representatives/committees
    67–68
satellite navigation (satnav) 201
scheduling software 201
Schengen Agreement 236–38
seat belts 267
secretaries, company 44–45
security of goods 335–36
self-employed
  defined 109
  income tax 152, 158, 159, 359
  National Insurance (NI) 81
senders
  responsibilities and liabilities 20–21
shared parental leave 97–98
shared parental pay (ShPP) 98
shareholders 46
shares 46–47, 53, 349–50
shop stewards 56–57
sifted encounters 224
signage 330, 338–39, **339**, 342–43, 344,
    367
Single Administrative Documents (SADs)
    232
sleeping partners 34
Slovakia, traffic rules in 328
Slovenia, traffic rules in 329
SMART objectives 188
Smoke-free (Premises and Enforcement)
    Regulations 2006 78–79
social institutions
  Advisory, Conciliation and Arbitration
    Service (ACAS) 59–60
  Central Arbitration Committee
    (CAC) 60
  Environment Agency (EA) 63–64

Health and Safety Executive (HSE) 62–63
trade unions 55–58
social law *see* drivers' hours; rights of
employees; social institutions;
tachographs
sole traders 29, 30–31, 52, 53, 348
income tax 152
individual voluntary arrangements
(IVAs) 49
National Insurance (NI) 81
Spain, traffic rules in 329
special interest 18–19
Special Types General Order (STGO) rules
253–54
speed limits 317–19, 322
staff development 189
standing costs 179
statements 162
stationery, company 41
statutes 9, 10
see also legislation
Statutory Declaration of Solvency 49
Statutory Off Road Notification (SORN)
144
statutory sick pay (SSP) 87
stock management 177–78
straight-line depreciation 183, *184*, 184–85
strikes 56, 57–58
structure of organizations 187–88
subcontractors 15
suspension 247
Sweden, traffic rules in 329
Switzerland, traffic rules in 329

tachographs
analogue 112–16, **113**
charts and records 115–16
company cards 121–22
digital 116–21, **117**
drivers' cards 117–18
drivers' responsibilities for 113–16,
118–19
equipment breakdown 122–23
exemptions 112
inspection and calibration 123
installation 123
loss of 133–34, 357
operators' roles and responsibilities
121–22
rules 112, 119–21
tax
corporation 153
motor vehicle taxation (VED) 140–44,
159, 360–61
see also fiscal law; income tax

TE160P forms 250
technical standards *see* dangerous goods;
weights and dimensions
technology 201–02
telemetry 201–02
temporary staff, health and safety and
74
terms of employment 83–84
testing
driver 312–15
vehicles 262–64, *265*
third-country traffic 230
third party auxiliaries *see* transport
auxiliaries
third-party insurance 197
through traffic 230
tolls 147–51, 157–58, 159, 359
torts 10
total costs 180–82
total share capital 46–47
trade licences 155–56
trade unions 55–58
trading and profit and loss (P&L) account
170–73, *171–72*, 205–06, 350
Traffic Commissioners 216–18, 225–26,
241
traffic rules
EU 322–31
UK 317–22
training 312–15
Driver Certificate of Professional
Competence (DCPC) 128–30
health and safety 73
staff development 189
transaction documents 161–62
Transfer of Undertakings (Protection of
Employment) Regulations (TUPE)
84
Transit Accompanying Documents (TADs)
232, 253
Transit Advice Notes (TANs) 232
transmission 258
transport auxiliaries 24–25
container movements 283
ferry movements 281–83
intermodel movements 283–84
Transport Security Directorate of the
Department for Transport
(TRANSEC) 292
Transports Internationale Routiers (TIR)
carnets 234–35
tunnel codes 291–92
type approval 260–61, 302–03, 306, 361,
362
tyres 267–68

unfair dismissal 90–92
United Nations Economic Commission for
      Europe (UNECE) 285
unwitting CMR 23

value-added tax (VAT) 137–40, 157, 159,
      359
variable costs 178, 180
VAT 137–40, 157, 159, 359
Vehicle Excise Duty (VED) 140–44
vehicles
      blindspots 266
      braking systems 266
      Construction and Use (C&U)
            regulations 265–68
      criteria for 257–58
      dangerous goods 286–89, 306, 363–66
      emissions 273
      insurance 197–98
      Lighting Regulations 268–72
      London, standards for operations in 266
      mirrors 266
      modifications 264
      noise 273
      notifiable alterations 264
      plating 261–62, 265
      seat belts 267
      security of goods 335–36
      taxation 140–44, 159, 360–61
      testing 262–64, 265
      type approval 260–61
      tyres 267–68
      visibility markings 269–70
      vocational driving tests 313–15
      see also maintenance of vehicles; weights
            and dimensions
VIN plates 261
visas 237

visibility markings 269–70
voluntary winding up of companies
      49–50
VTG6A plates 262

wage, minimum 86
wage slips 86
warehousing services 25
waste carriage 296–98
Waste Regulatory Authorities (WRAs)
      297
weights and dimensions
      abbreviations and acronyms 251
      abnormal indivisible loads (AILs)
            253–57
      diminishing loads 249–50
      enforcement 250–51
      European and international 251–53,
            252
      international operations 251–53, 252
      overhanging 255–56
      PG3 forms 250
      Special Types General Order (STGO)
            rules 253–54
      TE160P forms 250
      UK 247–51, 248, 249, 302, 306,
            361–62
winding up of companies 49–50
working capital ratio 166, 168–69, 205,
      208, 350
Working Time Directive (WTD) 84–85,
      108–09
working time rules 104–05
      see also drivers' hours

yellow lines 319–20

zero-based budgets 174